LEGITIMACY AND CONFLICT IN SOUTH ASIA

SOUTH ASIA INSTITUTE, NEW DELHI BRANCH
HEIDELBERG UNIVERSITY
SOUTH ASIAN STUDIES NO. XXXI

Legitimacy and Conflict in South Asia

Edited by

SUBRATA K. MITRA
AND
DIETMAR ROTHERMUND

MANOHAR

First published 1997
Reprinted 1998

ISBN 81-7304-200-4

Published by
Ajay Kumar Jain for
Manohar Publishers & Distributors
2/6 Ansari Road, Daryaganj
New Delhi 110002

Printed at
Replika Press Pvt. Ltd.
Plot No. A-229 DSIDC Narela Indl. Park
Delhi 110 040

Preface

The present volume contains the contributions to the International Colloquium on 'Legitimacy and Conflict in South Asia', held at the Internationales Wissenschaftsforum (IWH), Heidelberg, on 10 - 11, February 1995. The colloquium organized by Subrata K. Mitra and Dietmar Rothermund of the Südasien-Institut of the University of Heidelberg provided an opportunity to an international gathering of scholars to examine the theme of order, anarchy and legitimacy. This is also currently a major theme of interdisciplinary research at the Südasien Institut of Heidelberg.

The articles presented in this publication are based on the discussion papers, which were circulated during the colloquium. They do not appear in this book in their original order of presentation at the colloquium, but have been placed in a new, and in a more distinct way. Dietmar Rothermund has recorded the gist of the discussions. This was sent to all participants for their approval or corrections. He has also contributed an epilogue in which he highlights themes which have emerged from the conference.

International conferences involve rather complicated arrangements and coordination with colleagues who are separated by several time zones. First and foremost on our list of thanks are colleagues who interrupted their normal academic schedules to join us as authors, discussants and chairpersons and contributed lively and stimulating discussions over two days. This was made possible through the generous financial assistance of the Deutsche Forschungsgemeinschaft and the efficient organization of the colloquium by the staff of IWH and Haus Buhl. Monika Schlicher provided vital coordination from the beginning to the end. Other members of the department of Political Science - Evelin Hust, Sabine Klotz, Peter Lehr, Klaus Müller and Astrid Rüdiger - attended to every organizational detail with meticulous efficiency. Monika Ackermann and Ursula Schmitt-Köhler ran the conference secretariat with the right balance of general firmness and understanding for individual cases. The burden of preparation of the camera-ready copy has been cheerfully borne respectively by Mr. Ramesh Jain on behalf of Manohar in Delhi and Klaus Müller in Heidelberg. The index has been prepared by Astrid Rüdiger. Chitra Rothermund and Marie-Paule Mitra have added to the conviviality of the occasion by organizing *gemütliche* receptions. The editors wish to express their grateful appreciation to all who have helped to make the whole project a rewarding and pleasant experience.

Heidelberg,
August 1996

Contents

Introduction: Legitimacy and Conflict in South Asia

SUBRATA K. MITRA

Whether one looks at the horrors of civil war in Bosnia, communal conflict in Gujarat or insurgency in Punjab and Kashmir, the potential for disorder and outbreak of anarchy has emerged as the most important challenge to civilized human existence in the contemporary world. The tragic costs of violent conflict[1] necessarily points towards the salience of political order as a precondition for constitutional and concerted attempts to solve the outstanding issues of poverty, hunger and disease. This is not specific to any particular society but applies equally within any culture. Not surprisingly, political order has excited the attention of philosophers and analysts from Thomas Hobbes to Samuel P. Huntington, of statesmen from Curzon and Churchill to Patel, the 'Iron Man' of post-independence India, and aspiring advisors to princes like Plato, Machiavelli and the contemporary consultants in conflict management. Whatever one's ideological position or professional situation, the tragic costs of conflict in South Asia and in other regions of the world are eminently evident to all. This makes it imperative for both specialists of comparative politics and policy makers, from South Asia and those from the Western world who take a scientific, human or commercial interest in that region, containing a fourth of mankind, to join hands in finding an acceptable set of policies that will contribute to order and legitimacy.

The Problem Stated

Political order and challenge to legitimacy can be operationalised in terms of governance - measured by empirical indicators like violent deaths, criminal damage to property, riots, lawlessness, mandays lost in illegal strikes and other variables specific to particular political systems. However, as a conceptual variable, governance has the paradoxical attribute of being visible by its absence rather than its presence. In a world attuned to the horrors of Bosnia and Somalia, it is the outbreak of disorder rather than the patient everyday grind of the wheels of government which hits the headlines. The abrupt decline of governance thus comes virtually unannounced, with little advance warning to its tragic victims. But decline of governance is in fact neither irreversible nor inexorable. It is

1 Michael Cranna (ed.), *The True Cost of Conflict* (London: Saferworld, 1994).

the ignorance of the process that leads to the breakdown of order which makes it difficult for lawmakers and administrators to anticipate it and arrest the downward slide of the political system with timely intervention.

Neglected during the post-war decade of modernization and maligned in its stormy aftermath as an ideological façade for authoritarian rule, governance has emerged during the past decade as the new frontier of research on developing countries. However, scientific interest in order and legitimacy is encouraging because it draws attention to a problem of great political and theoretical significance. However, the tendency to identify governance as a problem typical of developing countries smacks faintly of a neo-Orientalist identification of non-Western cultures with the problem of governability. Governance can come to an abrupt end in places as different as Los Angeles, Bosnia, or Bihar for reasons that have very little to do with their native culture but a lot with their political structures and processes.

The objective of the conference was to analyse the problem of effective governance and legitimacy at the level of general and comparative theory, applied to the contemporary politics of South Asia. These issues were discussed on the basis of papers on theoretical exploration of the causes of political conflict that lead to the decline of legitimacy and the empirical investigation of cases from India, Pakistan, Bangladesh, Nepal and Sri Lanka.

State of the Art

In view of its importance, the theme of political order and conflict in societies in the process of rapid change has drawn the attention of several scholars. A quick overview shows that the literature consists of general contributions to the field such as those of Samuel P. Huntington, *Political Order in Changing Societies* (New Haven and London: Yale University Press, 1968) and Ted Robert Gurr, *Why Men Rebel* (Princeton: Princeton University Press, 1974) as well as a whole subfield of studies more directly concerned with South Asian experience. Important among those are Jyotirindra Dasgupta, *Language Conflict and National Development - Group Politics and National Language Policy in India* (Berkeley, Los Angeles and London: University of California Press, 1970), Atul Kohli, *Democracy and Discontent, India's Growing Crisis of Governability* (Cambridge: CUP, 1990), James Manor, *Power, Poverty and Poison - Disaster and Response in an Indian City* (New Delhi, Thousand Oaks and London: Sage Publications, 1993), Subrata K. Mitra, *Power, Protest and Participation - Local Elites and the Politics of Development in India* (London and New York: Routledge, 1992), Robert W. Jackman, *Power with-*

out Force - The Political Capacity of Nation-States (Ann Arbor: University of Michigan Press, 1993), Francine Frankel and M.S.A. Rao (eds.), *Dominance and State Power in Modern India: Decline of a Social Order, Vols. I/II* (Oxford: Oxford University Press, 1990), Paul Brass, *Ethnicity and Nationalism: Theory and Comparison* (New Delhi: Sage, 1991).

While these earlier studies have opened up new areas of research and made new information previously not accessible or not theorized available to the scientific community, in reading them one comes across a form of 'developmentalism' which seeks to explain non-Western experience on the basis of models derived from the historical experience of social and economic change in Europe. These historical experiences are then prescribed as normative for the purposes of nation-building and state formation in non-Western societies. However, when the political facts of non-Western societies prove to be impossible to explain away in terms of these models based on modernization theories, some theorists take recourse to a 'culturist' approach where the problems of disorder, conflict or underdevelopment are accounted for in terms of the innate cultural attributes of the country. This form of Orientalist scholarship is criticized by Edward Said (1979) and Ronald Inden (1990).[2]

Writers on the issue of political order have derived their reference points from a variety of sources, the most importants of which is Huntington's *Political Order in Changing Societies*. In drawing their inferences by basing themselves on institutions as the key marker, writers on governance unwittingly subject themselves to the same flaw that limits the utility of Huntington's model. For order is expected, rather wistfully, to emerge as an end state of a teleological process referred to as modernization. Failing this natural outcome (here modernization theory turns abruptly from an explanation of reality to a normative prescription), order is expected to be generated through requisite doses of authoritarian rule and, if need be, a restriction of participation (see Huntington, p. 55).

One consequence of this heavy reliance on Huntington's equation of institutions with order is the reification of institutions, which prevents them from being problematised with reference to the political context of societies in which they are ensconed. Those like Atul Kohli (1990) who point out 'deinstitutionalisation' as the main cause of the decline of orderly rule in India are neither able to account for the reasons of the decline of institutions except in a rather contingent fashion, nor to conjecture about the policy alternative that could restore a state of orderly rule.

[2] For an extended criticism, see Subrata K. Mitra, 'Flawed Paradigms: Some "Western" Representations of Indian Politics', in T.V. Sathyamurthy (ed.), *State and Nation in the Context of Social Change, Vol. 1* (Delhi: OUP, 1994), pp. 219-245.

On the basis of contemporary political analysis and application of the theory of games (Mitra, 1978) we assert that a high level of governance is possible when the rules of transaction are explicit, clear and generally obeyed. This, in turn, is possible when the alternative to rule bound behaviour is 'costly' in terms of its unpleasant implications for the actor. In a well governed society the managers of law and order see to it that social and economic reform make it unnecessary (or costly) for ordinary people to break the law. When they do, they are brought back to the ambit of rule bound behaviour by the near certainty of prohibitive penalties. Above all, the managers of law and order ensure that the other important reason for rule breaking - political acts and rules which offend one's notions of the sacred and non-negotiable for example - are removed through constitutional protection of sacred symbols. The conjectures arising out of these preliminary explorations are presented in greater detail in my chapter in this book.

Some Recent Conferences

The salience of legitimacy and conflict as a theme of research can be seen from several recent academic symposia on the issues of conflict, deriving out of ethnicity, class and identity in non-Western societies. Since the results arrived at in these conferences are important for the field as a whole, we thought it would be useful to inform the scientific community about their deliberations. Important among these conferences were the symposium on 'Changing Identities - The Transformation of Asian and African Societies under Colonialism', held at the Centre for Modern Oriental Studies, Berlin, 21-22 Oct. 1993; the symposium on 'Ethnicity and Identity' organized by the South Asia Centre of University of California, Berkeley in May 1994 and more recently, the symposium 'North-South Dialogue - Prospects for Development in India and Pakistan' organized by EUCIS, 5.-7. Oct. 1994 at Starnberg, Germany. While these important conferences have generated a useful body of information, three salient points need to be made regarding the nature of their deliberations:

(a) The conferences tended to emphasize the causes of conflict but not on analytical tools that could point towards a solution.

(b) An attempt was seldom made to establish a link between general theory of social change and specific policies meant for the orderly resolution of conflict.

(c) South Asia was often thought of as unique in its cultural context and, therefore, no attempt was made to undertake comparison across time and space and link South Asia with other regional conflicts through comparative politics.

The Heidelberg Symposium intended to bring the insights gained from our knowledge of the state of the art to a well focussed discussion of the subject of legitimacy and conflict, particularly by emphasizing the issue of governance and the impact of domestic and external politics on this issue. Naturally, this important issue needed to be addressed by a cohesive yet comprehensive group drawing on both the specialist as well as the generalist. These objectives could be specified in terms of the following questions:

Some Important Scientific Questions:

1. What are the cultural meanings and legal/institutional attributes of legitimacy in South Asia?

2. Why did India, compared to her neighbours and to the majority of post-colonial states, succeed in achieving a high level of governance following independence from British colonial rule? Why has this record of high governance registered a sharp decline in some parts of India during the past two decades?

3. How does the organization of the civil service affect the maintenance of law and order?

4. How do policies of economic reform affect law and order?

5. How do social mobilization and political organization on the basis of caste, language, religion, tribe and region affect political order?

6. Is military rule an effective solution to the problem of political order during the transition from agrarian to industrial society?

7. How does the confluence of domestic politics and regional conflict affect political order in South Asia?

Legitimacy, Governance and Rational Public Policy

The overall objective of the symposium was, thus, to examine the problem of social disorder and political conflict in South Asia not as symptomatic of its regional peculiarity or of its cultural uniqueness but, essentially as a political problem, brought about by forces of social and economic transition and political conjuncture, responding to a specific set of objective conditions. Our intention, therefore, was not merely to describe the condition of social disorder and political conflict in South Asia (without, necessarily, undermining the importance of accurate empirical description which is a necessary condition of any scientific research) but to draw on South Asian conditions to contribute to general social and political theory.

However, while our primary goal is scientific and theoretical (because, after all, we are a group of social scientists committed to research at the highest level on South Asian society, economy and the political process), we do not ignore the responsibility of the scientist towards the material welfare and security of people in everyday life. Society sustains scientific research by making resources available to the scientist. We believe, in return, scientists should make scientific knowledge of the causes of political conflict and conflict resolution available to policy makers and those in charge of the management of law and order. The result of this co-operation between the scientist and actors from the 'real world', we hope, will contribute to rational policies and action, and, the minimization of human suffering. The presence of policy makers and executives (who were invited to make brief presentations during the plenary session) also injected a sense of social realism without which scientific research runs the risk of becoming too abstract and lose the link with reality. Scientific research, on the other hand, is also a useful challenge for the policy makers whose normal tendency is to concentrate on the contingent and the *ad hoc* to the detriment of the long term and the comprehensive picture of reality. In uniting the social scientist and the policy maker on a common endeavour we expected to achieve a synthesis of theory and practice, to their common good. We hope some of our efforts will contribute towards the achievement of cooperation and just and humane governance in South Asia.

Conflict as a Challenge to Legitimacy: A Historical Perspective

DIETMAR ROTHERMUND

Conflict as a Challenge to Legitimacy

When discussing our theme we should state at the outset that we are concerned with the legitimacy of political power, that is the allegiance to a government which is based on the consent of the respective subjects or citizens. In juxtaposing legitimacy and conflict we indicate that we are interested only in a particular kind of conflict which arises from a challenge to 'legitimate' government. The challenger contests the legitimacy of the respective government and deprives it of his allegiance and consent. André Wink has tried to show that the term *fitna* is generally applicable to this kind of conflict from the disruption of the Islamic *umma* to the challenge posed by the Marathas to the Mughals and to the Mutiny of 1857.[1] The meaning of the term is a broad one, it could refer to schism, secession, sedition, i.e. to all attitudes or actions implying the rejection of legitimate authority. This broad meaning enables Wink to use *fitna* as a general category, he claims that it is *fitna* rather than legitimacy which is the pervading principle of political life because it embodies the particular as against the universal. *Islam*, the submission to the will of God, and *dharma*, the principle which upholds everything, are universal ideas which can only justify legitimacy in general, but not as applied to the actual control of a particular state. In giving too much prominence to *fitna* , Wink may have overstated his case. But it is a useful term for the kind of conflict with which we are concerned here. It highlights the old problem of the maintenance of political authority when it is challenged by forces opposed to it.

Ancient Indian political doctrine has dealt with this problem by obliging the ideal king to follow *dharma*, whereas for the actual preservation of the power of a particular king it has provided very pragmatic advice.[2] It equated *rajadharma* with *dandaniti*. In its literal meaning *danda* refers to a stick as the symbol of coercion, it could also refer to the army or, figuratively, even to the king himself. In keeping with this brutal realism, the very explanation of the rise of kingship was explained in terms of the *matsyanyaya*, i.e., without the authority of a king people

1 André Wink, *Land and Sovereignty in India, Agrarian Society and Politics under the Eighteenth Century Maratha Svarajya* (Cambridge, 1986).

2 R.P.Kangle, *The Kautiliya Arthasastra, 3 Vols.* (Bombay, 1962); see also Pandurang V. Kane, *History of Dharmasastra, Vol. III* (Pune, 1946).

would kill each other like the big fish which swallow the small ones. In Europe this theory found a belated echo in the teachings of Hobbes. It is presumed that this notion just like the Indian zero may have travelled to the West via several intermediaries.[3] The legitimacy of political power in a particular state is thus justified in a purely pragmatic way. Mao Tse Tung's famous dictum: 'Power flows from the barrel of a gun' is a perfect reflection of this type of legitimacy.

If we accept this we could stop here and analyse the relationship between legitimacy and conflict in terms of the mechanisms of coercion which help to suppress conflict and thus secure the legitimacy of the powers that be. But this would not be as realistic as it appears to be. Effective suppression is not achieved or maintained very easily. Moreover, once military power is seen as the only source of legitimacy, usurpers are practically invited to overthrow the established regime and replace it with their own power. Usurpers, however, are often most concerned with the aquisition of legitimacy by other means than only brute force. Indian history provides many examples of ursurpers who were very active in this way. In order to maintain their position they appealed to the religious belief of their subjects, built temples, advertised their measures of public welfare, etc.

The legitimacy of the king also depended on his resourcefulness with regard to conflict resolution within his realm. There is a virtuous circle in this respect. Those who are in conflict with each other will turn to the king to settle the issue because they recognize his legitimacy. The king reconfirms his legitimacy by promoting evenhanded justice. A case in point is the verdict of Bukka, the ruler of Vijayanagar, who was approached by Jains and Bhaktas (Shrivaishnavas) to settle a conflict which had arisen because both of them claimed to follow the right spiritual path. Bukka's verdict was that both their faiths were equally good.[4] Jains were an important community in Bukka's realm and he could not afford to alienate them. His verdict was wise and pragmatic, inscribed in stone it reminded the people of the conflict and its resolution and also served as a testimony of royal legitimacy. Legitimation is a process rather than a settled fact. Rebels, the very embodiment of *fitna*, were also aware of the need to acquire legitimacy. Usually they were not satisfied with a purely military challenge but contested the legitimacy of the powers that be by appealing to values held by the people. The 'mutineers' of 1857 were no exception to this rule. Their proclamations show this. Of course, they

[3] For the reference to the transfer of the idea of the *matsyanyaya* to Europe see J. Duncan M. Derrett, 'Social and Political Thought and Institutions', in A. L. Basham (ed.), *A Cultural History of India* (Oxford, 1975), p. 140.

[4] The inscription (AD 1368, in Kannada) is published in EC, IX ma 18 Vijayanagara Inscriptions. I owe the reference to an unpublished thesis on Penugonda by Prof. Vasantha, Anantapur.

rather wanted to restore Mughal rule than promote modern nationalism. Modern nationalists as rebels against British rule had to rely on different principles when trying to prove the legitimacy of their claims.

Indian Nationalists *versus* the British Raj

The contest between Indian nationalists and the British Raj provides a particularly interesting case study for our theme. To the British colonial rulers these nationalists were representatives of *fitna* (schism/sedition). *Danda* was firmly in the hands of the British who could even survive the challenge of the Mutiny. The nationalists had no military potential and yet ever since the proclamation of Queen Victoria which was later on followed by the Imperial *Darbar,* the British tried to stake a claim for the legitimacy of their rule beyond the display of brute force. In this they wanted to emulate the Mughal empire which had also relied on a kind of imperial charisma and not only on the superiority of the Mughal field artillery. In their initial constitutional reforms the British colonial rulers aimed at a *darbar* - style of politics rather than at introducing the kind of parliamentarism which they practised at home. In contesting the legitimacy of British colonial rule the Indian nationalists appealed to the values which had been introduced by British education in India. The concepts of the sovereignty of the people, of territorial representation, of parliamentary democracy and self-government were held against British rule in India which was called 'Un-British' by a leading liberal nationalist.[5]

In contesting the legitimacy of British rule the nationalists differed in their aims and their ideology. There emerged a radical wing of national revolutionaries who claimed that India had always been a nation and only needed to throw off the shackles of foreign rule in order to come into its own again. But there were also the liberal nationalists who argued that India was a nation in the making and needed the institutional framework introduced by the British in order to achieve its goal.[6] The ideological differences between these two strands of nationalism were very deep and are still significant today. The national revolutionaries did not stop at claiming that India had always been a nation, they tried to build national solidarity by reinterpreting the Hindu tradition. Thereby they necessarily left out the Muslims who were later on led to believe that there were two nations in India. The liberals on the other hand were very much aware of this problem and wanted to build a secular state based on a composite nation. These early controversies between 'Extremists' and

5 Dadabhai Naoroji, *Poverty and Un-British Rule in India* (London, 1901).

6 For an analysis of the different strands of Indian nationalism see Dietmar Rothermund, *Die politische Willensbildung in Indien, 1900-1960* (Wiesbaden, 1965).

'Moderates' receded into the background when Mahatma Gandhi took over the leadership of the national movement after the First World War. Gandhi was not a liberal. He did not believe in the beneficial effects of British institutions for India's political development, but he also disapproved of the national revolutionaries' flirting with terrorism. He contested the legitimacy of British rule by pointing out that this rule was not based on the consent of the Indian people who could prove this point by withholding all cooperation from the British in India. In this he was disappointed because a large scale demonstration of non-cooperation could not be achieved. But he was successful in defining the contest and broadening the social base of the national movement. John Rawls has coined the term 'overlapping consensus' with regard to the construction of solidarity in plural societies.[7] This is exactly what Gandhi tried to achieve first in South Africa and then in India.

The British colonial rulers took Gandhi's challenge seriously. They knew about their precarious position, but they were also aware of the fact that there were strata of the Indian people which had not been touched by Gandhi's message and could be rallied to support the British. The British tried to prevent the emergence of an 'overlapping consensus' among the elements of India's plural society. The Muslims, the princes, the peasants and the Untouchables were suitable targets for a policy of 'divide and rule'. Gandhi tried to counteract this in various ways. He joined the cause of the Muslims in the Khilafat movement, he restricted the national movement to British India in order not to drive the princes into the arms of the British, he helped the peasants by taking up their causes and he finally concentrated on fighting against the injustice done to the Untouchables. He could not be successful in all these spheres. The Khilafat movement got into a dead alley, the majority of the princes rallied around the British anyhow, the peasants benefited from agrarian legislation introduced by the British, and the Untouchables produced their own leaders who were jealous of Gandhi's attempts at adopting their clients.

In the late 1920s it seemed as if Gandhi was a spent force. But then the Salt March of 1930, a symbolic revolution which Gandhi staged with great skill, signified his political comeback. By coincidence the peasants were driven into the arms of the Congress by the impact of the Great Depression.[8] Gandhi's earlier work for the peasants now paid rich political dividends. His 'Epic Fast' of 1932 then created an awareness among Hindus of the plight of the Untouchables. In this way Gandhi brought about that the majority of the Untouchables remained in the Congress fold. To that extent Gandhi was successful in building a broadbased national party, however, he did not think of the Congress as a party but

7 John Rawls, *Political Liberalism* (New York, 1993), p. 150ff.

8 Dietmar Rothermund, *India in the Great Depression, 1929-1939* (New Delhi, 1992).

rather as a national parliament which should replace the artificial institutions which were set up by the British with a view to give legitimacy to their rule. Nehru's dictum: 'There are only two parties in India, the Congress and the British' reflected this contest of legitimacy. But Jinnah, the leader of the Muslim League to whom he addressed these words, could only take it as a confirmation of his fears that there would be no place for him and his party in an undivided India. Jinnah had started his political career as a liberal nationalist. He achieved his greatest success along this line with the Congress-League Pact of 1916. He was then pushed aside by Gandhi who regarded him as an outmoded elite politician. Jinnah resented this and criticised Gandhi's participation in the Khilafat movement. He saw that this movement was a manifestation of Islamic fundamentalism with which he did not want to be associated. Jinnah then appeared to be exactly the type of isolated elite politician which Gandhi had seen in him. In order to overcome this isolation, Jinnah had to strive for Islamic legitimacy and this is what he did in subsequent years.[9] He was driven to follow *fitna* with regard to the national movement - and the British welcomed this.

The Partition of India, Hindu Nationalism and Secularism

The partition of India was the final *fitna* (schism/sedition) which emerged from this contest of legitimacy. Unfortunately it did not provide a solution of the problem from which it arose. It led to the establishment of a two-winged Pakistan which made a further *fitna* inevitable. It gave rise to a permanent confrontation between India and Pakistan and it left India with a Muslim minority which was large enough to demand special attention but not big enough to stake a claim of its own in the Indian political system. Moreover, by the very logic of partition which separated the Muslim majority regions from India, the Muslims of India were bound to be a diaspora community which had no strongholds anywhere.

In this context the old controversies between 'Extremists' and 'Moderates', i.e. between Hindu-nationalism and a secular nation in the making re-emerged once more. Initially these controversies were muted by the stability of the Congress system which was supported by the linkage of state and federal elections and the peculiar working of the majority election law which did not produce a two party system in India but reinforced the central role of the Congress party flanked by opposition parties which were bitterly opposed to each other. But after Indira Gandhi delinked state and federal elections in 1971 and turned the federal elections into a

9 Stanley Wolpert, *Jinnah of Pakistan* (New York, Oxford, 1984).

populist plebiscite, the Congress system has never been the same again.[10] The plebiscitarian character of national elections has led to periodical swings of the pendulum for or against the Congress. Plebiscitarian campaigns shift the focus of legitimacy from a system to a person. Indira's campaign slogan 'Strengthen my hands' illustrated this very well. By winning the election she would regain legitimacy and confer it upon her party and her government.

Plebiscitarian campaigning has in recent years impaired the secular ideology of the Congress. The kind of 'overlapping consensus' which Mahatma Gandhi wanted to establish has been replaced by a personal equation. It is the leader who stands for the consensus, and this makes the consensus as vulnerable as the leader. But plebiscitarianism also had given the Congress a new lease of life. It has not given up its claim to represent the nation as a whole. Accordingly it would not think of joining a coalition with other parties. These parties on the other hand contest the legitimacy of Congress rule and try to replace it. This has led to the phenomenon of minority governments in recent years. The future of the Indian political system is not as clear as past experience seems to warrant. The smooth working of the democratic system seemed to indicate that this system as such rather than the Congress system had acquired legitimacy and would survive the transfer of power from one party to another. But in fact there has not been a real transfer of power so far but rather a sequence of *fitna* and coalescence. There has not yet been a Prime Minister of India who had not originally emerged from the ranks of the Congress. The democratic process embodies a management of conflict within a legitimate political system whose legitimacy is actually derived from this capacity.

The impressive record of parliamentary democracy in India has masked the viceregal heritage which comes into the limelight only occasionally when state governments which are not in the good books of the central government are eliminated by means of 'President's Rule'. Indian federalism which was introduced by the British in the course of the 'devolution of power' could be controlled by the Viceroy in this way. In independent India this device has been used to defend the Congress system. After her victory in 1971 Indira Gandhi argued that state governments which were run by parties other than the Congress had lost their legitimacy and should therefore be toppled. This impaired the legitimacy of federalism and damaged the capacity of the political system to survive transfers of power under adverse circumstances. There are many voices in India demanding the abolition of 'President's Rule', but so far no central government has dared to take this step. There are always imminent dangers which seem to require the retention of this viceregal *danda*.

[10] Paul Brass, *The Politics of India since Independence*, *The New Cambridge History of India*, Vol. IV.1 (Cambridge: Cambridge University Press, 1990), p. 83.

The 'Legitimacy' of Military Rule: Pakistan and Bangladesh

Whereas the viceregal heritage is restricted to 'President's Rule' in India, it formed the very basis of Pakistan, because of Jinnah's decision to opt for the post of Governor General rather than that of the Prime Minister of the new state. He had several reasons for this decision. First of all he did not like the idea of having Lord Mountbatten as joint Governor General of both India and Pakistan in the period of transition. In view of his terminal illness, Jinnah knew that his days were numbered. Therefore he wanted to secure the foundation of his new state in the short time that was still left to him. But the foundation which he created in this way was that of a presidential system based on the support of the army and the bureaucracy rather than a parliamentary democracy supported by the Muslim League. Therefore the Muslim League which had never been a very strong party anyhow withered away and was also not replaced by any other democratic party in the first decades of the new state. The presidential system without adequate party support could live on quite comfortably as it was in control of the levers of viceregal power. But it finally paved the way for military rule, because in times of trouble the army remained the only 'legitimate' representative of the nation.[11]

In keeping with this development military coups in South Asia have invariably been executed by the respective Chief of Staff. They were never products of *fitna* but could always claim to act in support of law and order. The typical military coup is led by colonels as they are in command of troops which are required if one wants to usurp power. In Pakistan and later on in Bangladesh only generals led successful coups. They then secured legitimacy as Chief Martial Law Administrators and proclaimed that they would only stay on until elections could be held. Subsequently they either adopted a party or founded a new one so as to be able to become presidents and thus acquire quasi-democratic legitimacy. It is only in recent years that political parties have emerged which seem to be able to challenge this alternating current of presidential and military regimes in Pakistan and Bangladesh. But it would be too early to predict that military rule will not raise its head again in these countries.

[11] Ayesha Jalal, *Pakistan. The State of Martial Rule: The Origins of Pakistan's Political Economy of Defence* (Cambridge, 1990).

The Patterns of Legitimacy and Conflict in Nepal and Sri Lanka

The remaining two states which have to be discussed here did not share the British Indian heritage. Nepal was a buffer state which the British did not subject to their direct rule, but its political system was nevertheless deeply influenced by its powerful neighbour. Sri Lanka was a British colony, but its political development differed from that of British India. For instance, Sri Lanka had universal adult franchise as early as 1931 when India still had to live with a severely restricted franchise. Furthermore, there was no freedom movement in Sri Lanka whose politics were dominated by a tiny elite inspite of universal franchise, because the political process was hedged in by all kinds of provisions. Independence was granted to Sri Lanka as a sequel to the transfer of power in India. Political conflicts emerged with a considerable time lag, but when they did come up they proved to be very virulent.

In Nepal the monarchy at first seemed to be rather 'progressive', providing legitimacy and support to a democratic process which was also favoured by India. This was due to the fact that the Nepalese monarchy owed its restoration to India, whereas the British had supported a dynasty of 'Prime Ministers' who had ruled Nepal like the *shôgun* had ruled Japan before the Meiji restoration. But the 'cohabitation' of monarchy and democracy was too good to be true. King Mahendra replaced parliamentary democracy with a type of 'guided democracy' which was also practised in Pakistan and Indonesia at that time. He recovered his *danda* in this way and could suppress any kind of *fitna.* But this system did not survive very long after his death. His son had to face revolts and make concessions to the extent of even swearing in a Communist government. It will be very interesting to watch the further political development of Nepal after this surprising turn of events.

Sri Lanka's political experience followed a very different pattern. It was initially in the hands of a Congress-type party, the United National Party (UNP), whose legitimacy was then successfully contested by the Sri Lanka Freedom Party (SLFP) under Solomon Bandaranaike who was himself a member of the old political elite but challenged the power of his peers by rallying the Sinhalese Buddhist electorate. In this he could draw on the support of the 'swabhasha educated', i.e. those who had attended Buddhist schools where Sinhalese was the medium of instruction and who were therefore excluded from careers which were open only to the English educated. This case was a classical example for a contest of legitimacy. The campaign for Sinhala as the only national language and for renaming Ceylon Sri Lanka were symptoms of this fundamental challenge to the prevailing political system. A tragic confirmation of the dynamism of this challenge was Bandaranaike's assassination by a Buddhist monk who thought that the Prime Minister was not going far enough towards a fullfledged Buddhist revolution. On the other hand he had gone far enough in alienating the Tamil minority of Sri Lanka.[12]

In subsequent years there seemed to be a surprising restoration of the legitimacy of the democratic process. UNP and SLFP took turns in forming stable governments, the transfers of power were peaceful. A serious *fitna*, the rebellion of a terrorist youth movement, was succesfully suppressed. But the Tamil minority was no longer part of this democratic process which included only the Sinhalese majority. This majority was less and less inclined to make any concessions to the minority. In this way those political representatives of the minority who still believed in the democratic process were more and more isolated while the radical advocates of secession rose to prominence and contested the legitimacy of the government by violent means. In this they were very successful, because they control a territory of their own in which their guerilla tactics make them practically invincible by outside military forces whether they are Sinhalese or Indian, as the frustration of the huge Indian Peace Keeping Force (IPKF) has shown.

The sending of the IPKF to Sri Lanka was by no means an exercise in political altruism. South Asian governments are in general not averse to encouraging *fitna* in their neighbour's territory if they can hope to derive some political advantage from this. Already Kautilya's *Arthashastra* contains a great deal of practical advice of this kind. But when the chips are down, all South Asian governments are *status quo*-powers and do not like to set examples which may encourage those who wish to contest their own legitimacy.

Conclusion: The Hidden Normative Agenda

In this short historical survey of the political experience of South Asian nations I have deliberately refrained from constructing a theoretical framework into which all this would have to fit and which would then also permit normative prescriptions. Nevertheless there is a hidden normative agenda and an attempt will be made to spell it out in these concluding lines.

There is an implict warning against all tendencies to restrict legitimacy to one particular party or to the guardians of order as defined in their own narrow terms, because this necessarily diminishes the potential of conflict resolution as political conflicts inevitably become contests of

12 Kingsley de Silva, *Managing Ethnic Tensions in Multi-Ethnic Societies. Sri Lanka 1880-1985* (Lanham, London, 1986).

legitimacy which may finally end in a violent showdown. Therefore the democratic process of conflict resolution itself must acquire legitimacy and must be respected for this. Politicians must be statesmen in order to act accordingly, they must resist the temptation of equating their own position with legitimacy and all challenges to this position as *fitna* which must be suppressed. There are, of course, limits to this approach to conflict resolution. The resistance to colonial rule or to dictatorship are instances where a contest of legitimacy is inevitable, but even in such a contest non-violent methods should be preferred to violent ones.

Legitimacy, Governance and Political Institutions in India after Independence[1]

SUBRATA K. MITRA

Conflict of interests and political competition following from it are characteristic of all political systems. The issue of legitimacy arises only when the values and rules that underpin the political system are contested. Despite the fact that problems of legitimacy very often characterize politics in post-colonial societies the issue is by no means unique to any culture or geographic area. It is of course a fact of contemporary political life that one is likely to come across the problem of political conflict over legitimacy more often in non-western societies, the successor states of the Soviet Union and Eastern Europe than in stable western democracies. But this has more to do with the rapid structural change that non-western societies are going through more than their innate or unique cultural attributes. Though this chapter draws its empirical reference mostly from India, its goal is to formulate a general model to verify this assertion. It does so by drawing on the interaction of legitimacy, governance and political institutions.

Many students of Indian politics regard the 1950s as a period of high legitimacy. Its sharp decline first manifested itself in the mid-1960s radical movements, communal violence, riots and violent political agitations. The Emergency of 1975-77 was a grim reminder of the fact that decline of legitimacy may be caused from above just as well as from below. The sharp variation of legitimacy has continued through the intervening period. The demolition of the Babri mosque of Ayodhya in 1992 and continued insurgency in Kashmir are urgent reminders of the challenges to legitimacy that haunts the politics of India today. The chapter addresses this broad theme, with rules and institutions as the main focus of analysis.

Rules, Institutions and Governance

Since rules are crucial for our understanding of spatio-temporal variation in legitimacy, it is important to have a clear definition of this concept at the outset. Rules, whether formal and legally binding or customary, with social sanction behind them, are, 'humanly devised constraints that shape

[1] I would like to thank the Nuffield Foundation (London) for a personal research grant which has been helpful in undertaking the research on which this chapter is based and Astrid Rüdiger for her comments on an earlier draft of this chapter.

human interaction'.[2] Rules have to be necessarily clear (or, at least equipped with rule interpreters whose job it is to clarify the rule for the benefit of those bound by it), consistent (i.e. invariant in time unless amended as prescribed under the constitution), universal (i.e. interpersonally non-discriminatory and applicable in a similar way to all who are equally placed) and effective (i.e., with a cost attached to non-compliance and a reasonable guarantee that these prices would be exacted should the issue be put to test). Institutions are clusters of rules, bound together in the minds of those who have to live by them. Seen in this light, institutions are more than 'recurrent patterns of behaviour'[3], for they exist not only in terms of their external appurtenances, but also in terms of their collective logic in the minds of those affected by them. The Indian Parliament is not only the elegant building in which the sessions of the Lok Sabha and Rajya Sabha take place or the uniformed servants of the state who conduct the many routine tasks associated with it; it is that, and the rules that govern conduct of parliamentary business. These are seen by the Members of Parliament and those who elect them as the main instrument of holding the government accountable to the people. The rules are the binding force that underpin an institution. Rules of functioning institutions become a part of everyday political life. As the experience of the defeat of Indira Gandhi's Congress party by the Janata coalition in 1977 showed, the supersession of the rules by any person or power can mobilize people who are normally divided on partisan lines to unite in their defence.

Now that we have clarified what rules and institutions are, let us look at what institutions do. Following North, besides constraining behaviour, institutions 'structure incentives in human exchanges, whether political, social or economic'.[4] They help measure what is valuable (i.e. the 'cost' of things and values in interpersonally meaningful ways); they protect rights and police and enforce agreements. They reduce uncertainty by providing predictability to everyday life. They are a guide to human interaction, so that when we wish to greet friends on the street, drive an automobile, buy oranges, borrow money, form a business, bury our dead, or whatever, we know (or can learn easily) how to perform these tasks'.[5]

[2] Douglass C. North, *Institutions, Institutional Change and Economic Performance* (Cambridge: CUP, 1990), p. 4.

[3] Samuel P. Huntington, *Political Order in Changing Societies* (New Haven: Yale University Press, 1969), emphasizes the central role of institutions in maintaining orderly governance. See ibid., p. 55, for the lawlike specification of the relationship between institutionalization and political stability.

[4] North, pp. 4-5.

[5] North, p. 3.

Legitimacy Defined

In its broadest sense, a society can be said to experience a high level of legitimacy when its rules are not explicitly rejected by any major social group. The decline of legitimacy is marked by political disorder. Once shorn of its moral imperative, political authority becomes mere force, which encourages men to behave in a manner which has the potential for reducing civilized society to a state of nature, where life becomes 'solitary, poor, nasty, brutish and short'. An orderly society is characterized by transactions based on rules that are clear and explicit to the actors, consistent across the political system and generally obeyed in practice. Orderly behaviour is a basic condition of organized political life. Its absence is marked by social chaos and political anarchy. When people cease to behave in a rule oriented manner, the consequences manifest themselves in the form of social pathologies ranging between electoral fraud, tax dodging, corruption and industrial unrest, to the breakdown of law and order, mass political violence and riots causing loss of life and property. The fabric of social life is torn apart in extreme cases of the decline of governance and life is reduced to the chaotic situation of a 'war of each against all'.[6]

Historical studies of the period of rapid social change in stable Western democracies are replete with spells of political disorder and disruption of social and economic life. Though in their contemporary form political systems in Western societies are not entirely immune from occasional spells of civic disorder, as a whole their level of governance provides a sharp contrast to most non-Western societies. However, riots, lawlessness and erosion of institutions, in the new states of Asia, Africa and Latin America has found their equivalence in Europe's own backyard following the end of communist regimes. While drawing many of its theoretical insights from a broad range of countries, this chapter concentrates on India for the detailed empirical verifications of an abstract general model of governance.

India presents the student of governance with a double puzzle. In the first place, India is virtually alone among post-colonial states to have sustained an orderly political process for over four decades following independence. That outstanding record, however, looks increasingly unsteady. The consequences of a precipitous decline in governance underpin much of the new writing on Indian politics. The leitmotif of practically all the major texts on Indian politics point towards the same question: Is India 'governable'?[7]

[6] The conceptual similarity between Hobbes's 'state of nature' from which these expressions are taken and *matsyanyaya* - the classic Indian concept which depicts a situation where big fish eat little fish - needs to be explored further. See Dietmar Rothermund, 'Legitimacy and Conflict in South Asia: A Historical Perspective', in this volume.

[7] The issue of India's 'governability' raised most recently by Kohli (1990) has a respectable genealogy. The distinction I would like to maintain between my use of governance and Kohli's governability is deliberate. The latter entails an implicit cultural baggage of European liberal

The question is inspired by armed secessionist movements in Punjab, Kashmir and India's North-East, and, violent communal conflict in parts of India where such incidents used to be relatively rare. The scale and intensity of these challenges to the authority of the state stand in sharp contrast to the record of the two decades since independence. During those early, trying years of the new republic, dominated by Jawaharlal Nehru, India stood as a beacon of orderly government to the vast majority of post-colonial states. In sharp contrast to this image, through the 1980s, the overall picture has been steadily replaced by the scenes of frenzied mobs taking the law to their own hands, a development that questions the images of orderly rule and democratic resilience of India.[8] Since some of these problems are thought of as cultural difficulties in sustaining rule bound governance, the chapter examines this question by first drawing on the cross-cultural experience of governance and then analyzing it on the basis of a formal model.

Is Governance a *Cultural* Problem?

A theoretical exploration of legitimacy needs to be based on the assumption that governance is a general phenomenon, related to factors like rules and legitimacy that are themselves general as well. The opposite position would suggest that governance and its underlying causes are unique attributes of European societies and culture. The latter view has much wider currency than one might suspect at the outset. In that, it is regularly reinforced by images of rampaging crowds and breakdown of political order in non-western countries and within peripheral regions and ethnic groups within stable, western democracies. Once again, while one can find many examples of this tendency to infer cultural causation from the correlation of the low levels of governance with non-western societies and non-European

---

democracy. As I see their argument, Western societies are 'governable' as they are; others need to acquire the institutions of governable societies for them to be able to enjoy the benefits of lawful and orderly rule. I would like to think of governance as a potential attribute of all societies. Changing environments require changes in the rules of government institutions. These changes in order, to be legitimate, need to be drawn from the political tradition of the given society. The point will be discussed further later in this essay.

[8] With the publication of Nehru's letter to Indira Gandhi, we are better situated now to evaluate the glorious years during which Nehru could do no wrong. A full evaluation would require further research on Nehru's private correspondence, but what is allready available is quite suggestive. Thus, Indira Gandhi, before she was inducted to high politics and gave full expression of her own authoritarian temperament, wrote to her father in a fit of outrage at attempts of a provincial government to take over the management of a newspaper. 'If you don't call (the Chief Minister) to order for interfering ... in the business of a newspaper, then please stop...talking about democracy and the freedom of the press in India. With all our other ills let us not also have hypocricy.' See Firdaus Kanga's review of Sonia Gandhi (ed.), 'Two Alone, Two Together, Letters Between Indira Gandhi and Jawaharlal Nehru, 1940-1964' (London: Hodder, 1992), *Sunday Times*, 19 July 1992.

societies, India presents a particularly good counter-example to this argument.

Since India's problems of governance are seen by some as unique (attributed to Hindu self regulation), it is useful to look into the past history of societies that now boast of fully fledged effective, democratic governments. For an effective antidote to the alarmist view of the current state of India's democratic institutions we can look at the history of popular discontent and disorder in England during the eighteenth century. The picture that we get from Ian Gilmore's *Riots, Risings and Revolution: Governance and Violence in Eighteenth-century England* (1993) would be familiar to students of contemporary Indian politics.[9] Rampaging crowds, criminals taking the law to their own hands, corrupt state machinery and ineffectual government at a scale that are familiar to parts of India were not altogether unknown in England barely two centuries ago. Benjamin Franklin, the London agent for the state of Pennsylvania in 1769 reported that within a year, he had witnessed 'riots in the country about corn; riots about elections; riots about work-houses; riots about colliers; riots of weavers; riots of coal-heavers; riots of sawyers; riots of chairmen; riots of smugglers in which custom-house officers and excisemen have been murdered and the king's armed vessels and troops fired at.' If Franklin were to look for examples of other disorderly instances, he would have noticed 'riots against turnpikes and toll collectors, press gangs and schoolmasters, French footmen and Irish labourers, theatre prices, bawdy houses and the naturalisation of Jews.'[10]

While in many of the eighteenth century English riots one social group vented its anger against another, the state was often embroiled in them, sometimes directly. Thus, an act passed in 1780 to give some minor relief to Roman Catholics provoked violent reactions from Protestant zealots: 'prisons and Catholic chapels were burned to the ground; the houses of politicians and judges were attacked; distilleries and shops were plundered. One mob attacked Downing Street; another mounted an assault upon the Bank. King George III, on the attorney-general's advice, eventually authorized army officers to open fire on the mob without the intervention of a magistrate. By nightfall on the last day of the violence, almost a thousand people had lost their lives.'[11]

If the state itself was the target of civil violence, the other noteworthy feature of these riots was the outright inaction or lukewarm performance of

[9] For European illustrations of taming of the crowd and the creation of order, see Charles Tilly, *The Formation of States in Western Europe* (1975) and Simon Schama, *Citizens: A Chronicle of the French Revolution* (Harmondsworth, 1989), particulary the chapter on 'The Cultural Construction of a Citizen', pp. 123-174.

[10] Gilmore, p. 16.

[11] Gilmore, p. 353. Jim Masselos' *Struggling and Ruling: The Indian National Congress 1885-1985* (New Delhi: Sterling 1987) is a pioneering analysis of the relationship of crowds, crowd-management and state formation in India.

the organs of law and order in putting them down. 'Throughout the worst rioting, Justices had been careful to keep out of sight. When they were found, being afraid of the mob's displeasure, they could not be prevailed upon to read the Riot Act. The Lord Mayor, who had once been a waiter in a brothel, when urged to do his duty, replied evasively that the mob seemed 'to have got hold of some people and furniture they did not like and were burning them, and where was the harm in that?'

The English case is not a unique example of social dislocation and political disorder in Western Europe. Tilly (1975) and Hobsbawm (1959) inform us of frequent food riots and other challenges to public order throughout early modern Europe. These examples should help us understand the political nature of European riots which left a historical residue in the form of the legitimacy of popular protest. They provided the backdrop against which the state, through the combination of redistributive policies and law and order management, sought to cope with disorder. The tragic lacunae of the scholarship on contemporary Indian politics is that having put its collective finger on the malaise of 'ungovernability', it has not been able to problematise it in a manner where it can draw on cross-cultural knowledge of coping mechanisms (policing, reform, and constitutional change) through which western states in course of their evolution have solved their problem of governance.

The issues of order and legitimacy have been the subject of extensive inquiry for students of comparative politics. The debate on governance in India which tends to draw on culture as an explanation could benefit from structural arguments employed by cross-national studies. Our objective in the next section is to examine some of these conventional explanations of decline of governance. However, since the theoretical literature has itself moved beyond conventional studies of legitimacy, we will also undertake a critique of conventional models from the perspective of rational choice.

Conventional Explanations of the Decline of Governance

It has already been mentioned that contemporary stable Western democracies have experienced considerable social turmoil, political disorder, graft and corruption during the periods of rapid social change. Even in more recent times, they have been rocked by violent revolts of the youth and other sections of the society. Social policies intended to contain such challenges are seen by those engaged in protest as repressive toleration. These acts of rebellion have spawned many theories to account for such conduct. There have been socio-psychological explanations, most famously by *Why Men Rebel?* (Gurr, 1974). At the heart of these themes are angry men and women, ennobled and empowered by righteous rage, taking on the might of the state and other powerful adversaries. A second source of theoretical explanations originates out of dialectical materialism which conceptualizes the decline of legitimacy in terms of the contradictory interests of classes, leading to revolutionary violence. Since these grand theories have influenced Indian writing on the subject, it is important to review them briefly at this stage.[12]

From the point of view of scholars and statesmen for whom a strong, modern state in India is a fixed point of analysis, all such outbreaks of public disorder and violent secessionist movements are misguided, and, are, possibly, 'acts of the foreign hand'.[13] However, seen from the perspective of the political actors, operating in the name of a wronged people who are their primary audience, sympathisers and occasional collaborators, each horrendous incident is a necessary step in the direction of a preferred future.[14] Though it is difficult to comprehend their action from within the paradigm of the modern state, these criminal-activists are only putatively anti-governmental. In a more profound sense, there is also a search for governance, perhaps underpinned by values and rules different from those that they contest. For, what else is government except the agency with which people give concrete shape to their political vision?

The violent articulation of demands by aggrieved political actors poses a difficult problem, both for the established authority as well as for the theorist who seeks to explain the politics of legitimacy and challenges to legitimacy in terms of the same model. Thus, if the wielders of power concede the point to those who challenge established values and norms, they risk losing their legitimacy. On the other hand, the failure to give satisfaction to the discontented might deepen their sense of outrage and alienation which can further reduce their legitimacy. This political dilemma has its parallel in the theoretical anomalies that analysts of the political process are faced with. Thus, for some, any challenge to authority is necessarily disfunctional, whereas, for some, such acts are necessarily just, practical and indespensable. Comparative studies of the political process have responded to the contestation of legitimacy in a variety of ways. Two of these are particularly interesting to the students of legitimacy and governance in India. The relative deprivation theory draws on the angry rebel as its main unit of analysis.

12 James Manor, 'Anomie in Indian Politics: Origins and Potential Wider Impact', *Economic and Political Weekly*, Annual Number, May 1983, pp. 725-734.

13 The point is made by Satish Saberwal, *India: The Roots of Crisis* (Delhi: OUP, 1986). The allegation of a conspiracy to destabilize India with the collusion of foreign powers dominated the political rhetoric of Indira Gandhi in the 1970s. See Bharat Wariavwala, 'Security Issues in Domestic Politics', in: Subrata K. Mitra and James Chiriyankandath (eds.), *A Changing Landscape: Electoral Politics in India* (New Delhi: Segment, 1992), pp. 125-136.

14 See Benedict Anderson, *Imagined Communities: Reflections on the Origin and Spread of Nationalism* (London: Verso, 1983). For a broad range of cross-cultural and historical evidence of the use of language, kinship and cultural networks as vehicles for political movements with a modernizing agenda see Eric J. Hobsbawm and Terence Ranger (eds.), *The Invention of Tradition* (Cambridge: CUP 1988).

Theories of group conflict, on the other hand, conceptualise whole collectivities such as class, caste, tribe and ethnic cluster as single political actors, striving to achieve their collective goals through the political process.[15]

Governance and the 'Irrational' Actor

In its typical form, the angry actor whose spontaneous fury is responsible for the breakdown of law and order, is motivated by a feeling of relative deprivation. In Gurr's account, relative deprivation arises out of a sense of being deprived of some resource to which the political actor is morally entitled. In Gurr's formulation, the transformation of personal rage to political action hangs crucially from individual perception of the immorality of his situation and not on the political context which makes collective action both feasible and rewarding. Since morality is a matter of individual perception, a sense of relative deprivation may arise out of what the individual perceives as the denial of material resources, as well as, cultural and religious identity. The latter is important for post-colonial societies whose political institutions often represent values and practices exogenous to the people for whom they are meant, or, are too closely identified with social elites to whom power was transferred by the departing colonial rulers.

Governance and the Rational 'Collective' Actor

Authors who concentrate on groups, whether primordial groups such as caste, tribe, community, or modern entities, such as class, conceptualise challenges to the authority of the state in terms of grievances collectively shared by the members of the protest group. Such grievances typically emerge from the perception of rules as discriminatory. The wronged people are galvanized into group formation and political action because of a shared sense of grievance against the state which either fails to deliver the resources that its rhetoric has led them to believe they are entitled to, but which are not delivered, or, a state which no longer provides the kind of security to the life style that the social group in question has been customarily used to. Faced with a situation where the group feels that it can rely on nobody else except its own resources, the only course of action is to challenge the rules in an act of rebellion.

[15] Gabriel A. Almond reports some of these controversies. See Gabriel A. Almond, Scott C. Flanagan, Robert J. Mundt (eds.), *Crisis, Choice and Change: Historical Studies of Political Development* (Boston: Little, Brown & Co. 1973).

Most radical scholars of Indian politics who use class conflict as their basic explanatory device come under this category. Also included here are studies of social conflict where caste is named as the main actor either as a vehicle of challenge from below or as a bastion of upper caste dominance, defending its traditional privilege in the face of such challenges.[16]

Both the approaches mentioned above have spawned considerable empirical research. But, the discourses generated by them have tended to go past one another rather than leading to cumulative growth of our knowledge of governance. As such, the empirical findings generated by them have not been properly integrated into a theoretical explanation that can account for the spatio-temporal variation in governance. Thus, on the face of it, the irrational actor explanation appears as a valid account of apparently irrational behaviour such as self-immolation of students protesting against the efforts by the government of India to augment caste quotas following the report of the Mandal Commission. However, the detailed planning that such action usually entails - the gathering of sympathetic audience and the grim paraphernalia for self-immolation - require considerable organization. That gives the impression of a broader strategy rather than the spontaneous outburst of rage by isolated persons acting out their sense of outrage in a spontaneous manner. In the same vein, though conflicts on caste or class lines mobilize support for the particular cause, it is rare to find the conflict engaging all the members of a particular social group. Nor does one find the same groups at other times locked in similar conflicts. For castes to come to a conflict which is centred on the rules of transaction that describe their normal behaviour, membership of a particular social group is not sufficient, and, probably not even necessary for individuals to be mobilized into action.

On the background of this unsatisfactory state of explanation, the need is clearly to start with an assumption that requires of politics no more than the fact that political actors seek to maximize their share of power. Just as unregulated competition for power creates a Hobbesian state of nature where life can be solitary, poor, nasty, brutish and short, given the effective constraint of institutions, civilized social intercourse and orderly rule become possible. A realistic model of governance cannot escape the need of political actors to amass power nor of the equally important necessity of institutions that constrain this competition for power.

16 Francine R. Frankel and M.S.A. Rao, *Dominance and State Power in Modern India: Decline of a Social Order, Vols. I/II* (Oxford, 1991), use such a framework. Also see Veena Das (ed.), *Mirrors of Violence: Communities, Riots and Survivors in South Asia* (Delhi: OUP, 1990) and Kalpana Wilson, 'Class Alliance and the Nature of Hegemony: The Post-Independence Indian State in Marxist Writing', in T.V. Sathyamurthy (ed.), *State and Nation in the Context of Social Change* (Delhi: OUP, 1994).

A Formal Model of Governance

In everyday life, a political system with a high degree of order indicates a situation where life and property are safe. Disorder, synonymous in our analysis with low governance, is indicated by a number of social pathologies, such as violent deaths, criminal damage to property, riots, lawlessness, illegal strikes and public corruption. For the purpose of constructing a formal model of governance, we shall assume that rational individuals will be governed if and only if they find being governed is worth their while, i.e. the expected utility of undertaking the transaction in accordance with the rule is higher than that they can expect to achieve by breaking the rule. Rules are thus a critical explanatory variable for governance. Governance is high when the rules of transaction are explicit, transparent, constitutional, comprehensive, implemented by functionaries and obeyed by those subject to them. On the basis of the above definitions, we can now operationalize governance in more technical terms, using, in the first instance, perception of actors through survey data, and, in the second instance, through aggregate indicators. The first can be done in a straight forward way by asking, in a survey context, about the respondent's perception of the state of the law and order at a given time and at a given place, in absolute terms, as well as the state of law and order at a given time and place relative to other times and places. The second measurement builds on the consequences of such events as violent deaths, public disorder, loss of property through public unrest, loss of mandays in illegal strikes, riots, public corruption, unpaid taxes and electoral fraud. These secondary effects of low governance can be measured through aggregate data. In order to link these measurements to the preferences and perceptions of political actors in the real world, we next turn to ideal type situations where two players, (who, in real life, might represent competing political forces) are engaged in guessing each other's options and choosing their alternatives in a manner that maximizes their expected utility.

The payoff matrix presented in situation (1) depicts the alternatives available to two actors each of whom has the choice of getting on with the transaction at hand according to the rule, or, of trying to maximize his expected gain by breaking the rule. For the sake of simplicity, we shall assume symmetry. So, when both actors obey the rule, each is likely to get K. (For the sake of simplicity we assume K as a payoff for each player but it needs not be, because, no interpersonal comparison of utility is involved and our objective is to show the likely choice of alternatives for each actor on the basis of his understanding of his expected utility calculus.) For a variety of reasons, however, actor 1 (and 2) might consider breaking the rule. The actor, in charge of some public function, might charge a fee for carrying out his public functions (rent-seeking); he may decide to help himself to the public resources that the rule requires him to disburse among potential beneficiaries (corruption); he may compromise the standards of bureaucratic neutrality in favour of his kin (nepotism) in a manner that the advocates of the moral economy argument are familiar with. Rule violation by those who should know better makes it economically necessary and morally feasible for others to do likewise. Thus, rule violations at higher reaches of the system cascades downwards with a cumulative multiplier effect leading to the collapse of law and order. Some of the likely situations are depicted below:

(1)

Actor 2

Actor 1	obey	not obey	
obey the rule	K, K	K-E, K+P	K-E
not obey	K+P, K-E	K+P/2-E K+P/2-E	K+P/2-E
	K-E	K+P/2-E	

(2)

Actor 2

Actor 1	obey	not obey	
obey	K, K	K-E, K+P	K-E
not obey	K+P, K-E	0, 0	0
	K-E	0	

(3)

Actor 2

		obey	not obey	
Actor 1	obey	K, K	K, 0	K
	not obey	0, K	0, 0	0
		K	0	

(4)

Actor 2

		obey	not obey	
Actor 1	obey	K-C, K-C	K-C-E P-E	K-C-E
	not obey	P-E K-C-E	P-E P-E	P-E
		K-C-E	P-E	

In each of the above situations, two players are considering their options. They can either carry out the transaction according to the rule or they can seek to get on with it in a manner not allowed under the rules or explicitly forbidden by the rules. The cells denote payoffs to the players. By convention the payoff to actor 1 is denoted first. The figures to the right of the matrix (outside the box) indicate the minimum payoff that actor 1 can expect out of a play; the figures at the bottom indicate minimum gains expected by actor 2. The rewards of rule breaking for actor 1 (and 2) are P, so that alternative 'not obey' can fetch K+P. However, the other actor might get wind of his rule-breaking activity. This creates some apprehension in the mind of the rule-abiding player because there is a possibility of some form of collective punishment from above. The closing of a fair price shop for example if it ceases to function properly, will get all the employees out of a job; so, the knowledge that one's colleague is not playing the game according to the rule is likely to have a small cost E to the rule bound player. So, when the rule breaker expects K+P (or, to be more rigorous, K+P-E), the rule abiding person expects K-E.

When both players for their own reasons decide to break the rule, the additional reward P being finite in nature, has to be shared out. We can anticipate the players to think in terms of a fraction of P (for the sake of symmetry, P/2) as the additional gain, less E, the cost of rule-breaking.

The minimum gains the players can expect are, K-E for rule-obedience and K+P/2-E for rule-breaking. It is easy to see that maximin players (i. e. players who choose their options in a manner that maximizes their minimum gain) will prefer rule-breaking to rule-obedience. So, rule breaking is the likely outcome of this two person non-cooperative game.[17]

Happily, the world does not always behave this way. Anarchy, resulting from general rule-breaking, while likely in principle, need not necessarily be the only result. The game presented in situation 2 depicts a situation where the two players form part of a small, enduring community and the game is iterated in their minds. They are aware of the fact that in the situation where neither player obeys the rule and *as a result*, the transaction ceases to take place (e.g. in the event of the closure of the fair price shop) $E \geq K$; there is no P (when there is no shop), so that the likely payoff is 0 or less. Since this is an outcome that neither player likes, the players themselves are likely to generate resources for rule maintenance. Self-policing will thus lead to general rule-obedience.

The same outcome can be expected when a third party is entrusted with the responsibility of law and order management. Thus, in situation 3, the outside law enforces guarantees that whoever breaks the rule gets at least 0 or worse. Once again, the likely outcome is general rule-obedience.

From the point of view of the state, orderly rule and high governance are desirable. But they are possible only under strict policing (physically impossible as an exclusive strategy because no society has the necessary resource to police every transaction and who will police the police anyway?) or when transactions are ensconced within small, enduring social units where the communal network also functions as the instrument of law and order management. This is likely to be less and less frequent when social change enhances the frequency of transactions, increases the number of people involved in transactions and puts people from different social groups together as partners and adversaries.

The likelihood of rule-obedience gets further complicated in a fourth category of situations (see situation 4) where actors perceive rule-breaking as a good in itself. This is likely to be the case when the rule violates a deeply held belief. If one's sacred belief or sense of identity is violated by a rule, then the act of rule breaking gives an arbitrarily large satisfaction P to

[17] See Steven J. Brams, *Rational Politics, Decisions, Games & Strategy* (San Diego, 1985), pp. 139-167, for illustrations of Prisoner's Dilemma Games.

the actor. Rule breaking also has a cost: one has to forego the fixed reward K of getting on with the transaction, plus the likely punishment from the keepers of the law. However, if many people start breaking the rule for the reason, (jail *bharo*: fill in the jails movement, for example),[18] this will appear less likely. Once again, the maximin player is called upon to choose between K-C (C, the cost of rule obedience in this context being social disapproval, meted out to scabs, black legs, collaborators, compradors and so on) and K-C-E where the cost of obedience by player 1 has been further enhanced by E, the additional cost of the decline of rules due to player 2's disobedience; or, getting O+P-E when he disobeys the rule when 2 obeys and getting P-E when both disobey the rule. When both violate the rule, the chances of being penalized are less likely though the pleasure of breaking the rule remains undiminished. The least that the actor can expect now is:

obedience K-C-E
disobedience P-E

If P>=K [e.g. for some Sikh militants defying the Indian state could be more rewarding than holding on to a job or bringing the wheat crop in (K)] then it can be shown that a collective outcome of rule breaking is both feasible and probable. In this situation, rational actors, who are motivated by the sole desire of maximizing expected utility, are likely to disobey the law.

The moral of the story for the keepers of the law is quite straightforward. Situations 2 and 3 suggest that a combination of law and order management and social and economic reform will, respectively, enhance the value of K (the reward of transacting according to the rule) and diminish the profits to be made out of law-breaking (reward of rent seeking, nepotism and corruption) and enhance the E, the cost of rule breaking by making punishment both severe and likely.

The implications of situation 4 are more complex. The most important lesson here is to make sure that the constitution upholds values considered sacred by the citizens. That will make the rewards of law breaking less tempting. Compare the rewards of law breaking before and after the creation of linguistic states from the point of view of those agitating for giving the mother tongue centrality in the public affairs of the state.[19]

The policy advice that hardpressed governments can get from the situations depicted above is to enact policies based on the strategic combination of law and order management which reduces P to zero or less, reform which increases the value of K and constitutional incorporation of sacred beliefs which strengthens the moral basis of law and makes the psychological rewards of law breaking negative, rather than positive.

[18] See my *Power, Protest and Participation* (London: Routledge, 1992) for survey reports of the use of protest movements as a political resource by local elites in Gujarat and Orissa.
[19] See Jyoti Dasgupta, *Language Conflict and National Development* (Berkeley, 1970).

There are, however, two boundary conditions, exogenous to the game situations depicted here. In the first place, the rule violators, rather than being interested in policy outcomes, might simply wish to be rid of the specific governing elites concerned. If one were an East Bengali politician in 1971, with one's country ravaged and community devastated, the top priority might be to get the existing government, seen as aggressors, out of one's soil. The contestation of legitimacy under these circumstances leads to a situation where no orderly transaction is possible, particularly if there is no overlap between entrenched elites and their challengers. However, if there is an intersection between the two, then, depending on the relative weight of the intersection, it is possible to anticipate an orderly rather than a disorderly *coup d'état*, rebellion or riots. Following from this conjecture, policies based on regular elections, electoral reform and creation of new political arenas which facilitate the recruitment of new elites would enhance the legitimacy of political institutions.

Elite Succession and Political Order

A: existing elites B: contending elites

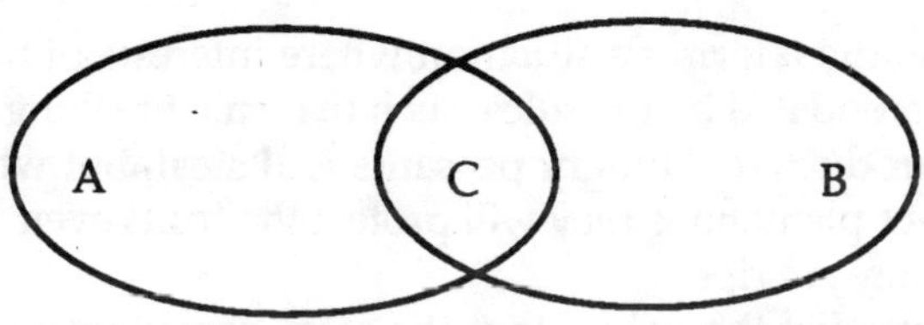

If B+C>A then 'normal' succession, i.e. new elites replace established elites.

If B+C<A then status quo prevails and protest continues.

If the intersection is empty, i.e. there is no overlap between established elites and their challengers, then only a 'disorderly' succession is possible.

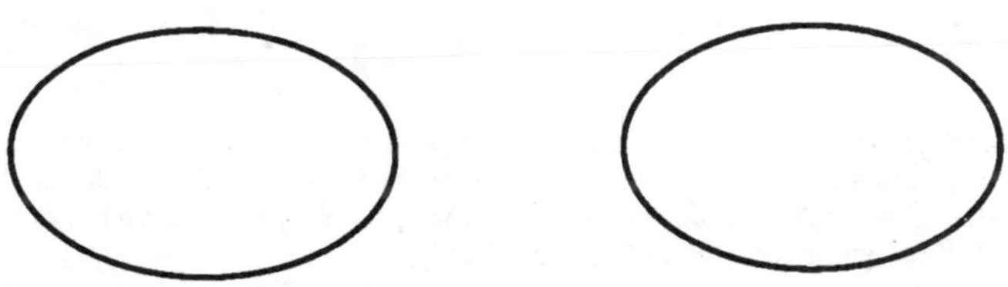

Another exogenous factor that affects legitimacy and political order is geo-political in nature. If a neighbouring state exports disaffection downstream through 'agents provocateurs', or armed secessionists and encourages law breaking by providing sanctuaries, then there is not much that can be done by the government in terms of domestic public policy. This is an area where the comparative politics of governance finds common cause with the problem of global and regional security.[20] Since the main objective of this chapter is to formulate hypotheses on legitimacy and political order from the angle of domestic politics and policy, this geo-strategic factor will not be further pursued here.

On the basis of the above discussion, the main reasons for which rational expected utility maximi zers do not necessarily end up in an anarchic situation, is because in the real world their options are constrained in a variety of ways. These constraints are crucial for the existence of order, rules and institutions. These can be specified in the form of the following conjectures:

1. Law and order management - a Hobbesian solution where the state mana ges to convince rational players that disobedience will be punished, i.e. $P <= 0$.
2. Social control - a Lockean solution (greatly enriched by Axelrod[21]) where actors are aware that disobedience in the long run will lead to anarchy, i. e. $P < 0$.
3. Social and economic reform - a situation where interests of the players are effectively accommodated by the rules, such that rule breaking is seen as costly and counterproductive. Hungry peasants will steal, but when transformed into owners of plantations they will protect the fruits even from their own children until they are ripe.
4. When rules contradict the values that the actor considers sacred, non-negotiable and transcendental such that their violation is a good in itself ($P>K$), legitimacy is enhanced by incorporating the values of the actors in the rules of the game.
5. The recruitment of new elites and creation of new political arenas can lead to the incorporation of new interests into a status quo or, the rapid, lawful replacement of existing interests by those of emerging elites, which makes K, i. e. the reward of rule-bound transaction attractive to the contesting elites and reduces the value of P in the eyes of these newly enfranchised actors.

[20] The complementarity of domestic and international politics in this context would be familiar to students of the politics of sub-nationalism. See Subrata K. Mitra: 'The Rational Politics of Cultural Nationalism: Sub-national Movements in South Asia in Comparative Perspective', *The British Journal of Political Science*, Vol. 25 (1995), pp. 57-78.

[21] Axelrod suggests that in a situation where two rational players share proximity, knowledge of each other and are engaged in a recursive as opposed to an end-game, they will find it to their advance to cooperate. See Robert Axelrod, *The Evolution of Cooperation* (London, 1990).

A Rational Choice Critique of Conventional Theories of Conflict

A model of governance which can successfully mitigate challenges to legitimacy should incorporate at least four sets of parameters: a bureaucratic state machinery that combines policy responsiveness with the law and order management; contribution to agenda setting by local protest movements; political elites using two-track strategies that combine protest and participation; and, constitutional change as a political resource, to be treated along with other explanatory factors as a conceptual variable. This model, which approaches the problem of challenges to legitimacy from the perspective of methodological individualism, contrasts sharply with existing literature.

The literature on crisis of governability is vast and fast growing. Atul Kohli (1990), in his important contribution to the research on mass political discontent and the problem of governability, differs significantly from other commentators by bringing about the necessarily political as opposed to cultural (Saberwal, 1986), socio-psychological (Kothari, 1988), economic (Bardhan, 1984) character of the 'governability crisis'.

> 'Detailed investigation of local, regional, and national politics leads to the proposition that the roots of India's growing problems of governability are more political than socio-economic; that is, they are located mainly in India's political structure. A highly interventionist state dealing with a poor economy has become an object of intense political competition. The spread of egalitarian political values and the opportunities provided by democracy have, in turn, helped to transform what was once a heterogeneous social structure into many groups of mobilised activists. Failure of leaders to make timely concessions has only intensified political demands and activity. And, finally, the growing weakness of fragmented political parties, which both reflects and exacerbates this process of overpoliticization has made it difficult for leaders to rule effectively.'[22]

There are of course no objective criteria to decide at what level political demands become 'overpolitical' except the threshold of what is considered tolerable by the modern state and experts who speak in its name. Ironically while Kohli's formulations indicate a new point of departure by restoring a sense of autonomy to the political process, it also indicates the limitations of an approach that remains beholden to the government, operating within the constraints of a liberal democratic constitution as the only legitimate agent of political action.

[22] Kohli (1990; p. ix). For the concept of the responsive state, see G. Hage, R. Hannemann and E. Gargan, *State, Responsiveness and State Activism* (London: Unwin Hyman, 1989).

Once we conceptualize the political process - law and order, policy making and constitution - as an explanatory variable, the discourse on governability reveals a number of interesting factors, including civil disobedience, riots, caste and tribal conflict, insurgency and terrorism.[23] What unites these rather disparate acts is the fact that the government is invariably a key player at which the agitations are aimed. Underneath the challenge to the government of the day there usually lurks a political agenda which wholly or partly questions the legitimacy of the established authority and institutions of the state. For that very reason, the articulation of such demands takes place outside conventional political institutions. In a broader sense, thus, the agents responsible for 'governability crisis' are political actors - a status that the representatives of the state resolutely try to deny them until they cannot do otherwise.

In the event of the outbreak of the problems of governance, one of three things is likely to occur: persistent crisis which slowly brings most social institutions to a standstill leading to a radical change in the constitutional rules governing conflict, e.g. take-over by a military dictator; quick escalation of the crisis into violent conflict leading to civil war or military insurgency; or, political accommodation of the agenda of the challengers through state action - administrative, legal, or constitutional. Liberal democratic theory holds that the probability of the breakdown of law and order is low in a situation where political parties and pressure groups which act as intervening structures between government and society, are capable of articulation and aggregation of political demands. The state and the constitution within which it is embedded provide an overarching framework which acts as the boundary condition to the competition, collaboration and occasional conflict of the concerned actors. An intelligent and effective government, i.e. one that listens to the society and where the bureaucracy manages to implement that which is legally ordained can be presented in terms of the following model:

Figure 1
The Liberal Model of State-Society Linkage

Society ⟶ Parties
Pressure Groups ⟶ State

[23] Such an approach treats the micro-actor as the unit of analysis in order to explain variations in the micro-structure in contrast to approaches such as Huntington's (1968) which treats the political system as both the unit of analysis and the field of investigation.

The political process described in figure 1 becomes problematic in post-colonial societies where rapid economic and social change combined with inadequate institutionalisation and parties with narrow social base can lead to violent protest, crisis and decline of legitimacy. This theoretical linkage postulated by Huntington (1968) and Kohli (1990) is further reinforced by the suggestion of Gurr (1970) that discontent is felt most intensely by people experiencing relative deprivation as a result of rapid change. The implications of these observations can be specified in the form of a model presented in figure 2. The factors that Kohli points out in his account of political change in India leading to the governability crisis, namely 'the deinstitutionalizing role of national and regional leaders, weak political institutions, 'the undisciplined political competition', politicization of 'all types of social divisions, including caste, class and ethnic cleavages', and, numerous strategies, including the use of violence (which) have been used to gain access to the state's resources'[24] are consistent with the Huntington-Gurr Model.

Figure 2
The Huntington-Gurr 'Polarisation Model'

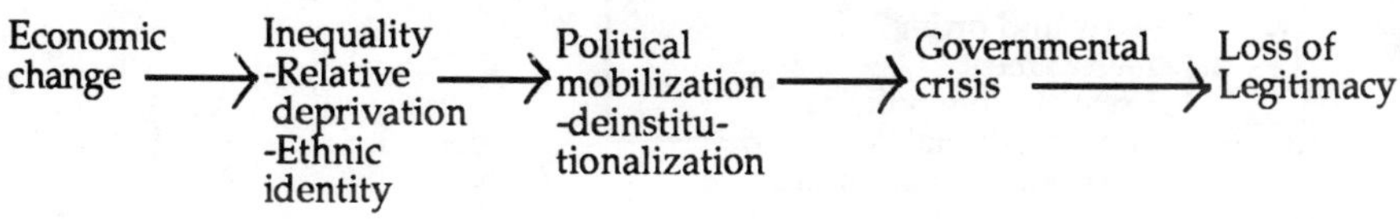

While Kohli makes these general points about India as a whole based on his diachronic analysis of five districts that Myron Weiner studied two decades earlier (Weiner, 1965) the more interesting point of his contribution is the comparison of the levels of governability crisis in different States of India. Thus, whereas he finds Bihar virtually in a state of war of each against all and Gujarat caught in intense political conflict on communal lines, West Bengal provides a contrasting case because of generally successful conflict management. A reform minded political party with a cohesive leadership, disciplined rank and file has managed to firmly plant itself between the people and the government. The West Bengal situation, thus, resembles that of the model presented in figure 1.

24 Kohli (1990; p. 385). See Jan Breman, *Of Peasants, Migrants and Paupers: Rural Labour Circulation and Capitalist Production in West India* (Delhi: OUP, 1985) for field data on the hard negotiations that characterize peasant-state and peasant-labour relations in an environment of expanding agrarian economy. For a discussion of the two-track strategy used by local leaders in order to get the best terms from the state, see my *Power, Protest and Participation*.

How did West Bengal achieve this level of conflict management, leading to orderly and lawful government? By Kohli's own reckoning, political parties are only intermediate level variables. In other words, rather than asserting the reform minded Communist Party of India (Marxist) as the 'cause' of West Bengal's governability, we need to understand the ensemble of factors that created the environment within which the left front government could carry out its policies in West Bengal. Comparative analysis is important in this context in order to reveal the organisational role of political parties as compared to their ideological profile. Thus, the Congress machine in Maharashtra could fulfil the same function as intermediary institutions between the state and society as the Communist party in West Bengal. These factors can be specified in terms of the model presented in figure 3.

Figure 3
How political systems cope with discontent

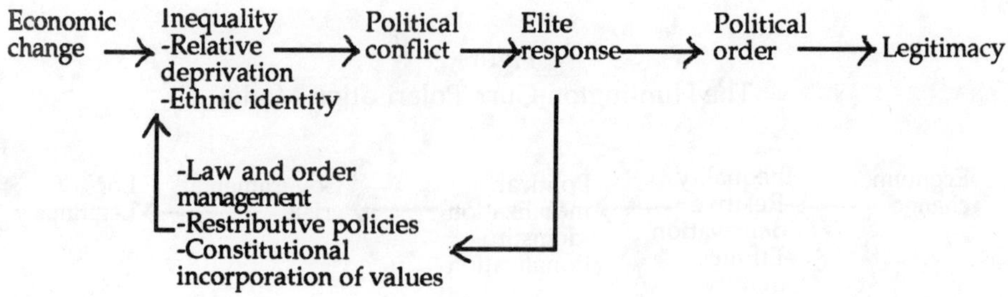

Once again, the fixed perspective of the modern state and its apologists set the criteria to distinguish 'undisciplined' political mobilisation from legitimate political participation. A degree of reality and dynamism can be added to a model of governance by leaving open the criteria of legitimate political action to political actors at the local and regional levels. The response of the government, in terms of law and order management, redistributive policies and constitutional change acts as a feedback loop that affects the perception of the people at the local and regional levels. The perception of a flexible, manipulable and 'responsive' state lowers the level of relative deprivation. Compared to the model presented in figure 2, that in figure 3 introduces a few additional parameters such as the presence of a 'responsive' state with which competing elites seen here as rational actors who choose their options in a manner that maximizes benefits and minimizes costs of transaction, negotiate on the basis of a complex repertoire that combines instruments of rational protest with elements of participation such as contacts with higher level decision-makers, lobbying, voting and sending petitions. India's significant achievement in the area of positive discrimination which has successfully severed the cultural and emotional links between caste and occupation, and legislation which has transformed social privilege into a politically contested concept bear ample testimony to the change that has come about democratically. When the results are redistributive policies and constitutional change, it leads to the reduction of perceived inequality and provides necessary political accommodation to such 'transcendental' issues as that of group identity.[25] Once the transcendental issues are incorporated into the constitution through appropriate changes in the rules of the game and creation of new arenas, politics within the reconstituted units reverts back to the transactional themes of material benefits.

A Dynamic Model of Governance

The model, as it stands, is a model of static equilibrium because while it considers the creation of new rules a feasible alternative, the rule creators, namely government elites, are themselves exogenous to the models. In some conflicts their existence itself is the focus of the contention (part of the payoff to contending actors). To develop a model of dynamic equilibrium, the existing model will need to be revised and a theory of succession should be incorporated into it as it stands.

The empirical verification of the model suggested in diagram 3 would involve four sets of independent variables, which alone or in combination, account for the variation in governance.

These are:

(a) law and order management: Who are the managers? How are they trained, equipped, paid, supervised and held politically accountable? Methods of conflict adjudication at local, district, regional and national levels.

(b) redistributive policies: What kind of legislation is made which makes it unnecessary for reasonable people to break the law? Of interest here are labour laws, agrarian reform, tenancy legislation, minimum wages laws, welfare legislation, positive discrimination and methods of minimizing rent-seeking behaviour.

(c) constitutional sanction for 'sacred beliefs': Non-negotiable values such as group identity, ethnicity, shared religious ideals. Communal accommodation as the basis of constitutional solution of confessional politics in divided societies.

25 This point has been made in Subrata K. Mitra, 'Desecularising the State: Religion and Politics in India after Independence', *Comparative Studies in Society and History*, Vol. 33, No. 4, October 1991, pp. 755-777.

(d) rules of succession, recruitment of new elites and political order: The variables to be investigated would include elections as a method of elite recruitment and the effectiveness of election commissions in maintaining free and fair competition, and, creation of new political arenas which create more effective intermediate institutions.

The statistical model, specified above, can be tested on the basis of data derived from interviews with political actors and data pertaining to the policy process. The chapter will next undertake a critical review of the literature on governance in India from the perspective of the model advocated here.

Governance as a Problem of Deinstitutionalisation

When Nehru inaugurated the Republic of India with his famous speech on Freedom at Midnight, he rested the task of laying the foundations of a modern state squarely on the institutional structure of the new republic, namely, the Parliament, the bureaucracy and the courts. Their capacity to carry this burden was questioned right at the outset by Selig Harrison whose *India, the Most Dangerous Decades* remains a landmark study of governance from the early decades of the republic. More recently, Manor (1983), Saberwal (1986), Morris-Jones (1987), Kothari (1988), and Kohli (1990) have added their voice to it.[26] Not to be outdone by academia, specialized organizations like Amnesty International and the popular press in the west and in India have also joined in.[27] One could, of course, trace the genealogy of the doomsayer much further back into history. During the early years of the Raj, it was generally asserted by the British administrators that without the firm and guiding hand of the colonial power, India would revert back to her natural state of internecine conflict and petty tyranny.[28] With the steady accumulation of evidence about government in ancient India following the translation of the Arthasastra into English and local self-government the conventional idea of India's natural ungovernability looked increasingly like an ideological justification for British rule. As the national movement be-

26 For the rise of lawlessness and the 'criminalization' of politics, see Paul Brass, *The Politics of India since Indepencence. The New Cambridge History of India, Vol IV. 1* (Cambridge: CUP, 1990), and Smitu Kothari and Harsh Sethi (eds.), *Rethinking Human Rights: Challenges for Theory and Action* (Delhi, 1989). For a report on the increase in 'violence, defiant indiscipline and lawlessness' by 'not just the armed militants of the Jammu and Kashmir Liberation Front or the Khalistan Commando Force, but but ordinary people, lawyers, policemen, shopkeepers, civil servants, students, trade unionists', see *India Today*, 31 August 1990.

27 See Amnesty International, *India, Torture, Rape & Deaths in Custody* (London, 1992), W.H. Morris-Jones, *The Government and Politics of India* (Wistow, Huntingdon: The Eothen Press, reprint 1987), p. 260.

28 See Karl A. Wittfogel, *Oriental Despotism* (New York, reprint 1981), p. 262, for India's natural ungovernability.

came increasingly more strident, the pressure for gradual transfer of power grew in volume and intensity. But when such powers were ceded to Indian hands, it was more a part of a larger strategy to buy time than the result of a conviction about India's readiness for self-government.[29]

Not much progress has been made since in the theory of governance in India. The real irony of the situation is that the uncritical acquiescence in Nehru's brand of parliamentary democracy following independence finds a parallel in the pre-independence refusal of the colonial power to recognize the indigenous people's ability at sustaining self-rule. No attempt was thus made to derive government out of the cultural and institutional heritage of governance in pre-colonial India. India was independent; the British had gone home; Nehru and the Congress party were safely ensconced in the Parliament. So there had to be a government by Indians and that was that. Faced with such an unproblematic conception of government from the early years, it is hardly surprising that the political analysis of the problem of governance in India gets very rapidly transformed into a moral discourse about the motives and methods of India's political elites.

With the possible exception of Rudolph and Rudolph (1987) whose views will be examined subsequently, the specialists of government and politics in India are very much in unison in their diagnosis of the malaise affecting governance in India. Voicing this common concern, Morris-Jones questions the 'complacent view' of the incremental evolution of the modern state and traditional society in India. 'The process of peaceful interpenetration is certainly present but its character has become hugely conflictual and frequently manifested in violence.' Morris-Jones finds evidence of lawlessness in the 'blood spilt on the streets of Ahmedabad in Gujarat where upper caste students became enraged when the state government, backed by the votes of the numerous "backward" castes, announced enhanced proportions of students vacancies for these castes in engineering and medical colleges. [Further] In parts of Bihar a condition of intermittent civil war has become virtually normal, with caste-based "armies" serving the interests of landlord groups by carrying out terrorist killings designed to discourage low-caste sharecroppers and untouchable landless labourers from getting ideas about land reform and cultivators' rights above their station and from daring to organize in order to press their claims.'[30] Under the impact of this growing, violent conflict over the allocation of material benefits as well as issues of

29 Rajni Kothari, 'Decline of the Moderate State', in Kothari, *State against Democracy: In Search of Humane Governance*, (Delhi: Ajanta, 1988) p. 34. Kothari concludes the essay with a discussion of the 'moral dimension' of Indian politics.

30 Morris-Jones (1987), p. 262. He adds 'the draconian measures of autocratic rule were well received in certain rural elite circles. Threatened by the rising political influence of the middle level industry, they welcomed a regime which checked politicization, above all at the level of local government.' See Morris-Jones, 'Shaping the Post-Imerial State', in M. Twaddle (ed.) *Imperialism, the State and the Third World* (London, 1992), p. 343.

ethnic identity, political institutions have decayed, the 'centre' does not any longer 'hold'. Joining Morris-Jones here are Paul R. Brass who talks about the criminalization of Indian politics and Rajni Kothari (1988) who presents a picture of increasingly violent, authoritarian state turning against the democratic aspirations of upward mobility by underprivileged social groups.

Kothari's views on the collapse of the democratic structure in India deserve careful consideration, not only because of their intrinsic interest but also because their status as the representative exemplar of a mode of thinking that has dominated the scholarly view of Indian politics for over a generation, both within India as well as among the larger community of scholars of Indian politics. During the 1960s, in a series of influential articles and more specifically, in his *Politics in India* (1970), Kothari described the process of political change and integration in India in terms of the 'Congress System' where the Indian National Congress acted as the intermediary between the modern state and traditional society. The decline of Congress, both the facilitator and the beneficiary of the interpenetration of the state and society and the rise of popular authoritarianism under the leadership of Indira Gandhi became a puzzle that the 'Congress System' framework of analysis could not solve. Kothari's response to this challenge to his earlier explanation consists mostly in evocation of the need for morality in politics: 'Central to the moderation of State power is this insistence on a larger ethical code without which politics is bound to degenerate into a cold and cynical exercise in control and manipulation and ultimately its take-over by musclemen and mafias. This is what has happened over the past few years.'[31]

As Kothari, the 'fairly severely analytical political scientist of the early years has become subsequently something of a seer with a mission'[32], his understanding (and that of other influential writers) of the problems of government in India has been increasingly dominated by a new essentialism constituted of the secular, modern institutionalism of Nehru. Following his disenchantment with the radical liberalism of Indira Gandhi as she split the Congress party and allied herself with the Congress Young Turks and the broad left outside the Congress in 1969 eventually leading to the imposition of the Emergency of 1975, Kothari has increasingly placed his trust in political action by grassroots movements and allied himself with the concept of partyless democracy and non-party political processes. In Kothari's more recent writings, the gentle reminder of the salience of moral concerns in politics has gained in salience.

> 'Fascism in many ways is not only an Orwellian new speak. It is more in the nature of a vitiated language seeking to hide in the noise of slo-

[31] Rajni Kothari (1988), p. 34.

[32] Morris-Jones (1992), p. 342.

gans. The epitome of such slogans, "Plan your family", "one man, one tree", "marry without dowry", or "work more, talk less". Or the more lurid texts of the highly provocative advertisements of the Congress (I) on the "last drop of my blood" in true resonating in the funeral songs of *khoon ka badla khoon*. Or the invocations of *badla* in the maiden public speech of the new Prime Minister. [The reference here is to Rajiv Gandhi.] They all attested to the fact that the pathology of politics inevitably reflects itself in language.'[33]

Kothari's reservations against the use of *bazaar* language as key categories of political campaigns or more sophisticated arguments about the 'deinstitutionalisation' of Indian politics ignore two important facts. In the first place, the language of Indian politics increasingly reflects the efforts of political actors to integrate local and regional cultural symbols, modes of speech and practices into their political campaigns.[34] Secondly, there was a consistent element of support from below for the type of popular authoritarianism embodied in the politics of Indira Gandhi. Her defeat in the election of 1977 was not so much the result of loss of popular support as the harnessing of anti-Congress votes by the coalition of opposition parties that subsequently came to be known as the Janata party. Those who had equated the success of the Janata party in 1977 and subsequently in 1989 with the victory of 'value based politics' must have had second thoughts as the 'cold and cynical exercise of control' that Kothari vehemently criticized in the politics of Indira Gandhi increasingly asserted its presence within the Janata government as well.

Moral platitudes, alas, are no substitute for political analysis. The indiscriminate use of the concept of deinstitutionalisation, which is nothing short of thinly disguised moral rhetoric, conducted in terms of acquired, liberal, constitutional essence which denies agency to actors who do not articulate their arguments in this particular form does not by itself constitute an explanation. It is a formidable obstacle in the path of the specification of India's problems of governance in terms of detailed empirical inquiry. That the essence of modern secular institutions, a fixed point in deinstitu-tionalisation discourse is not germane to the life world of the actors, who articulate agendas born out of their immediate, relatively unmediated perception of reality, is a matter of great importance for the understanding of the politics that issues out of it. The inability to register this point also accounts for the failure to come up with a serious, theoretical account of the rise of popular authoritarianism in India.

33 Rajni Kothari, *Politics and the People: In Search of a Humane India, Vol. 2* (Delhi: Ajanta, 1988), p. 455.

34 For an analysis of the categories of Indian political discourse see T.V. Sathyamurthy (ed.), *State and Nation in the Context of Social Change* (Delhi: OUP, 1994).

Institutionalisation, both as a measure of governance and the method of achieving it, has been the main contribution of Huntington. In relying on institutions for the same purpose, writers who formulate the problem of governance in terms of deinstitutionalisation face the same problem that Huntington's model (1968, p. 55) faced in the years following its publication. How was one to achieve institutionalisation except through the restriction of participation and hence, limit the political mobilization of people lower down the social scale? The feasibility of the authoritarian model for the restriction of participation as a solution to the problem of governance appears unlikely in an age of democratization when enfranchisement, empowerment and entitlement have become part and parcel of the political process at all levels of the system.

Further complicating the sustainability issue is the problem of values. In stipulating institutions as the critical variable underpinning his model, Huntington merely asserts that institutions are important without trying to derive them from within the life world of actors whose movements were meant to be constrained by those rules. The problem has been commented on by Saberwal who describes India's crisis of legitimacy 'as a consequence of our collective difficulty in working with institutions of Western derivation which have been implanted in India during and after the colonial period: legislatures, courts, universities, banks and so forth. Our difficulty arises perhaps in a lack of fit between the principles which have gone into the designing of these institutions over many long centuries in Europe, and those informal institutions to which we in India have traditionally been heir: family, caste, village, pilgrimage centre, little kingdom, and so forth.'[35] Nehru who was aware of the problem, and, as the *Letters to Chief Ministers, 1947-64* indicate, spoke tirelessly about it. With hindsight, the startling conclusion one comes up with is how little public debate there was about the lack of fit between acquired institutions and the political culture. There appears to have been this naive belief that Nehru and the congress party would somehow transform both alien institutions and endogenous culture magically and create a modern state which is harmonious with traditional society.

No consistent attempt has, however, been made to derive nor to adopt the principle of government to local and regional cultural and political traditions. The result, as Inden (1990) argues, is a 'nation-state that remains ontologically and politically inaccessible to its own citizens. Its government continues to be, just like its immediate British Indian ancestor, merely a neutral enforcer of unity on a morselized society, continually in danger of being pulled apart by 'centrifugal' forces. It remains the instrument of an agent, a 'divinity' that stays beyond the reach of its own people and institutions. That divinity no longer has an external home country as a platform from

[35] Satish Saberwal, *India: The Roots of Crisis* (Delhi: OUP, 1986), pp. 197-198.

which to enforce its impartial unity. What the Indian nationalists substitute for the transcendent divine kingship of the British Raj is the equally transcendent *idea* of Indian unity.'

Nationalist discourse around the nascent Indian state, immaculately conceived (or imagined by its modern 'builders') and delivered by Nehru (one hears very little of Gandhi or Patel) has invented a new essence - a 'civilization united by 'social' harmony as its legitimizing myth. The unproblematic 'civilisational state' has replaced problematic and divisive caste, religion, region and community. This idea of a modern, secular state has become a 'non-sectarian transcendent Dharma', an 'essentialised ideal Oneness, dichotomously contrasted with ... immanent divisiveness of India's social and religious 'reality', 'which would somehow be transformed by a bureaucratic state grounded in a world-ordering reason that India had lost but would regain from the west.' (198) Inden goes on to show how this modernist project, sponsored by the advocates of the modern state denied agency to non-state actors as well as to *themselves* in the name of a substantialized essence, an idealized *Bharatmata* - Mother India - which reduced problematic concepts of local, regional and sectarian politics to an unproblematic nationalism. 'Since that Dharma or Spirit is the premise and guarantee of the Indian nation-state itself, specific here-and-now agents could not negotiate with it or construct it... National historians could 'discover' it in India's ancient past, and nationalist politicians could invoke it and mobilize people in its name, but none of them could make it. Which is to say the nationalist have Indianized that old religious and scientistic dream of so many Europeans and Americans - a 'society' that would be free of politics because it hung from some immobile point in heaven or rested on an indisputable foundation.' [36]

It should be clear from the above that deinstitutionalisation merely describes the state of low governance. It does not by itself constitute an explanation of the state of affairs. A second aspect of the decline of governance that needs to be pointed out is that in spite of an impression of rising lawlessness and erosion of the norms of orderly behaviour in public life, the level of governance tends to vary both in time and space. This is discussed at greater length below, which will help us move in the direction of a theoretical explanation of the crisis of legitimacy from a rational-institutional perspective.

[36] Ronald Inden, *Imagining India* (Oxford, 1990), pp. 197-198.

The Cycles of the Crisis of Governance in India

The problem of legitimacy and governance in India is complex. Far from being uniform, it is historically variable and, often in contradiction with the prediction. While the Indian state and government are often faced with serious problems and appear to be on the brink, they confound predictions of disaster by somehow bouncing back. Thus, high governmental stability of the fifties was followed by the rapid rise and fall of governments and the first indications of the use of crowds by opposition parties to press their demands for political change in the sixties. Indira Gandhi's populist rhetoric, authoritarian politics and use of mass mobilization as an alternative to parliamentary approval of her policies characterized the 1970s. The 1980s brought India back to the niceties of parliamentary democracy and saw the loosening of government control over the economy, particularly imports. But it also witnessed the mobilization of large crowds on the rampage, intent on the assertion of the power and territorial exclusiveness of their communal identity. In retrospect, through its double achievement of liberalization for economy and restoration of orderly rule, the government of Narasimha Rao can claim to have restored India to a level where she ceases to be the subject of dire predictions.[37]

The position of the Rudolphs provides an interesting and useful contrast to the main thrust of the governability discourse. Though they also talk about deinstitutionalisation of Indian politics, they find in the tensile character of the Indian state the necessary political resources to secure high stateness and effective government. In the Rudolphs' characterization,

> 'Like Hindu conceptions of the divine, the state in India is polymorphous, a creature of manifold forms and orientations. One is the third actor whose scale and power contribute to the marginality of class politics. Another is a liberal or citizens' state, a judicial body whose legislative reach is limited by a written constitution, judicial review, and fundamental rights. Still another is a capitalist state that guards the boundaries of the mixed economy by protecting the rights and promoting the interest of property in agriculture, commerce, and industry. Finally a socialist state is concerned to use public power to eradicate poverty and privilege and tame private power. Which combination prevails in a particular historical setting is a matter for inquiry.'[38]

37 See my review of James Manor, 'Nehru to the Nineties: The Changing Office of Prime Minister in India', *The Journal of Commonwealth & Comparative Politics*, Vol. 33, No. 2, (July 1995), pp. 295-298.

38 Lloyd I. and Susanne H. Rudolph, *In Pursuit of Lakshmi: The Political Economy of the Indian State* (Chicago, 1987), pp. 400-401.

The Rudolphs' state is both essence and agent and as such, is at least partly contestable. Its stateness[39] is surrounded by a zone of grey that admits actors whose political idiom may be putatively anti-state but whose substantive contribution to state formation is more positive than what one might conclude at the first encounter. However, while this characterization of Indian politics points in the direction of an explanatory model of state formation and government, the specific empirical parameters remain at best implicit.

Though the governability discourse of the writers discussed above provides no sustained explanation for the regenerative ability of the state in India, many among them make assertions to this effect on intuitive grounds. Several conclude their studies of political decay and governability crisis by a routine affirmation of the resilience of Indian democracy and the intrinsic ability of Indian culture to absorb conflict by accommodating differences. Kohli (1990) repeatedly asserts that his is not a doomsday scenario. The best is from Morris-Jones (1987): '[The] sombre picture of social conflict and institutional decay as the heightened features of recent years [presents] some contrast with the earlier post-independence decades. But a sense of proportion requires that at the end one should say of India what Galileo said of the earth: 'Eppur si mouve' - 'still, it moves'. Certainly nothing in this epilogue should incline the reader to imagine that changing India has become anything other than what it has ever been: by turns infuriating and fun to be with, always an absorbing delight to try to understand.'[40]

Conclusion: Why do we have Institutions, sometimes?

In order to understand the puzzle of institutional change within the context of general theory, it is necessary first of all to put the key terms of reference such as rules, actors (both individual and collective), and political forces of a complex society within the framework of a political system. At its most general level, a political system is bounded by a constitution, written or unwritten. The rules of the constitution serve as the ultimate arbiters for determining the winner at the highest level of the political system, for deciding who the legitimate players are, what kind of payoffs can be expected and what the ultimate prize is. There are similar games within the political system at the level of subsystems, both spatially and functionally defined. These games are tied together in a manner where the games at the higher

39 For the concept of stateness see J.P. Nettl, 'The State as a Conceptual Variable', *World Politics*, Vol. 20 (July 1968), p. 566.

40 Morris-Jones, *The Government and Politics of India* (Wistow, Huntingdon, 1987).

level gain precedence over the lower games in case of conflict. We can thus specify the political system and its subsystems as a set of hierarchic games.

A political system with a high degree of legitimacy is one at a state of static equilibrium where successive players reinforce the constitution. The pendulum, the transformation of the British welfare state to a property owning democracy by Margaret Thatcher is an example of this kind of equilibrium. The political system can be said to be at a state of dynamic equilibrium if a particular play results in disturbing the constitutional rules of the game, leading to the creation of a new constitution. The transformation of the French Fourth Republic to the Fifth is an example of a dynamic equilibrium. A political system in disequilibrium is one where each play results in a disturbance to the constitution which becomes cumulative in a way that causes the system to degenerate to anarchy, a situation which is best exemplified by the successor states of the former Soviet Union.

One of the advantages of the analytical distinction made above is that it helps us transform legitimacy into a dependent variable which is scaleable, and can be measured using the indicators mentioned earlier, using countries or other geographic areas as units of measurement. Though the Kashmir valley probably constitutes an exception, India's average level of legitimacy puts her in the category of dynamic equilibrium.[41]

This section will conclude with some comments on how we can draw on this discussion of legitimacy to help the policy-maker construct institutions with a greater degree of legitimacy. Since India is the empirical focus of this paper, we shall once again return to North who provides important theoretical insights for the analysis of dynamic equilibria. 'Institutional change is a complicated process because the changes at the margin can be a consequence of changes in rules, in informal constraints, and in kinds and effectiveness of enforcement. Moreover, institutions typically change incrementally rather than in discontinuous fashion. How and why they change incrementally and why even discontinuous changes (such as revolution and conquest) are never completely discontinuous are a result of the embeddedness of informal constraints in societies. Although formal rules may change overnight as the result of political or judicial decisions, informal constraints embodied in customs, traditions and codes of conduct are much more impervious to deliberate policies. These cultural constraints not only connect the past with the present and future, but provides us with a key to explaining past historical change. 'The resultant path of institutional change is shaped by (1) the lock-in that come from the symbiotic relationship between institutions and the organizations that have evolved as a consequence of the incentive structure provided by those institutions and (2) the feedback pro-

41 These concepts are derived from William Riker and Peter Ordeshook, *An Introduction to Positive Political Theory* (Englewood Cliffs, N.J., 1973).

cess by which human beings perceive and react to changes in the opportunity set.'[42]

The 'locked-in symbiosis' referred to above suggests a close relationship between 'sacred beliefs' of important groups in society and their main interests. As long as this convergence holds fast, these groups do not question the legitimacy of the rules of the game. To this familiar concept of the close relationship of the substructure and the superstructure which Marx alludes to, we shall add a third variable, namely, law and order management which persuades *individuals* within these groups not to take the path of the free rider so far as abiding by the rules is concerned. For the benefit of unreconstructed functionalists who might argue that rule obedience originates from political culture, one can point out that neither values nor interests are constant in time. Both of course play an important role in politics. Legitimacy of the political system requires that their effect be continuously reflected in appropriate changes in the constitution. But this 'feedback' may not take place for a variety of reasons. Thus, the original impetus for Pakistan was created through a fortuitous convergence of Islam and a good career move for Muslim elites of British India, but, when the equally important Bengali nationalism and the resentment of the Bengali elite against the quasi-monopoly exercised by the West Pakistani elite over the economy and administration manifested themselves, these changes were not effectively communicated into Pakistan's high politics. Within India, the emergence of Tamil and Telugu nationalism have found an institutional home within the Indian Republic but the same cannot be said about Sikh nationalism which is still testing the limits of India's secular state. Nor can this be said of Kashmiri nationalism which, basically for reasons of the institutionalized hiatus between the political and economic market of Kashmir and the rest of India in the form of Article 370 and the systematic rigging of Kashmir polls in the past stopped an emergent post-independence generation of Kashmiri elites from getting into power (like in other regions of India). As such, the political process of Kashmir has not succeeded in finding its home within the constitution of the Indian Republic despite the repeated claims of India's leadership about Kashmir being an integral part of Indian territory.

Turning now to the general literature of conflict resolution, one can identify two solutions that have been tried to achieve legitimacy: firstly, the removal of the causes of challenges to the constitution by the simple expedient of getting rid of the groups who engage in or are likely to engage in such activities; and, secondly, by accommodating the values and interests of as wide a spectrum of groups as possible. There are several variations on these two main themes. Thus, McGarry and O'Leary, with exemplary methodological rigour and empirical exactitude, have identified eight modes of conflict regulation, which, in their usage, includes both conflict management

[42] North, p. 7.

and termination. The methods of eliminating differences include genocide, forced mass-population transfers (better known to mass publics as ethnic cleansing), partition and/or assimilation, and, integration and/or assimilation. The methods for managing differences include hegemonic control, arbitration (third party intervention), cantonization and/or federalization, and, consociationalism or powersharing.

The Indian expedient at independence was to combine the formal rules of a liberal democratic constitution with the informal practices of a consociational state. Her leaders who had tenuously fought any formal concessions to group identity in the form of communal representation had, through an intricate form of quotas in the distribution of 'tickets', managed to recreate an effective replica of Indian society within Indian polity. This arrangement was reflected in what has been referred to by Morris-Jones and Kothari as the 'Congress system' of India. McGarry and O'Leary call it 'hegemonic control': 'The most common system of managing as opposed to eliminating ethnic conflict practised in multi- or biethnic states is that of "hegemonic control", a concept first developed by Ian Lustick (1979, 1987). Hegemonic control has been the most common mode through which multi-ethnic societies have been stabilized in world history, imperial or authoritarian regimes controlled multiple cultures within their territories through coercive domination and elite cooption. They suppressed latent divisions between ethnic communities which might otherwise have been manifested, especially in connection with economic modernization. The control was hegemonic if it made an overtly violent ethnic contest for state power either unthinkable or unworkable on the part of the subordinated communities.'[43]

Limitations of space preclude the possibility of a detailed discussion of the complex factors that underpin the legitimacy of the state in India. But it can be broadly suggested that the decline of the Congress system has removed the extra-constitutional means of generating a wide acceptance of the rules of the game. Perhaps the time has now come in India to think of other, formal ways of solving the problem of legitimacy. Taking a cue from more recent sub-regional members of the Indian federation such as Gorkhaland and Jharkhand, which institutionalise tribal as opposed to linguistic identity, that have been added to the Indian Republic, it is well worth exploring 'cantonisation' as a general solution. 'Under cantonisation the relevant multi-ethnic state is subjected to a micro partition in which political power is devolved to (conceivably very small) political units, each of which enjoys mini-sovereignty... Cantonisation decomposes the arena of ethnic conflict and competition into smaller more manageable units: it involves a negotiable form of internal secession.' I broadly agree with the conclusions of McGarry and O'Leary: 'The best normative case for consociational arrangements is

[43] John McGarry and Brendan O'Leary (eds.), *The Politics of Ethnic Conflict Regulation* (London: Routledge, 1993), p. 4.

that they involve the self-government of the relevant communities, and they are better than the alternative: majority domination, bloody partition, secessionist warfare and the unthinkable options of forced population transfers and genocide.'[44] But two conditions are necessary for this to work. Most important of all is 'the rival segments must not be unreservedly committed to immediate or medium term integration or assimilation of others into their "nation" or to the creation of their own nation-state. Also, leaders of the relevant ethnic communities must enjoy some political autonomy themselves so that they can make compromises without being accused of treachery.'[45]

Oscar Wilde is said to have exclaimed from his death-bed: 'I don't like the wall paper; one of us has to go'. If there is a conflict between rules and a significant number of political actors, then one of the two has to go. The critical threshold that determines what is a significant level will depend upon the nature of the political system. The analyst in search of political resources on which to build a solution for a specific context has to turn to the culture and history of the society in question. The theory of constitutional change in post-colonial societies is, in this sense, an integral part of a search for an endogenous modernity.

44 McGarry and O'Leary (eds.), p. 36.
45 ibid., p. 36.

Hindu Nationalism, the Politics of Nation-Building and Implications for the Legitimacy of the State

PARTHA S. GHOSH

Introduction

One of the challenges faced by developing polities is as to how to reconcile the ideal of separating the state from religion to the phenomenon of political use of religion. While it is relatively easy to technically achieve the ideal, say, by declaring the state as secular through the constitution, it is not easy to separate politics from religion which on its part keeps threatening the constitutional commitment. The problem basically lies in the fact that almost every individual invariably subscribes to one religious faith or the other and this rather habitual orientation largely determines his social interactions. As society and politics are inseparable, so are politics and religion.[1] The lesser a society is politically developed, the greater is the relationship.

For Islamic societies the question is probably less relevant. In those societies generally, on the one hand, there is no conceptual contradiction between state and religion as Islam does not distinguish between the two, and on the other, since some are politically less developed there is not much of a demand for this either. But even in these societies the political use of religion can be destabilizing. Leave aside the danger that Islamic fundamentalism poses to the state,[2] political crises may arise from sectarian conflicts (Shia versus Sunni) or from decisions to brand some groups as non-Muslim (Ahmedis in Pakistan). Who should have the final say in interpreting the Quran itself is potentially contentious. These conflicts have often been so violent that they negate the idea of Islamic solidarity and brotherhood.

For a multi-religious democratic society like India the question is a most crucial one. This is so not because religion plays a dominant role in

[1] According to Indian sociologist T.N. Madan, '. . . it is important to remember that the traditional conception of religion in India . . . equates it with the totality of life. . . . Politics and economics are neither autonomous domains nor are they contradictory of religion: they are simply encompassed by religion. The religious and the secular cannot be separated, therefore, in other words, religion cannot be in any meaningful sense privatized.' 'The Historical Significance of Secularism in India', in S.C. Dube and V.N. Basilov, *Secularization in Multi-Religious Societies: Indo-Soviet Perspectives* (New Delhi: Concept, 1983), p. 12.

[2] The OIC Summit held in Marocco in late 1994 adopted a code calling on the organization's 51 members to cooperate among themselves to deal with the threat of Islamic fundamentalism to their political stability. See Sybil Bebermeyer, 'Muslim Nations See Extremism as Main Threat to Stability', *The Asian Age*, 29 Dec 1994.

Indian politics which is true only to a certain extent but because of the fact that as a politically more developed state India contains powerful interest groups which are opposed to any link between politics and religion. The apprehension is that it is not only harmful to India's liberal democratic tradition but also disruptive of the inter-communal societal balance so critical to the survival of the nation. The fact that certain Hindu chauvinistic groups have started questioning this wisdom and more so the fact that their logic that the Indian nation should actually connote the Hindu nation is gaining in popularity makes the discourse more acrimonious. This debate is what the present paper is all about. The central issue here is how can the Hindus and Muslims, or for that matter the Buddhists, Christians, Sikhs, and everybody else, coexist peacefully as Indian citizens without anyone having the feeling of a second class citizen.

The Backdrop

The debate whether Indian nationalism has a territorial, and, therefore, civilisational content, or it has a cultural connotation, is not new. All these years, however, the protagonists of the civilisational school were firmly in the saddle. But of late the other school also have gained in strength. The rise of the Hindu chauvinistic Bharatiya Janata Party (BJP) as a political force to reckon with characterizes a phase in Indian politics without any parallel in the past. This is the backdrop of our analysis.

The demolition of the sixteenth century Babri mosque on 6 December 1992 by a fanatical Hindu mob can be called a watershed in Indian politics. The fact that the demolition was not the result of a sudden outburst of emotions but was a pre-planned design worked out by several Hindu organizations and that it was accomplished in the presence of state power raised questions with far-reaching implications. The BJP which had either masterminded the operation or had at least given a tacit approval to the plan was not only a recognized political party that had sworn in the name of the secular constitution of India but was also in power in U.P. where the mosque was situated. In the elections of 1989 and 1991 it had significantly enlarged its popular base—from bare two seats in the parliament in 1984 to 85 and 117 seats in 1989 and 1991 respectively. No wonder that many started viewing the party as one in the waiting list to capture power at the centre.

The demolition seemed to indicate two inter-related trends. The first was that the Hindu nationalists were no longer on the fringes of Indian politics and were actually able to call the shots, and secondly, the state was not serious enough to honour one of its basic commitments, that is, the protection of the constitution. Doubtless, the omission of the Congress-ruled union government to save the mosque amounted to a crime no less deplorable than that of the BJP. Some even suspected the hidden hand of Prime Minister Narasimha Rao behind the event for it was argued that he had exhausted all his cards to clinch the issue politically and hence he waited helplessly for the inevitable to happen.[3]

It was only after the demolition that the state reasserted itself and the people also seemed to realize the damage it had caused to the Indian polity. The Rao administration dismissed all the three BJP governments in Himachal Pradesh, Madhya Pradesh and Rajasthan (the BJP government in U.P. had already resigned), banned several religious and fanatical organizations belonging to both Hindus and Muslims which were deemed potentially disruptive of communal peace, and unequivocally promised to rebuild the mosque. At the intellectual level there was an outcry against the demolition and BJP seemed to be on the defensive. In the assembly polls held in November 1993 the party suffered reverses in all the four States that it had ruled prior to the demolition.

These positive indicators notwithstanding, nagging doubts persist about the future of secularism in India. Given the volatility of Indian politics marked by growing casteism and localism and the probability of an impending rift within the Congress, BJP seems to have a future. That by the time the next general election is held in 1996 it would recover its lost ground is the calculated guess. What its ideology, agenda and strategy would mean to the Indian state is the vital question.

The Ideology of Hindu Nationalism

The essential element of the ideology of Hindu nationalism is that India is for the Hindus. The unity of Hindus alone can ensure the integrity of the nation. The non-Hindus, most notably the Muslims, have indeed the right to live as full citizens and enjoy the benefits of development but they must shed their sectarian identity and extra-territorial mindset. Prior to the partition it was the Islamic identity of the Muslims alone that used to concern the Hindu nationalists but after the creation of Pakistan the element of extra-territoriality in that ideology has been added to the fear. The rise of fundamentalism in many parts of the Muslim world, the growth

[3] In the context of the growing rift between Rao and Arjun Singh, till recently the Minister of Human Resource Development Minister in the Rao cabinet, the latter is alleging that the Prime Minister did not take necessary steps to preempt the demolition although Singh had categorically cautioned him. Text of Arjun Singh's letter in *The Hindu* (New Delhi, 25 December 1994). Sonia Gandhi who is emerging as a political force within the Congress seemingly subscribes to this. See *India Today* (New Delhi), 31 January 1995, pp. 60-69. Logically, the Muslims had reasons to suspect Rao's inaction as an unfriendly act. For an analysis of how this kind of suspicion is constructed in a communal situation, see Beth Roy, 'Of Cabbages and Kings and Why the Sea is Boiling Hot: How Communities Decide to Fight', *International Journal of the Sociology of Law* (London), Vol. 20, (1992), pp. 285-293.

of an international political Islam, and Pakistan's involvement in the secessionist movements in the Punjab and Kashmir have accentuated the anxiety.

Viewed from historical and global perspectives one must concede that there is nothing extraordinary in the Hindu nationalistic ideology. Everywhere in the world nations have been conceived and formed around the nucleus of the majority group and wherever necessary the religious beliefs and practices of that group have been used as the rallying point. In India too when the seeds of Indian nationalism started sprouting the thrust was on Hindu nationalism. Whether it was the literary writings of Bankim Chandra Chatterjee, Maithilisharan Gupta or Bharatendu Harishchandra, or the history texts meant for the schools, the emphasis was on Hindu consciousness. While the British rule was the target of attack the argument was often built around the Hindu-Muslim cleavage in which the latter were seen as responsible for all that went wrong with the Hindu self respect. Since there was a simultaneous growth of Muslim self-consciousness as well both communal ideologies throve at each other's success.

The concept of Hindu nationalism was based on the concept of *Hindutva* which had its origin in the theories of nation-building propounded by the Arya Samaj, the Hindu Mahasabha, and the RSS. Unlike the concept of Hinduism which is concerned with the theological and spiritual aspects of the religion, *Hindutva* encompasses the entire spectrum of cultural, social, political and linguistic aspects of the Hindus of which the political aspect is the most dominant. Actually *Hindutva* is, like political Islam, political Hinduism, that is, the quest for power and influence through the use of Hindu religious, historical, and cultural traditions.

In view of the nationalistic thrust and the historic period in which these Hindu organizations were born they were expected to fight the British colonial yoke. But they made the Muslims their real targets considering them as the bigger enemies than the British, for after all the latter had not claimed India to be their homeland. As such there was no room for the participation of Muslims in India's nation-building. This dogmatism blinded their objectivity to such an extent that in his 568-page book *Six Glorious Epochs of Indian History* the Hindu Mahasabha leader V.D. Savarkar did not even mention the three-century-long Mughal rule during which the Indian empire was at its zenith.

While this was the reality with the hard-core Hindu nationalists, the leaders of the mainstream of the Indian National Congress were also making use of Hindu traditions and customs to articulate their version of Indian nationalism. For example, Bal Gangadhar Tilak's emphasis on Ganapati and Shivaji festivals, Mahatma Gandhi's talk of Ramrajya, Harijan, etc. were clearly directed to mobilize Hindu support for the freedom movement.[4] Indeed there was a strong undercurrent of Hindu nationalism in the Congress and leaders like Lala Lajpat Rai, Govind Vallabh Pant and Sardar Vallabhbhai Patel were known sympathizers of the cause. After the partition and the resultant Hindu-Muslim riots Patel was of the view that the Muslims were disloyal to the country and that the Mahatma was closing his eyes to this reality.

The Nuance

But a subtle distinction here must be made between the communalism of the Hindu nationalists and the communalism of the Congress nationalists. To build the Indian nation the former visualized the role of only the Hindus and ignored that of the Muslims who formed about 25 per cent of the population of undivided India. In the process they showed an utter indifference to a community which was not only large in number but also possessed a distinct identity in terms of religion, culture, personal law, food habit, language, and so on. In the argumentation of the Hindu nationalists there was no idea as to what would happen to this community if India became independent by following their model.

The communalism that the Congress subscribed to was aimed at placating and mobilizing both the communities.[5] It realized that India was a traditional society in which religion played an important role in the life of the people. It also recognized the distinct cultural identities of Hindus and Muslims which could not be easily bridged but certainly helped to coexist if a suitable political climate was created. An a-religious political strategy, however, desirable it may be in the modern context, would not, therefore, work. We have already noted how Hindu cultural traditions were selectively employed to arouse Hindu nationalism. The same was done to mobilize the Muslim community as well. This found expression first in the Congress support for the Khilafat movement and later in its commitment not to disturb the Muslim personal law.[6] In essence, the biggest difference between the Hindu nationalists and the Congress nationalists was that the latter were not driven by any hatred *per se* for the Muslims

[4] Partha Chatterjee, 'History and the nationalization of Hinduism', *Social Research* (New York), 59 (1), Spring 1992, pp. 130-134. Christophe Jaffrelot, 'Hindu Nationalism: Strategic Syncretism in Ideology Building', *Economic and Political Weekly* (Bombay), 20-27 March 1993, pp. 518-519.

[5] That Congress was open to all communities was evident not only from the fact that many Muslim leaders had become its presidents, even Europeans and Christians like Annie Besant and Nellie Sengupta had held the post. Now they are talking about Italian Sonia Gandhi as the Congress president.

[6] For more on the Congress view of the Muslim personal law, see Partha S. Ghosh, 'Political Hinduism in India: Genesis, Prognosis and Implications', Occasional Paper of Stiftung Wissenschaft und Politik (Ebenhausen, 1995), pp. 21-29.

although the Hindu cards were selectively used for political and electoral gains.[7]

Hindu Muslim Coexistence

Commenting on the Hindu-Muslim conflict in India political scientist Gopal Krishna had once written: 'The inescapable truth seems to be that Hindu India cannot escape the consequences of its medieval defeat, however much it may try, and Indian Islam cannot overcome the consequences of the failure of its mission of conquest in India whatever it might do. The result has been on both sides frustration, hatred, and apparent powerlessness to alter the situation.'[8] Given the realities that the country has been divided on communal lines, that India and Pakistan have been on conflictual terms ever since independence on the question of Kashmir, that Hindus and Muslims have made it their pastime to indulge in riots at almost regular intervals, etc., there cannot be any doubt that there is enough grain of truth in what Gopal Krishna said. But what he has not emphasized is equally important. It is true that Hindu-Muslim relationship is problematic, but is it not also true that it is one of the most enduring intercommunal coexistential experiences, despite the creation of Pakistan, which not many comparable societies can boast of? The factors that contributed to this would explain the rationale behind the Congress ideology of bi-communalism and debunk the theory of Hindu communalism as propounded by the Hindu nationalists.

There are essentially three factors that contributed to the millennium-old Hindu-Muslim coexistence without any mentionable disruption of peace. In the first place, prior to the British rule, to whatever community the rulers belonged - in large parts of India they were Muslims while in some places Hindu - they seldom interfered with the personal faith of the masses. There was hardly any organized move to convert the Hindus to Islam or vice-versa (Hinduism any way does not recognize the idea; the Arya Samaj did introduce it through the ritual of *shuddhi*, but it had little impact). Since Hinduism was a syncretic, non-proselytizing, non-congregational, non-mono-scriptural, and an extremely individualistic and pluralistic faith it neither threatened the Muslim rulers nor was it itself

7 It is not necessary that the Hindu card has to be used only against the Muslims or other religious minorities. It can be used against any ideological challenger as well. For example, in the Faizabad by-election to UP assembly held in June 1948 when the UP Congress under the leadership of G. B. Pant decided to defeat the break-away Congress leader Acharya Narendra Dev, a socialist by conviction, all kinds of Hindu religious forces were unleashed.

8 Gopal Krishna, 'Communalism Revisited' (in two parts), *Times of India*, 23, 24 July 1974.

threatened by the latter's presence. Mutual non-interference seemed to suit both the communities best.[9]

The other important thing that the Muslim rulers did not do was to interfere with the Hindu personal law and thus avoided pricking Hindu cultural sensitivities. All those Hindus who these days feel so strongly about the anachronism of Muslim personal law must not lose sight of the fact that Hindu personal law had survived a thousand years of Muslim rule and two hundred years of Christian rule. Even its codification in 1955 was not a smooth affair as no less important a Hindu than Dr. Rajendra Prasad, the first President of the Indian Republic, was opposed to it.

In addition to the above two factors there was the critical element of isolation. Both on account of lack of communication as well as absence of an international political Islam the Muslims of India of the medieval times did not look beyond the Indian borders for ideological support. Inspite of the fact that they had come from outside they had made India their home. Actually many of the Muslim traditions of India, notably those introduced by Indian Sufis were indigenous to India. As a result there was not much of an allegation of extra-territoriality against medieval Muslims as is so common these days against the present Muslims.

This coexistential structure, however, teetered towards the end of the nineteenth century more on account of developmental reasons. As the Indian society became more modern with greater participation in education, administration and professions based on open competition, and less on birth, a growing number of Hindus and Muslims started considering that competition in communal terms. The British government which received different sets of demands from the two communities were all too willing to exploit this cleavage to its political advantage thus vitiating the relationship.[10]

Nation-Building: Congress Style

The Congress strategy of identifying itself with both the Hindu and Muslim communal sentiments found its expression in the constitution of India, not necessarily in its provisions but also in the absence of some of them. The most notable absence was that of the term secularism. The constitution that was introduced in 1950 was the blueprint of a modern Indian polity

[9] Till the reign of Shah Jahan there were even thousands of cases of Hindu-Muslim marriage without either person converting to Islam. Shah Jahan, however, put an end to it by requiring Hindu men having married to Muslims to convert into Islam but not the other way round. *Shah Jahan Nama*, p. 139, cited by Harbans Mukhia, 'Communalism and the Indian Polity', *South Asia Bulletin* (London), Vol. 11, No. 1&2 (1991), p. 65.

[10] The pro-Muslim Communal Award of 1932 angered even a universalist like Rabindranath Tagore and a secularist like Sarat Chandra Chattopadhyaya.

based on the principle of separation of religion and politics but it did not mention secularism. Twice the term was debated in the Constituent Assembly but on both the occasions it was rejected. Even Pandit Jawaharlal Nehru who was an agnostic did not feel the necessity of giving secularism a constitutional status. He was not sure of its efficacy in the Indian socio-cultural milieu. Later, in defence of his use of the word he said that it was closest to what it should mean in the Indian context, that is, politics and religion should be two different domains of people's activity.[11]

The government was conscious of the religious and cultural sentiments of both Hindus and Muslims. The way the Somnath temple and the Babri Masjid issues were politically handled indicated this. Since there was widespread Hindu sentiment in favour of rebuilding the Somnath temple, ransacked and destroyed by Muslim plunderers from outside India, a trust was created through the good offices of the government to rebuild the temple. Funds of course were raised from the public but once the temple was ready it was inaugurated by the President of India.

With regard to the Babri Masjid the Nehru government's action was most appropriate keeping in view the communal harmony. In December 1949, Hindu-Muslim riots had broken out in Ayodhya following the clandestine installation of an idol of Lord Ram in the Masjid. Nehru took personal initiative in the matter and under his express orders the mosque was sealed and a police guard posted. Litigation over rights of entry to the shrine continued without adjudication till as late as 1985.

At the micro level, probably even without the endorsement of the top leadership,[12] the Congress strategy was to identify with some of the Hindu and Muslim communal interests. The reason for the failure of the Hindu-nationalistic Bharatiya Jana Sangh to make any dent in the Congress constituency and its lacklustre performance in all the five parliamentary elections held between 1952 and 1971 was that its Hindu communal plank was virtually stolen by the Congress. Whether it was the anti-cow slaughter movement, or the cause of Hindi vis-à-vis Urdu, or the anti-Pakistan posture, Congress left no stone unturned to prove its credentials as a champion of the Hindu cause as much as the Jana Sangh.[13] The result was the systematic marginalization of the latter. By the time the sixth parliamentary elections were held in 1977 the Jana Sangh had been

[11] M.C. Setalvad, *Secularism* (Patel Memorial Lectures, 1965) (New Delhi: Government of India Publications Division, January 1967), pp. 17-21.

[12] Nehru had bemoaned that although 'the Congress stood for a secular society, the workers were slipping away from the Congress principles of secularism and becoming more and more communal minded.' *Congress Bulletin* (New Delhi), 5 May 1958.

[13] B.D. Graham, *Hindu Nationalism and Indian Politics: The Origins and Development of the Bharatiya Jana Sangh* (Cambridge : Cambridge University Press, 1990), pp. 255-256.

so much emasculated that it had no choice but to merge with the newly-formed Janata Party.

Simultaneously, Congress saw to it that some of the Muslim leaders who commanded respect among their co-religionists were elected to the parliament. It did not want to take any risk in this regard. For example, in the case of Maulana Abul Kalam Azad it was feared that a pre-dominantly Hindu constituency would not elect him. Therefore Azad was always fielded from constituencies with a significant number of Muslim voters - either urban Rampur or rural Mewat. This had made Dr. Zakir Hussain, the then vice president of India, to lament in his lecture at the National Integration Conference in 1961, that if a person of Azad's calibre and secular credentials had to be returned only from such a constituency having a large number of Muslims one could well imagine the fate of secularism in India.[14]

The policy of the Congress to keep the Muslims in good humour also found expression in its high profile anti-Israel and pro-Arab stance. There was a broad foreign policy rationale to follow such a policy but much of its diplomacy in West Asia was also geared to play to the domestic Muslim gallery. The idea was also to challenge Pakistan's diplomatic offensive in the region as the Rabat OIC episode of 1964 showed. Starting from the days of Mahatma Gandhi till recently Congress was ever conscious of the extra-territorial emotional bonds of the Muslims and considered it politically prudent to advertise its respect for them.

Post-Nehru Drift

After the death of Nehru (1964), and more so after the Congress split of 1969, the nation-building strategy of the party underwent a change. Actually, the national integrative strategies that Indira Gandhi followed during her twenty years of Congress leadership (1966-1984) were often in sharp contrast to those of her father both in respect of democratic norms as well as secularism. The policy of identifying itself with both the Hindu and Muslim communal sentiments was maintained but it was now tilted more in favour of Hindu interests. It must be underlined that neither Indira Gandhi nor Rajiv Gandhi were narrow-minded Hindu communalists but in search of easy acceptability among the masses they took recourse to all types of populism in which patting the Hindu ego was also one.

[14] Bidyut Chakrabarty, 'India's Secularism: Tolerance and Coercion?,' in Bidyut Chakrabarty (ed.), *Secularism and Indian Polity* (New Delhi: Segment, 1990), p. 99. Probably the party was not wrong in its political calculations. During the elections of 1962 and 1967, Congress found it difficult to get its Muslim nominees elected in northern India. Correspondingly the Jana Sangh votes increased in the region. See Mohit Bhattacharya, 'Secularism and State Building in India', in ibid., pp. 181-182; Graham, *Hindu Nationalism*, p. 265.

In the seventies, owing partly to the two wars with Pakistan (1965 and 1971) and the steep rise in the price of oil following the OPEC decision of 1973 the economic condition deteriorated. These developments coupled with the dictatorial style of functioning of Indira Gandhi resulted in widespread disaffection in the country resulting in a mass movement which rocked the politics of almost the entire Hindi belt. To prevent the political ground under her feet from slipping further she retaliated by declaring the Emergency thereby suspending all democratic and civil rights of the people. To advertise the move as a preemptive operation aimed at disallowing the 'reactionary' forces from taking over the Indian government she introduced two new words into the constitution—socialism and secularism, as if by just adding them to the document India's commitment to those ideals became total. As one scholar put it, secularism became 'a victim of its official success.'[15]

During the Emergency an extra-constitutional authority developed in the person of Indira Gandhi's younger son Sanjay Gandhi who had no qualms to tamper with the texture of Indian politics. Some of his actions caused considerable alienation of the Muslims from the Congress. His over enthusiasm for the family planning programme resulted in forcible sterilization in which Muslim males often became the victims. Similarly, the Sanjay Gandhi-inspired demolition drives against unauthorized structures that took place on a massive scale in Delhi targeted some of the Muslim-inhabited areas in particular. All this coupled with the common knowledge that Sanjay was hobnobbing with the RSS made the Muslims suspicious of Congress intentions. No wonder that they voted almost *en bloc* against the party in the 1977 elections although the erstwhile Hindu nationalistic Jana Sangh was one of the important constituents of the coalition which ousted the Congress party.

In the general elections of 1980 and subsequently in the J&K assembly elections of early 1983 the Congress strategy was to identify itself with the general Hindu fear that the nation was in danger from centrifugal forces most of which were non- or anti-Hindu in their orientation. It had been Indira Gandhi's policy to boost the Hindu ego by projecting a high-profile external posture - recall how the Jana Sangh leader Atal Behari Vajpayee had likened her to Goddess Durga, the destroyer of all evils, after India's victory over Pakistan in the Bangladesh war. It was in tune with this policy that she allowed the first nuclear test to be conducted in 1974 which had otherwise little foreign policy or military strategic rationale. In Indira Gandhi's reckoning, an India poised to emerge as a military power would attract international notice and respect which would reduce Pakistan's nuisance value in the region deemed to be behind much of India's

[15] Ashutosh Varshney, 'Contested Meanings: India's National Identity, Hindu Nationalism, and the Politics of Anxiety', *Daedalus* (Summer 1993), p. 245.

integrational problems. One of her important campaign rhetorics against the Janata Party in 1980 was that the latter had so much compromised on the foreign policy front that India's image as a great power had been tarnished—'even tiny Bhutan is sneering at us', she taunted.

During Pandit Nehru's time, as we have noted, the Congress was stealing the Hindu nationalistic platform at the micro levels. During Indira Gandhi's time the same was done at the macro level. By projecting India as a great power particularly vis-a-vis Pakistan and by aligning with communal forces depending upon the then political requirement she tried to ensure the safety of her regime by sheer *realpolitik*. In the Punjab, for example, she propped up the extremist Sikh leader Jarnail Singh Bhindranwale as a countervailing force to tackle the growing popularity of the Akali Dal. When Bhindranwale proved to be a Frankenstein he was crushed. Operation Blue Star which killed Bhindranwale satisfied the average Hindu ego. In the Muslim-majority J&K, she identified herself fully with Hindu sentiments of the people of Jammu. The Muslim-dominated National Conference of Farooq Abdullah of course retaliated in kind and won the election but the real and long-term success went to Indira Gandhi. It did not only result in the total eclipse of the BJP in Jammu, Congress emerged as somewhat of an overt champion of the Hindu cause. The policy paid handsome electoral dividends to her son Rajiv Gandhi in the election of 1984 which was held soon after her assassination by her Sikh bodyguards which led to a Hindu backlash killing thousands of Sikhs in Delhi and other parts of the country. At the back of the mind of the majority of Indians was the spectre of further disintegration of India by non-Hindu forces. The stealing of the BJP's Hindu platform was now complete - Congress won an unprecedented four-fifths majority in the parliament while the BJP was reduced to a non-entity with only two seats.

Rajiv Gandhi inherited the political strategy left behind by Indira Gandhi. He fanned the Hindu fear of possible disintegration of the country to counter the forces opposed to the concentration of power at the centre. To do this he even used temples and gatherings of *sadhus* (hermits) to make a political point or a high-voltage anti-Pakistan statement. Since abusing Pakistan is the most non-controversial pro-Hindu posture that any Indian leader can assume he frequently took recourse to this strategy. On 15 August 1988, while delivering the Independence Day speech from the ramparts of the Red Fort in Delhi he thundered that if Pakistan attacked India they would be made to remember their grand-mothers (literal translation of a Hindi slang meaning that the retaliation would far outweigh the aggression). In tune with his mother's policy of projecting India as a power to reckon with he launched a high-profile peace offensive demanding universal nuclear disarmament but actually justifying India's refusal to sign the NPT. In the neighbourhood India's military muscle was displayed to dictate politics in the region as was done in Sri Lanka. (India's intervention in the Maldives is also seen in this light by some commentators but since it was in response to an SOS sent by the Maldivian president Mohammad Abdul Gayoom it cannot be viewed that way.)

The Congress government's identification with Hindu sentiments went hand in glove with a growing public exposition of anti-Muslim feelings at the mass level. The Meenakshipuram incident of 1982 in which two hundred Harijans were converted to Islam was blown out of proportion by Hindu organizations to raise the bogey of 'Hinduism in danger'. Although the enquiry committee report on the incident revealed that the converts had done so to get rid of the social discriminations perpetrated by caste Hindus the Hindu zealots had already extracted the maximum political mileage from it. In 1983, the theme of the VHP-sponsored Ekatmata Yagna was once again the same : 'Hinduism is in danger and India cannot be kept united without uniting the Hindus.' The religious leaders who took active part in the march made provocative anti-Muslim speeches and threatened all the politicians who 'pampered' that community. It was increasingly becoming clear that a Hindu vote bank comparable to the proverbial Muslim vote bank was emerging and whosoever could grab it was sure to make it to power. The obvious contenders were the BJP and the Congress.

Advantage BJP

In this competition the Congress had an inherent handicap. Being the ruling party as well as one traditionally committed to take care of both the Hindu and Muslim communal interests it was not only expected to uphold the rule of law but also to avoid appearing overtly sympathetic to the Hindu cause. As a result it could not match the BJP's no-holds-barred pro-Hindu rhetorics allowing the latter to increasingly steal the show as the real champion of the Hindu cause. They used the Babri mosque-Ram Janmabhoomi issue and the Shah Bano case to embarrass the Congress as much as possible.

The *Hindutva* forces knew that the above issues would charge the Hindu sentiments. BJP leader L.K. Advani later admitted that following the passage of the Muslim women's bill 'the mood of the Hindus began building up'.[16] Claiming that 'we have now decided to create a strong [Hindu] vote bank' the VHP challenged all political parties to either support the *Hindutva* forces or lose these votes.[17] BJP unequivocally demanded that the mosque site must be handed over to the Hindus as the issue in question was the faith of the majority and not the legal claim over the struc-

16 *Sunday Times of India*, 14 October 1990.

17 Dagmar Markova, 'Babar's Mosque versus Ram's Birthplace: A Case Study of Misuse of Religion', *Archiv Orientalni* (Prague), Vol. 59, No. 3 (1991), pp. 271-273.

ture. The Congress which emphasized the legality of the issue could not withstand the onslaught of the BJP bandwagon.

Still, the Congress did not give up its efforts to enlist the Hindu communal support. In the electoral campaign of Allahabad by-election of 1988 it extensively used the cine actor Arun Govil who had portrayed Lord Ram in the popular TV serial *Ramayan* to drive home the point that the Congress was also pro-Ram. In the parliamentary election of 1989 the party launched its campaign from Faizabad, the U.P. district in which Ayodhya was located. There Rajiv Gandhi tacitly supported the Ramshila programme by allowing the foundation stones for the proposed Ram temple to be laid adjacent to the Babri mosque. He also promised Ramrajya. Party workers at the local levels used these to drive home the point that their party was as much in favour of the temple as the BJP. As one Congress activist put it: *Samajhnewale samajh gaye* (the message has been conveyed to those for whom it is meant).[18] But in the prevailing Hindu mood this kind of tongue-in-cheek commitment was not enough particularly when there was another party available with an unambiguous pro-Hindu commitment.

BJP's Hindutva Ideology

In analysing the ideology of the BJP the theories of Hindu nationalism as developed by itself as well as organizations like the Hindu Mahasabha, the RSS and in recent times the VHP, the Bajrang Dal, etc., who together constitute the so-called *Sangh Parivar*, should be read together. Although it has been the constant effort of the BJP to clarify that it is not in favour of establishing a Hindu theocratic state, in its political strategy to reach the masses it has always emphasized the indispensability of one's commitment to Hindutva to build the Indian nation upon.

BJP's emphasis on Hindutva is couched in the slogan of 'genuine secularism'—a Hindu state cannot be anything but secular because Hindus are essentially secular. The party is not against minorities but against 'minorityism', claim its ideologues.[19] The ideology traverses slippery ground when it argues that Indian tradition and Hindu tradition are one and the same thing and whosoever subscribes to the Indian tradition is a Hindu. Since tradition and history cannot be separated the concept breeds confusion of the worst type. D.P. Chattopadhyaya, an Indian philosopher, has argued that 'if culture is enfolded history, history is unfolded culture' and

[18] Prakash Chandra Upadhyaya, 'The Politics of Indian Secularism' *Modern Asian Studies* (Cambridge), Vol. 26, No. 4 (1992), p. 8.

[19] See interview of K.N. Govindacharya, all India general secretary of BJP, *Statesman* (New Delhi), 10 April 1993.

since cultural and historical realities are the same thing representing merely 'two views, one synchronic and the other diachronic, of one and the same reality respectively, there is no scope of segregating Indian culture from Indian history'.[20] Can, therefore, Hindu and Indian cultures be synonymous when Hinduism has a history of three-four (or even more) thousand years while Islam, and for that matter Christianity too, has also a history and tradition on the Indian soil for at least a thousand years. As Romila Thapar puts it: 'Tradition is not something which is handed down in its pristine form through generations. It is that which is chosen from the past, imbibed with a meaning which derives from the present, or, even be an invention of the present which is legitimized by an association with the past. . . . To be steeped in tradition is frequently to be seeped in what one believes or would like to believe, is the tradition. The appropriation of tradition also becomes a matter of political importance.'[21]

As its action plan BJP demands a uniform civil code for India thus doing away with the Muslim personal law, abolition of Article 370 of the constitution which gives special status to the Muslim-majority state of J&K, rewriting of the history of India which, according to it, has an unhistorical pro-Muslim bias as it has been written by 'pseudosecular' historians, and above all construction of the Ram temple at Ayodhya. All these demands can be met only if the BJP captures power at the centre. But as the ruling party in some of the states it has demonstrated that it has the willingness to take up its agenda if voted to power. The demolition of the Babri mosque comes to one's mind first in this regard. In U.P. and M.P. it also took up the task of rewriting of school history textbooks with alacrity.[22]

Another point that the BJP has dinned into willing Hindu ears is that the population of Muslims in India is increasing at a much faster rate compared to that of the Hindus thereby disturbing the present demographic balance. They attribute this to both a relatively less controlled birth rate among the Muslims as well as constant unauthorized entry of thousands of Bangladeshis into India. There is some truth in both the allegations but the facts have been blown out of proportion.[23] The charge of 'minorityism',

[20] D.P. Chattopadhyaya, 'On the Alleged Unity of Religions', Radhakrishnan Memorial Lecture, Indian Institute of Advanced Studies, Shimla, 1991, p. 4.

[21] Romila Thapar, 'Religion, Culture and Nation', *Monthly Public Opinion Survey* (New Delhi), April 1991, pp. 3-4.

[22] For details, see Ghosh, 'Rise of Political Hinduism', pp. 33-35.

[23] Some relevant literature in this context are: Nafis Ahmad Siddiqui, *Population Geography of Muslims of India* (New Delhi: S. Chand, 1976); Ashish Bose, *From Population to People* (New Delhi : B.R. Publishing, 1988), pp. 363-377; R.B.N. Sinha, 'Attitudes of Hindus and Muslims to Family Planning', *The Journal of Family Welfare* (Bombay), Vol. 37 No. 2 (June 1991), pp. 47-49; Malika B. Mistry, 'Hindu-Muslim Fertility Differentials in India', *New Quest* (Pune), No. 94, (July-August 1992), p. 236; Pravin Visaria and Leela Visaria, 'Demographic Transition: Accelerating Fertility Decline in 1980s', *Economic and Political Weekly* (Bombay), 17-24 December 1994, p. 3286.

that is, that the Muslims are pampered is just not true as all social indicators reveal.[24]

The Legitimacy Debate

The debate over nation-building naturally boils down to the question as to who has the legitimate means and goals to rule India. Although both the Hindu nationalists and the Congress-type secularists accuse each other of following disruptive means and each claims to follow the right track towards building the Indian nation, going by the changing electoral graphs of India it seems that people have not yet made up their mind as to who is right. In a democracy, that too in a pluralistic society, if just the logic of numbers is accepted as the criterion of political legitimacy it would create havoc with the societal balance. Actually the strength of a democracy does not lie in how much care it takes of the majority interests. Its strength lies in its capacity and commitment to safeguard the rights of the minorities and provide them with a sense of security. Viewed from this perspective the logic of the Hindu nationalists does not seem to be tenable. By creating the situation that led to the destruction of the Babri mosque they have subscribed to nothing but mobocracy. Similarly, by putting all their ideological eggs in the Hindutva basket they have rationalized what may be characterized as majoritarianism. Both mobocracy and majoritarianism are anathema to democracy.

By mob one may mean a large collection of people who are temporarily charged with emotions to do or undo a particular act beyond the institutional or legal norms. While democracies must permit the expression of all such views they are not obliged to implement all those views. Likewise, although democracy is all for majority rule it must never presuppose one group as a permanent majority and others as permanent minorities which is bound to be the case if the majority-minority parameters are drawn on ethnic or communal lines. As it has been put: 'Democracy must keep open the possibility of the continuous restructuring of the ruling group in majority. A person in the minority today must have a reasonable hope of being in the majority tomorrow. Likewise, the group currently in the majority must be aware that in future it may sit on the back-benches, lie on the fringe. In short, a society where a group is permanently entrenched as the politically

[24] Although Muslims have held very responsible positions in the government such as presidents, cabinet ministers, cabinet secretaries, army generals, defence research scientists, Supreme Court Chief Justices, etc., so far as general employment in civil and military sectors are concerned they are under-represented. For various kinds of statistics in this regard, see H.Y. Siddiqui, 'Quest for a Secular Society—Challenge and Response', in Chakrabarty (ed.), *Secularism*, p. 240; *Muslim India* (New Delhi), No. 141, September 1994, pp. 413-414; *India Today*, 31 January 1993, pp. 36-37.

relevant majority cannot be a democracy. For quite simply, there exists no permanent majority within a democracy.'[25]

But if the BJP variety of majoritarianism is repugnant to democracy the Congress variety of secularism based on bi-communalism or multi-communalism does not augur well for the future of Indian democracy either. Each category would try to thrive at the cost of the other making the debate ever more acrimonious and the political competition cut-throat. Against the background of major electoral reverses for the Congress in Andhra Pradesh and Karnataka and impending elections in politically important Bihar, Gujarat and Maharashtra the party is frantic to win back the Muslim sympathy which it has been losing over the years. The recent reimposition of the ban on the VHP under the Unlawful Activities (Prevention) Act of 1967, the indication that Prime Minister Rao has given that the Terrorist and Disruptive Activities Act (TADA) should be repealed in Gujarat and Maharashtra as it is being misused there against the Muslims,[26] the way the promotion of Urdu has been subjected to electoral calculations in Karnataka, etc., point to the party's hot pursuit of the Muslim votes. Yet on one of its most important commitments made after the Babri mosque affair, that it would be rebuilt, the Congress is evasive. This reflects its ambivalence—it does not want to appear as totally impartial on the Hindu-Muslim question which has the political danger of being interpreted by communal Hindus as pro-Muslim while at the same time it does not want the Muslims to be totally alienated either. That the Muslims would not be enamoured by the Congress gimmicks, at least in the near future, is almost certain.[27]

Legitimacy is essentially a political concept. Unfortunately, however, the Congress is shying away from taking political positions on certain issues which can be resolved only that way. Had Nehru not closed the Babri Masjid in 1949 it would have led to communal violence. But the present Congress leadership is throwing things to the judiciary for decisions which the latter is not even competent to handle. The presidential reference under Article 143 of the Indian Constitution to the Supreme Court for its opinion

25 Rajeev Bhargava, 'What is Democracy?', *Seminar* (New Delhi), No. 389, January 1992, pp. 37-38.

26 Rao's interview in the *Times of India*, 25 January 1995. That there is a clear strategy to woo the Muslim voters in these states is evident, for barring J&K where the people arrested under the act have to be Muslims in other parts Muslims are only a few. Out of about 68,000 so arrested only 3,416 are Muslims. See Arun Shourie, 'Tada is a Decade Old, So Why has Rao Suddenly Discovered it Must Go Now', *The Asian Age*, 20 January 1995.

27 Some Muslim organizations in Bombay and Imam Bukhari of Delhi have called for a boycott of the Congress in the forthcoming elections. Reportedly, groups of Muslim youth are being sent to Bihar, Gujarat and Maharashtra to campaign among Muslims against the Congress. Ironically, the Muslims of Maharashtra are supporting the BJP-Shiv Sena combine to defeat the Congress. See *The Asian Age*, 13, 18, 22 and 25 January 1995. Also see Asghar Ali Engineer, 'The Muslim Vote in Maharashtra', *The Hindu*, 19 January 1995.

whether any temple existed in Ayodhya at the spot of the Babri Masjid before it was constructed fell in such a category. Knowing that the issue was political the Supreme Court very rightly refused to answer the query and returned the reference.[28]

Communalism of All Sorts

The hard reality of Indian political culture is that India has not yet become a society where the individual is an autonomous political unit, although both constitutionally and electorally it is supposed to be so. During the drafting of the Indian constitution when there were discussions to emulate the traditional Indian style of governance by going back to village-oriented administration, both modernists like Nehru and the spokesman of the depressed classes and the chairman of the drafting committee, B.R. Ambedkar, were opposed to it. While concluding the debate, Ambedkar had said: 'I hold that these village republics have been the ruination of India. I am therefore surprised that those who condemn provincialism and communalism should come forward as the champions of the village. What is the village but a sink of localism, a den of ignorance, narrow-mindedness and communalism? I am glad that the draft constitution has discarded the village and adopted the individual as its unit.'[29] Ambedkar had hoped that by making the individual an autonomous political unit the scourge of casteism, communalism and localism would be done away with. But after about half-a-century of India's independence the experience seems to be quite different. In the mass politics of the country what has become more important is not the individual but the caste or community he belongs to resulting in all sorts of inter-caste and inter-communal bargainings.

The stratification of Indian society is at multiple levels - religious, linguistic, casteist, gender-related, and over and above economic. The overlapping nature of these stratifications both at the horizontal as well as vertical levels makes things difficult to analyze but there is an inherent logic. Anthropologist Ajit Danda has shown that not only ethnic or other identities of individuals matter, they are also extremely elastic as several identities make up for a complete personality.[30] Therefore, one need not be

[28] It was a vindication of the BJP stand that the issue could not be settled through the court as Hindu faith was involved. It may be relevant here to mention that in 1988 the Muslims had demonstrated in Murshidabad (West Bengal) against the ruling of the Supreme Court in the Babri Masjid case. In 1991, the Blacks in the United States had revolted against the judgment of a district court in the Rodney Jones case leading to widespread riots. On the so-called 'faith' argument as viewed from a comparative international perspective, see Varshney, 'Contested Meanings', pp. 250-251.

[29] Quoted in S. Gurumurthy, 'State and Society', *Seminar*, No. 417, May 1994, p. 16.

[30] Ajit K. Danda, *Ethnicity in India* (New Delhi: Inter-India, 1991).

apologetic about the current backward classes movements and the resultant inter-caste tensions. Given the hierarchical nature of Indian society this was bound to happen one day. From these conflicts only would emerge a more democratic socio-political order.

What Indians are increasingly getting used to is neither the Hindu nationalism of the Sangh Parivar nor the bi-communalism of the Congress but some sort of multi-communalism where each of the constituents is fractured by intra-community tensions. The political alliance between the backward castes and the Muslims in Bihar and U.P. has emerged as such a formidable force that both the BJP and the Congress have started feeling the brunt. No wonder that the BJP has included in its political lexicon such themes as equity and justice for them.[31] Muslims and Christians also have realized the worth of collective bargaining and just like the Hindu backward castes they too are demanding job quotas or some such affirmative actions from the state. There is no doubt that as the Hindu nationalists would come more and more to the vicinity of power the sheer logic of numbers would make them shift their strategies. During the Aurangabad municipal elections of 1988 when the Shiv Sena assumed a more militant Hindu posture and caused reversals for the BJP the latter castigated the Sena for its most dangerous use of the communal card.[32] Now the two are together for the Maharashtra assembly polls. But if the Muslims there feel more comfortable with them than with the Congress they would take little time to change their rhetorics. Already the emphasis has shifted to economic issues.[33] In Gujarat there are reports that inner tensions are building up between the BJP and the RSS.[34] So far as the BJP-VHP relations are concerned the BJP has strictly confined its agenda to the Ram temple in Ayodhya alone and not to Kashi and Mathura which are the VHP's next targets. In the Muslim society also there are internal debates and introspection. The so-called modernists and traditionalists are vying with each other to capture the attention of the masses.

The end result of all these 'million little mutinies', to borrow V.S. Naipaul's phrase, would have to be a more secular polity which should be defined as 'the mode of reconciliation of identity groups in the process of democratic transformation based on reason'. The basic assumption is that 'it is part of the struggle against social and class domination and the under-

[31] For details, see Ghosh, 'Rise of Political Hinduism', pp. 49-51.

[32] Asghar Ali Engineer, 'Secularism and Emerging Challenge of Communalism: Practical Aspects', in Chakrabarty (ed.), *Secularism,* p. 249.

[33] Following the Telugu Desam Party's model to come to power in Andhra Pradesh the BJP and the Shiv Sena have also promised cheap food for the poor and houses for the slum dwellers. *Times of India,* 22 December 1994; *The Asian Age,* 21 January 1995; *The Hindu,* 26 January 1995.

[34] *The Asian Age,* 23 January 1995.

lying concept of rationality is not positivist rationality but democratic rationality.'[35]

Conclusion

Hindu nationalism is a permanent fixture in Indian polity. But now that the Hindu nationalists are dreaming for the first time of capturing political power there is a visible shift in their strategies to accommodate the various social classes in governance and for the distribution of justice. But all these are still piecemeal and ad-hocist. There is hardly any effort to integrate them into a grand strategy for nation-building. At this juncture the Muslims might have probably considered it tactical to vote for the BJP in Maharashtra but so long as the ideology of *Hindutva* would be the guiding spirit of the party it is most unlikely that the Muslims would feel comfortable with it.

For building the Indian nation Hindutva indeed has a role but its undercurrents can be more forceful than its overt display. So long as the Congress understood this its record was better. But from the time it switched to a strategy of playing to the Hindu gallery it became a victim of its own folly. It not only alienated the Muslims but also gave respectability to an ideology the ultimate beneficiary of which became the Hindu nationalists for they had both the organization as well as the jargons to outsmart the Congress in this game.

The only way India can achieve secularism in the real sense when the rule of law would rule the roost is through intra-social conflicts of all kinds. In the short run it may look disruptive but given the historical experience of India there do not seem to be any short-cut. Before individuals become the autonomous political units the stage to be undergone would have to be the federation of communities. India has achieved the political federation - a union of states - which is a vertical contraption. To complete the process a horizontal federation would as well have to be achieved. The dalit, backward caste and minority rights movements that are now rocking the country would eventually be the catalysts. That would complete the process of legitimacy of the Indian state.

35 Manoranjan Mohanty, 'Secularism: Hegemonic and Democratic', in Chakrabarty (ed.), *Secularism*, p. 8.

Understanding Order and Legitimacy in Punjab since 1984

GURHARPAL SINGH

In the general discussion of legitimacy in South Asian politics the issue of disorder and the maintenance of order in peripheral regions has largely been neglected. Most South Asian states face regional and sub-national movements that stubbornly resist the transformation of order into routinised legitimacy. Some of these challenges (Kashmir, Sindh, the Tamil Movement in Sri Lanka) are so profound that they question the very bases of the state system; others (Punjab, Assam, Nagaland) at best have been 'managed' and would appear to provide useful lessons that might have some value in policy research and more detached reflection on the wider subject of political legitimacy.[1] The developments in Punjab since 1984 seem to fit into the latter category for, from being almost a pathological case of disorder for nearly a decade, the situation in the state, it is argued, has been 'transformed' in the last two years into one of near 'normalcy'. Punjab today is being projected as 'model'[2] - with all-India implications - where the Indian state has successfully overcome one of the most difficult confrontations since independence.

The aim of this paper is to critically examine the explanations being offered for the transformation of Punjab's political crisis into a managed model of orderly rule. This will be done by focusing on developments from 1987 to 1995. After outlining the scale of disorder and reviewing the flawed attempt to reconstruct the state's political system under the Rajiv-Longowal Accord, we will examine perspectives which underpin the dramatic change: (i) effective anti-terrorism; (ii) Punjab's social structure; and (iii), the case of 'managed disorder'. None of these perspectives is exclusive and there is considerable overlap. The paper will conclude with a reflection on the implications of achieving 'order' for future politics in the state.

[1] Political order and challenges to legitimacy in South Asia have recently been operationalized in terms of 'governance,' see for example, Atul Kohli's *Democracy and Discontent: India's Growing Crisis of Ungovernability* (Cambridge: Cambridge University Press, 1990). In South Asia's peripheral regions it is perhaps more appropriate to see 'governance' as a continuum with disorder and legitimacy at the extremes and order occupying an intermediate position. The term legitimacy as used in this paper will refer to rule bound behaviour which commands majority consent freely and willingly given and is underpinned by 'normative agreement' on how rules are constructed. For discussion of the latter see David Held, *Political Theory and the Modern State* (Cambridge: Polity Press, 1990), ch. 4.

[2] See H.S. Sodhi, 'Punjab: The Trendsetter', *Defence Today* (New Delhi), August 1993, pp. 21-31.

I

The magnitude of the disorder in Punjab can be appreciated by the scale of violence. Since 1981 almost 25,000 people have been killed.[3] In addition the number of involuntary disappearances and illegal detainees remain unknown although the latter are estimated to vary from 20,000 to 45,000. At its peak between 1989-92 the insurgency by Sikh militants campaigning for a separate Sikh state of Khalistan threatened to completely overwhelm the security forces and effectively sidelined the moderate Akalis - the mainstream Sikh political party. From May 1987 to February 1992 Punjab was under President's Rule, witnessed quasi-militarisation and de facto 'police raj.' A series of special laws not only suspended the normal political process in the state but empowered the security forces to take draconian measure in the containment of disorder and insurgents. The level of violence increased dramatically from 1987 onwards with the death toll rising from 1,333 (1987) to 2,432 (1988) and peaking at 5,265 (1991), before falling to 3,883 (1992) and 871 (1993).[4] During these years Punjab was often referred to as 'an area of darkness' where virtual civil war conditions prevailed.[5]

In contrast to the events leading up to Operation Blue Star, the period since 1984 has received little scholarly attention.[6] To be sure the stress has been on the causes of the 'Punjab problem' rather than factors that sustained the political structure in the state during this period. Some scholars have now begun to explore the strategies of conflict management pursued by the Centre since 1984, but even here the emphasis is on broad policy - or the lack of it - than on local conditions or anti-terrorist strategy.[7] One explanation for this omission could be the obvious: that this area of research has hitherto been neglected. But a more plausible answer, however, probably lies in the fixation with the Rajiv-Longowal Accord as a kind of 'social contract' of Punjab politics.

Indeed, most conventional writing on the Punjab problem since 1984 suggests that the subsequent causes of the troubles lay in the inability of

[3] *India Today* (New Delhi), 15 June 1993.

[4] The figures are cited in *The Week* (New Delhi), 5 June 1994.

[5] *India Today*, 15 July 1992.

[6] For two recent contributions see Joyce Pettigrew, *The Sikhs of Punjab: Unheard Voices of State and Guerrilla Violence* (New Jersey: Zed Books, 1995a), and Gurharpal Singh, 'The Punjab Crisis since 1984: A Reassessment', *Ethnic and Racial Studies*, Vol. 18, No. 3, July 1995, pp. 476-493.

[7] See Gurharpal Singh, 'Ethnic Conflict in India: A Case Study of Punjab', in John McGarry and Brendan O'Leary (eds.), *The Politics of Ethnic Conflict Regulation* (London: Routledge, 1993), pp. 84-105.

the Centre to deliver on the accord.[8] Completed against the backdrop of Indira Gandhi's assassination, the election of Rajiv Gandhi as Congress-I leader, and the latter's landslide victory in the 1984 elections, the Rajiv-Longowal Accord appeared to mark a new departure in regional policy. The territorial, economic and religious demands that had fuelled the Sikh agitation before 1984, and were held to be non-negotiable by Indira Gandhi, were recognized by the accord. For the moderate Akali Dal Longowal AD(L), the accord provided a return to democratic politics; for Rajiv Gandhi it represented a dynamic breakthrough, a befitting start to his premiership.

Yet in retrospect the accord far from marking a new departure in Punjab politics was a continuation of the Centre's policy, dating from the late 1940s, of symbolic agreements accompanied by non-implementation.[9] Hastily formulated by Rajiv's advisors, the AD(L) party to the agreement was assiduously groomed by New Delhi along the familiar pattern of tactical concession of political power at the state level as quid pro quo for deflection, diffusion and de-emphasis on ethnic demands. As a wit has aptly put it, this effort was a continuation of a process in which 'secular' and (Indian) 'nationalist' Sikh leaders have been regularly 'hailed' by New Delhi only to be 'nailed' when they have served their purpose.[10] That this role proved difficult for AD(L) was soon to become apparent. The AD(L) government which came to power in September 1985 rapidly disintegrated as Rajiv's commitment to the accord waned and the Congress-I government at the Centre reverted to interference in the AD(L) administration for short-term gain. Whereas the Centre increasingly viewed the AD(L) administration in terms of containing militancy, its capacity to do so was undermined by the reluctance of the Centre to implement provisions of the accord. The transfer of Chandigarh, scheduled for 26 January 1986, was first delayed, then postponed, and eventually suspended for an indefinite period. Other provisions of the accord were either nullified or produced outcomes incompatible with the original agreement.[11] The ultimate reversal of policy was marked by the Congress-I factional penetration of AD(L) government from April 1986 onwards, the appointment of a highly partisan governor (Ray), and the instalment of Julius Ribeiro as the Director General of police with a wide brief to undertake anti-terrorist operati-

[8] See Atul Kohli (1990); Paul R. Brass, *Ethnicity and Nationalism* (New Delhi: Sage, 1991).

[9] In a sense a systematic analysis of the Rajiv-Longowal Accord would locate it in the context of other Punjab accords since 1947 and the strategies of ethnic conflict management followed in Punjab by the Centre since independence. As argued in Singh (1995), the main strategy has been one of 'hegemonic control' (1947-1984), collapsing into 'violent control' after 1986. For a discussion of 'hegemonic control', see McGarry and O'Leary (eds.), (1993), pp. 1-40.

[10] See Gurharpal Singh, 'The Punjab Problem in the 1990s: A Post-1984 Assessment', *The Journal of Commonwealth and Comparative Politics*, Vol. 29, No. 2, July 1991, p. 188.

[11] Singh (1991), p. 178.

ons. The AD(L) government was eventually dismissed in May 1987 when President's Rule was imposed on the grounds that there was 'chaos and anarchy in Punjab.'

II

Following the imposition of President's Rule anti-terrorism became the main instrument of the Centre's policy in Punjab. Despite the misgivings of most analysts about this policy it appears to have succeeded without making major political concessions, either to militants or moderate Akali leadership. What factors account for this success? As noted above there are three different interpretations that require further examination.

(i) Effective Anti-Terrorism

The most public explanation of restoration of order in Punjab claims the main credit for the effective anti-terrorist policies of the security forces. Although anti-terrorism had become the main thrust of the Centre's policy after May 1987, it was in mid-1992 that the security forces achieved an impressive breakthrough.

Nevertheless pre-1992 anti-terrorism as policy was vigorously pursued. Pronounced in Ribeiro's words as a form of 'bullets for bullets,' it led to a number of major changes. The security apparatus in Punjab, particularly the Punjab Police, was reorganized.[12] In addition to the Central Reserve Police Force (CRPF), the Border Security Force (BSF) and the regular use of the Army, the Punjab Police was strengthened with the creation of new senior posts and mass recruitment at constable and special constable level. Anti-terrorist legislation - National Security Act (1980), Punjab Disturbed Areas Ordinance (1983), Terrorist Areas (Special Courts) Act (1984), and the Terrorist and Disruptive Activities (Prevention) Act (1985) - was rigorously enforced with official approval for 'shoot to kill' where known offenders were apprehended. Moreover, counter-insurgency was given a high priority with the employment of irregular hit squads intended to infiltrate and liquidate terrorist organizations.[13]

The political backing for anti-terrorism began to waver with the election of the National Front government in November 1989 and 8 Sikh radical MPs from 13 Lok Sabha seats in Punjab. Whilst the National Front government of V. P. Singh sought to introduce more accountability into the

[12] The size of Punjab Police increased from about 20,000 in the early 1980s to approximately 60,000 in 1992. Expenditure on the police increased from 200 million Rupees in 1981 to 7,000 million in 1993. See *The Tribune* (Chandigarh), 5 March 1993.

[13] See Singh (1991).

operation of the security forces, its successor led by Shekhar opened a dialogue with the militants that eventually culminated in the agreement to hold Punjab Legislative Assembly (PLA) elections in June 1991. During this period, it is argued, the moral of the security forces plummeted as some former terrorists prepared to capture power through the ballot box in a contest that was boycotted by the Congress-I.[14] Thus the timely assassination of Rajiv Gandhi, the massacre of 76 passengers on two trains, and the election of a Congress-I government at the Centre in June 1991, provided a set of circumstances that led to the reinforcement of political will and commitment to anti-terrorism.

In the autumn of 1991 several measures were taken to 'pacify' Punjab. K. P. S. Gill, the former chief of police who had acquired the reputation of 'Governor-General' and, had ruthlessly prosecuted the anti-terrorist campaign, was reinstated. Simultaneously, further nine divisions of the Indian Army were moved into the province to contain militancy.[15] The army deployment at its peak in February 1992 blanketed the state with security for in addition to 120,000 army personnel, the security forces could call on 53,000 Punjab Police, 28,000 Home Guards, 10,000 Special Police Officers and over 70,000 paramilitary personnel. Unlike previous deployments, in Operation Rakshak II (November 1991 onwards) the army took a backstage role by providing support to the police and administration to re-establish the authority of the state. This was done by freeing the police from routine duties to undertake more offensive actions and by sealing the Indo-Pakistan border.[16]

Further support for the policy came with the victory of the Congress-I in the February 1992 PLA elections which were boycotted by the mainstream Sikh political parties. As the main raison d' être of the new administration was to combat militancy, it gave a free hand to the security force to 'systematically plan for five years to rid Punjab of militancy.'[17] Gill bolstered the Police with further recruitment. Incentives were offered for the elimination of suspected terrorists and police tactics were reevaluated. Massacres by terrorists were countered by massacres by the security

14 In an earlier article, Gurharpal Singh, 'The Punjab Elections 1992: Breakthrough or Breakdown?', *Asian Survey*, Vol. 32, No. 11 (1992), pp. 998-999, I have provided a typology of Sikh political leadership at the time. Had the elections taken place - elections boycotted by the Congress-I - the 'democratic militants' would have formed the government.

15 After 1984 the army was deployed in Punjab in Operation Rakshak I (May 1990). During this deployment its role was to seal the border with Pakistan and assist the police in anti-terrorist operations. In May 1991, the army was asked to withdraw from the border districts. In Operation Rakshak II (November 1992 onwards), troops from I, II and VI corps were used to swamp the state with a security cordon prior to the holding of PLA elections in February 1992. See R. Nath, 'In the Eye of the Storm', *Defence Today*, August 1993, pp. 32-45.

16 See Manoj Joshi, *Combating Terrorism in Punjab* (London: RISCI, 1993), pp. 12-13.

17 See *Jane's Defence Weekly* (London), 23 June 1993.

forces. The new mood of determination was aptly summarized by Gill who now declared an 'open season on terrorists'.[18]

The first results of aggressive anti-terrorism became evident in the middle of 1992: several leading figures of militant organizations were killed. Thereafter, despite the efforts of the militants to regroup and target families of the police, the security forces gained the upper hand. This turnabout was marked by a number of well publicized 'surrender ceremonies' of terrorists and the death of Manochahal, the leader of Bhindranwale Tiger Force, in February 1993. The latter's death marked the elimination of most top-ranking militants and with their departure their organizations rapidly disintegrated.

Aggressive anti-terrorism, however, was not without its limitations. For one though its effectiveness against leading militants was quite marked, it lacked subtlety in dealing with the militants' support structures. One set of figures available suggests that the casualty rate between 1984 and 1994 was 60.8 per cent terrorist, 31 per cent civilian and 8.2 per cent the security force.[19] Thus the main victims of violence in Punjab were not the security forces, but civilians and terrorists. A more detailed assessment of the figure for the elimination of terrorists in the first six months of 1992 suggests that the killing ratio of hardcore terrorists to non-hardcore terrorists varied from 1:9 to 1:18, respectively.[20] This may have been done for sound operational reasons - to instil fear and discourage further recruitment by militants - but its outcome suggests a more of a blunderbuss approach. Concern at such 'effectiveness' was expressed even by sections of the army.[21] More significantly, however, the cost of counter-insurgency in Punjab since 1984 has been variously estimated to be around Rs 60,000 millions, a figure which excludes certain hidden costs and the operation expenditure of the army. While it might be justified to argue that this expenditure was necessary to fight the 'nation's war', we need to examine the implications of entrenching a 'security state' that has become one of the main consumers of Punjab government expenditure.[22]

(ii) Punjab's Social Structure

A more interesting perspective on how order has been re-established in Punjab locates the role of counter-insurgency in a broader context. It sug-

18 *India Today*, 15 April 1993.

19 *The Week*, 5 June 1994.

20 This based on data cited in *The Tribune*, January-June 1992.

21 *India Today*, 30 April 1991.

22 For a discussion of the economic implications of counter-insurgency in Punjab see, Shinder S. Thandi, 'Counter-insurgency and Political Violence in Punjab 1980-1994', in Gurharpal Singh and Ian Talbot (eds.), *Punjabi Identity: Continuity and Change* (New Delhi: Manohar, 1995).

gests that the success of anti-terrorism was not simply the function of actions taken by the security force. Rather the failure of the militants - and therefore the success of the security forces - can be explained by the characteristics of Punjab's social structure, and in particular the values of *Jat* Sikh society.

As the militancy was largely based among the *Jat* Sikh peasantry, this fact has drawn the attention of some social anthropologists.[23] Historically, studies of *Jat* Sikhs have shown the continuation of certain types of social behaviour dating from the past. Prominent among these is the high propensity to factionalism, competitiveness, egalitarianism, and the pursuit of vertical linkages to enhance the accumulation of property and prestige.[24] These values, it is further suggested, are not purely the outgrowth of Sikhism but are rooted in Punjab's agrarian society. Economic development, including the Green Revolution, has done little to change Punjab's social values and has in fact introduced further competition, factionalism, rivalry and enmity by atomizing village society. In short, *Jat* Sikh society - apart from its religious institutions - has developed few associations of horizontal nature, and is characterized essentially by vertical linkages which, in times of crisis, can easily become porous and provide little opportunity for acting as structures of resistance, opposition and mobilization.

From detailed studies now being done of militants and their organizations[25] it is becoming apparent that their mode of functioning was heavily influenced by the existing social structure. As well as utilizing cultural Jat Sikh history - heroism, resistance, and inevitable will to power - the militants in their daily operations became ensnared in existing social networks - in local feuds and factional enmities, in kinship retribution, in the social underworld of criminality, in the private accumulation of wealth, and in the personal pursuit of aggrandizement. The militants pursued multi-functional tasks

> involving themselves in family disputes, maintaining contacts with kin, and with business partners or contacting the police for information on disappearing persons... Instead of maintaining exclusivist, single purpose ties, guerillas became involved in the networks of rural society inevitably perishing at their hands.[26]

23 See, Joyce Pettigrew (1995a), and Joyce Pettigrew, 'Achieving a New Frontier: Rural Political Patterns and their Impact on the Sikh Independence Movement', *International Journal of Punjab Studies*, Vol. 2, No. 1, April 1995b.

24 See Joyce Pettigrew, *Robber Noblemen* (London: Routledge, Kegan and Paul, 1975).

25 See Pettigrew (1995a and 1995b).

26 Joyce Pettigrew, 'Defeating an Independence Movement: The State and Local Groupings in the Sikh Rural Areas Post-1984', in Singh and Talbot (eds.), (1995).

Or to put in other words:

> The movement (militancy) had been ideological in intent and a people's struggle. What distorted it was that rural society, where it was located, gave primary importance to the personal bond and to the individual...Guerillas working within a framework based entirely on personal connections rather than associational ties were fighting a modern war with primitive forms of organisation.[27]

These characteristics made the militant movement easy prey to infiltration, counter-insurgency and manipulation by the security forces. Local and personal vendettas were skilfully exploited by the police and the unofficial counter-insurgency forces. In fact it is suggested, as we shall see below, the whole militancy movement was thoroughly infiltrated by the counter-insurgency agencies.

This perspective has some tangible appeal insofar as it conforms to the 'iron law of *Jat* Sikh politics': that is, the more ideological a cause the more likely it is that it will generate intense factionalism. Indeed, there is a powerful logic in the explanation for it draws attention to the way *Jat* Sikh politics have been 'managed' by the Congress since 1947 through a skilful exploitation of factional rivalries. And if under the disturbed conditions of 1984-95 the use of the same tactic led to disorder, anarchy and the loss of innocent lives, then its advocates insist, it must be situated in the 'rough and ready culture of Punjab [where] people find nothing extraordinary in the implementation of the maxim that 'those who live by the sword shall perish by the sword.'[28]

(iii) 'Managed Disorder'

The relative ease with which the security forces penetrated the militants can perhaps be attributed to the social structure. It has also, however, revived speculation that troubles in Punjab were carefully orchestrated, representing a form of 'managed disorder.' Such conspiratorial explanations would be difficult to entertain were it not for the strange congruence in events before and after 1984 and that this view is strongly held by the main political force in the state - the Akalis.

Whereas most serious analyst agree that the role of Pakistan and the Sikh diaspora in supporting the militants' insurgency was a contributory factor to the troubles, few have ever doubted the Indian state's *capacity* to impose its authority in the province. Unlike other peripheral regions of

[27] Ibid.
[28] Joshi, p. 20.

the Indian Union, Punjab hardly constitutes ideal territory for guerilla warfare. Moreover, previous examples of insurgency (Babbar Akalis, Communists, Naxalites) in the province, before and after 1947, provide ready case studies of the failure of what the novelist Jaswant Singh Kanwal has called 'revolts of the blood.'[29] What was different about the militants' campaign for Khalistan was that elements within the Centre actively support the secessionists only later to put them to the sword. The Machiavellian manoeuvres of Indira Gandhi and events leading up to Operation Blue Star have been well documented.[30] Even if militants led by Bhindranwale had developed a 'relative autonomy' of their own, they could not avoid the final reckoning.

The policy of infiltrating and using militant organization by elements of the Centre and security forces was not abandoned by the Rajiv-Longowal Accord but continued thereafter. Evidence now emerging of the 'secret war' against terrorism points conclusively to the direct involvement of sections of the security and counter-insurgency intelligence agencies in the setting-up, control and actions of certain militant organizations.[31] This involvement cannot be dismissed purely in terms of the 'necessary requirements of counter-insurgency': the exact extent of the influence might never be known, but what is certain that those who could have been in a position to provide some answers - militant leaders - have been killed with ruthless efficiency.[32]

The case of 'managed disorder' is further supported by circumstantial evidence. Little systematic research has thus far been undertaken into the various 'operations' and strategic acts of 'terror'. Many of the security operations (e.g. Operation Black Thunder) were stage-managed or deliberately of limited nature (Operation Rakshak I).[33] More crucially perhaps the test of 'Who benefited?' by some of the acts of timely terror (e.g. almost prior to each successive renewal of President's Rule, postponement of June 1991 elections, the Akali boycott of 1992 PLA elections and so on) has hardly been undertaken. Any such assessment would have to evaluate a number of inconsistencies, not least between the militants' goal of building a people's movement and the use of terror as strategy. Although formally

29 See J.S. Kanwal, *Lhue de Lohe* (New Delhi: Arsi Publishers, 1982 (Punjabi).

30 See Mark Tully and Satish Jacob, *Amritsar: Mrs Gandhi's Last Battle* (London: Jonathan Cape, 1985).

31 This point is forcefully made by Pettigrew (1995a, ch.3). For confessions of a former police 'black cat' see *The Tribune*, 10 November, 1994.

32 Speaking of the security forces ability to control the militants, Kanwar Sandhu, correspondent of *India Today*, commented: 'When it came to the bit, Gill was able to control militant activity within three months. When the police wanted to control it, they did.' Quoted in Pettigrew (1995a), p. 123.

33 For detailed account of the Centre's efforts to split the militant leadership before Operation Black Thunder, see Gurmit Singh, *History of Sikh Struggles*, Vol. IV (New Delhi: Atlantic Publishers), ch. 5.

the Congress-I has been the main proponent of anti-terrorism, its pursuit of this policy has 'fortuitously' coincided with the resurrection of its political fortunes in the state.

The case for 'managed disorder' also highlights a parallel example: Assam, it is suggested, was the forerunner of the 'Punjab model' and, interestingly, many of the leading administrative and security personnel were transferred from Assam to Punjab.[34] More significantly interviews with leading 'moderate' Akalis indicate their dismay that the '10 per cent government' - reference to the Congress-I victory in the 1992 PLA elections - was able to so effectively and quickly deal with the militant threat. Either the militants, they contend, were 'paper tigers' or Congress 'agents' whose actions directly or indirectly benefited only one party. Of course reality might not be so simple and the charge of Congress agents against militants has been the regular retort of moderate Akalis. The truth probably lies somewhere in between for as the *Economic and Political Weekly* has noted both the militants and the security forces certainly succeeded in 'terrorizing the people of Punjab.'[35]

III

Whatever perspective is held to be critical in undermining militancy in Punjab, a number of implications arise for the political system in the state and for the management of regional conflicts generally.

First, effective anti-terrorism creates more problems than it resolves. In addition to the high costs of such a policy - costs might or might not be justified - there is the obvious brutalization of administration and civil society, catalogued extensively by human rights agencies in the case of Punjab.[36] Such brutalization cannot be sustained simply by the argument that it is the result of the conditions in the 'war against militancy.' To pose it differently, a liberal-democratic system that replicates the methods of terrorists in its anti-terrorist policies threatens to undermine its own foundations. As a perceptive observer of the Punjab scene has noted:

> The free hand given to the Punjab Police may become a 'model' for application elsewhere, and, more dangerously everywhere in the country. Unchecked by a political system...it could mean the collapse of democracy as witnessed in Sri Lanka in the 1980s.[37]

34 See Shekhar Gupta, *India Redefines its Role*, Adelphi Paper 293 (Oxford: OUP, 1995).

35 *Economic and Political Weekly* (Bombay), 23 September 1989.

36 For example see, *Asia Watch Human Rights in India: Punjab in Crisis* (New York: Asia Watch, 1991).

37 Joshi, p. 28.

Indeed, the 'security state' in Punjab succeeded in establishing a degree of paramountcy over the civil administration that has been resented both by the state's bureaucracy and, to some extent, the Beant Singh administration since 1992. It openly justified the coercion of non-militant opposition politicians and resents formal scrutiny, either by its own internal systems or outside bodies such as the judicial system or human rights organizations.[38] Perhaps the major limitations of the kind of 'effective anti-terrorism' practized in Punjab, however, is its capacity for *repetition*. Underpinned - like Operation Desert Storm - by the assumption of overwhelming use of force, it will require a high level of commitment, both in political and financial terms, if it is ever to be replicated. In the shortterm horizons that dominate most leadership in Punjab and the Centre, such commitment may not be always forthcoming.

Second, if there is some validity in the social structure and 'managed disorder' perspectives, then despite the reservations about the *repeatability* of effective anti-terrorism, one conclusion is obvious: problems of legitimate governance apart, the state has an enormous capacity to *impose* and *sustain* order in the social conditions pertaining in Punjab where the threat from militancy arises from one community that itself is a minority in the all-India context and is heavily integrated into the local and national state structure. Set against these overwhelming odds it seems militancy is unlikely to succeed unless there is a set of concurrent crises - lack of cohesion and indecisiveness at the Centre, a generalized geo-political conflagration and, above all, a high degree of political unity among Sikhs.

Third, in light of the above arguments we must also reflect on the ability of the Congress-I government in Punjab since 1992 to convert 'order' into 'legitimacy'. So far this exercise has been relatively problematic with the capital of 'defeating terrorism' wasted in scandals, corruption, and the continued use of coercion to intimidate mainstream Akalis. Whilst the government has had some success in the municipal and panchayat elections, the relatively non-partisan nature of these elections and the extensive use of security personnel and civil administration to influence the outcomes has been well noted. Surprisingly, the Congressites are split between those who want to sustain the anti-militant coalition, and continue to malign the Akalis with it, and those who recognize that long-term political stability in the Punjab necessities that the political voice of the Sikh peasantry should also be articulated. In the short term, however, the anti-militant rhetoric is likely to remain as a substitute for policy because of the ideological investment of the Punjab Congress-I leadership in the strategy, the absence of fiscal room for manoeuvre to pursue a so-

[38] On 28 August 1993, the Punjab Civil Service leadership demanded a judicial commission into the rise and decline of militancy during President's Rule vis-a-vis the role of the police. Cited in Pettigrew (1995a), p. 134.

cial/development policy, and the potential mobilizatory threat from the Akalis. In the medium term the possibility of change cannot be ruled out because of change of leadership in the national Congress-I, especially if Singh displaces Rao.

Finally, given the difficulties of Congress-I government in constructing legitimacy, the question arises as to whether normal rules of the game can be re-established in Punjab. Does it require, for example, a new Rajiv-Longowal Accord? Or has the Congress-I succeeded in reconstructing not only order but the Sikh political system?

The argument presented so far contends that within the Punjab political system fundamental issues of legitimacy remain. They remain not only because the current 'order' is constructed on political pillars of sand without seriously addressing the central concerns that caused the Punjab troubles, but also because maintaining lasting legitimacy requires confronting the values of the Sikh political system. I have argued elsewhere that the relationship between the Indian state and the Sikh community since 1947 has been characterized by 'hegemonic control', and one of the main factors contributing to the revival of militant politics among Sikhs was continued ethnic negation in the pursuit of factional instrumentalism.[39] Support for this interpretation can also be discerned in the writings of 'state revisionists' who, though coming from a different direction, call for a basic reassessment of the nature of the Indian state. As Mitra has persuasively argued:

> defending a strong central government at all costs in Punjab, and more recently Kashmir, is enough to demonstrate the need for greater accommodation of regional and religious interests. A modern secular state as the lowest common denominator of regional and religious differences can generate neither the strength nor the legitimacy adequate for the task. A sense of organic unity and political coherence in a regionally diverse state can be created through the better integration of the sacred and secular sources of authority in India.[40]

The case for such an accommodation is surely overwhelming in the few regions where India's minorities are in the majority because the intra-consociational features of the old 'Congress System' have long disintegrated and central government is increasingly perceived as alien, if not an occupying, force. Whether a-symmetrical neo-federalism can accommodate some of these demands remains a moot point as the issues are less of territoriality and region than religion. To paraphrase Mao, the maintenance of

39 Singh (1995).

40 Subrata K. Mitra, 'Desecularising the State: Religion and Politics in India After Independence', *Comparative Studies in Society*, Vol. 33, No. 4, October 1991, pp. 755-777.

a modern secular system in South Asia's peripheral regions may require that political power grows out of the 'barrel of a gun' rather than consent freely and willingly given.

IV

In conclusion it needs to be noted that the issues of order and disorder in the case of Punjab, and probably elsewhere in the peripheral regions in South Asia, are intimately intervowen. What is perhaps problematic is not 'disorder' but how 'order' has been maintained, justified and, sometimes, legitimized. Clearly the 'efficient secret' and 'mystique' associated with the maintenance of order since independence is now increasingly transparent as South Asia's peripheral regions have become the battlegrounds for low-intensity conflicts. In these conditions disorder is likely to create new opportunities for those over whom order is exercised and create severe difficulties for those who are entrusted with the task of maintaining it. This realization should call for a better understanding of conditions that can contribute towards sustained normative legitimacy and acts of political closure that abort, limit and restrict transactional politics.

Democracy, Development and Federalism: Some Implications of Constructive Constitutionalism in India

JYOTIRINDRA DASGUPTA

New democracies of recent decades have been more fortunate than their older counterparts in developing countries. Academic as well as popular attention to the newly democratizing countries have tended to be more enthusiastically positive compared to the cold and negative treatment received by their predecessors.[1] Even now the rising tide of studies addressed to the new 'wave' cases rarely refer to the developing democracies that have endured in defiance of grim predictions made in the literature during the earliest decades of their emergence.[2] Nearly five decades of enduring democratic development in a vast country like India, confronted with an incredible complexity, rarely evokes interest in comparative studies addressed to the issues of durability of institutions to promote stability and capability in the course of new democratization. In fact, the wide variety of its social divisions usually scare observers who are often prone to fall for a general presumption of crisis in multi-ethnic developing democracies.

Why is it so difficult to notice the positive elements of democratic development in settings that were indeed supposed to offer less hospitable conditions than in many cases included in the new wave? While the new wave literature gropes for ways to ensure a stable and progressively constructive democratic transition, what makes it so unreceptive to the lessons of five decades impressed in the institutional history of India, for example? Why does developmental scholarship tend to set its gaze in a negative manner mainly on some disquieting elements in the history of the evolving process of coordination of multiple sub-national units to the exclusion of many positive elements encoded and practiced in the history of the federal constitutional system in India (Harrison, 1960)? Is there a constructive responsibility implied in comparative studies of democratic transformation in developing countries that calls for identifying the positive institutional designs and conducts that have in a fair measure stood the test of

[1] The positive tone is impressed in a growing body of literature beginning from O'Donnell (1986). The negative tone associated with the earlier literature produced during the beginning decades of the 'second wave' democracies (1947-1962) was a prominent part of the modernization literature. For an early example witness, Shils (1960).

[2] There are exceptions like Diamond (1989), for example. The reference to 'wave' is taken from Huntington (1991).

several decades in a vast political space? This is not a question of endorsing particular designs or practices. The constructive academic responsibility may be exercised at least by reading history with a more balanced and fair sense of reasonable expectation.

II

The purpose of this paper is to focus on one aspect of constructive constitutionalism[3] that is concerned with the coordination of sub-national divisions for the purpose of ensuring a durable coherence for pursuing national development. This can be described as a federalizing institutional enterprise for promoting development in a cooperative manner at national, regional and sub-regional levels. My interest in developmental federalism stems from a sense that when federalizing institutions are deployed to serve a constructive function involving *simultaneous* processes of social, economic and political development of the entire nation they deserve a different name and criteria of accomplishment than when they are used simply to create a balancing mechanism of governance. Given the simultaneity of multiple goals in an initial situation of grossly underdeveloped stock of resources, the issue of relative authority exercised by different levels of the system may require a different kind of appreciation than what is offered by the conventional literature on federalism (Elazar, 1987).

It is from this perspective that the Indian experience of developmental federalism is examined here in an understandably brief analysis beginning from the initial constitutional design to five decades of evolution and practice. The purpose, of course, is not to offer another historical study. I am interested in the story of the federal practice because of what it can clarify in terms of the connections between a democratic way of designing a constitutional system and making it work for facilitating the realization of national cohesion, economic and human resource development, and social justice. I would hope that the story will show that constitutionalism in a developmental context can perform an *enabling*[4] and *energizing* function in addition to the *limiting* role that has been normally ascribed to it in the conventional literature mainly reflecting the experience of the West (Offe, 1991).

In this sense, my account will indicate the importance of institutional enterprise in creating a mutuality between democratic processes and devel-

[3] This term and the emphasis on the constructive aspects can mean many things. My specifically developmental use will be elaborated shortly. For some recent uses in other contexts see Elkin (1993), esp. pp. 32-35 (S. Elkin, 'Constitutionalism: Old and New').

[4] These aspects of democratic constitutional systems are discussed in Offe (1991), pp. 145ff.

opmental accomplishment in a developing democracy. How the Indian system was inaugurated apparently had something important to do with how it was valued by the participants so that its basic purpose could be realized. Even a relative success at each phase reinforced the need to sustain and renew the vitality of the institution. In the process, the system has survived its founders and their successors indicating an institutional health over a long run despite many discontents and periodic anxieties regarding deinstitutionalization (Rudolph, 1987). The fact of life is that it has proved to be a reasonable system, far from being ideal but apparently more assuring to most people than what other realistic options could possibly offer.

III

What are the constitutive principles of the Indian federal system? How has the system served the nation in terms of meeting the common national as well as the specifically regional developmental needs? Our major focus is on the developing institutional network that has helped or hindered the federal processes to serve the diversified needs of national development at different levels including the regional and sub-regional[5] levels. The question of needs is treated here in terms of their articulation at respective levels over different points of time. In other words, the subjective nature and the expressive *variability* of the needs are also taken into our account as being normal parts of the democratic developmental system. How has this network worked? What are its prospective contributions?

The basic principles of the federal system in India can be discerned well if one goes beyond the constitutional documents and concentrates on the long evolution of the national discourse and practice of political construction. A proper long view (Braudel, 1986), in fact, should take us back into the pre-colonial lineage of evolving political values concerning large scale political conciliation and coordination of authority. Scholarly dependence on the dominant discourses of modernity and modernization has led most accounts of political development to ignore the long view. But the long view spanning the history of Indian state formation from the early days of large scale empires predating the Christian era is important for understanding the nature of the historical recall and the cultural subsoil that offer important elements of sustenance of contemporary institutions. When the long lineage (Tambiah, 1987; Geertz, 1980; Stein, 1989) of the

[5] Sub-regional, for example, would refer to the level of action conducted at the points of urban and rural local government; inter-regional would refer to modes of cooperative action involving some states with common interests shared by them, e.g. Hindi language planning action on the part of states in the Hindi speaking areas. See, for instance, Robinson (1988); Eames (1988); Dasgupta (1990a).

historical modes of large scale governance in India is traced, one can find a persistence of preference for a loosely textured coordination between the reigning centre and the regional authorities that prevailed through a variety of precolonial political systems (Wallace, 1985).

Even at independence the inheritance of the colonial territory was not transmitted in one seamless piece. It came in more than five hundred widely dispersed pieces, including British India and the princely states that were formerly under British suzerainty. As the founding moments of Indian independent statehood recede in memory, people tend to forget the unusually violent and disorderly initial situation that set the disquieting context of the new institutional construction. The disorder was not limited to the unprecedented violence connected with the partition of the country. It was also evident in the colossal task of integrating more than five hundred princely administrative systems into one national system. The long story of the process of bringing order to the territorial system need not be recounted here. We should note, however, that the process of integrating transition at least from 1947 to 1956, involving a massive rearrangement of hundreds of administrative systems into one durable institutional pattern, called for a tremendously capable national authority at the very inception of independent statehood.

This almost impossible task required that the design of the political system should be one which will assure the diverse components of the country of an *acceptable mode of combination* of national coherence and regional autonomy. A long history of affinity for a principle of constitutional order based on the assent of the component units had, fortunately, marked the evolution of the nationalist movement associated with the Indian National Congress. The organizational constitution of the Congress and its institutional practice from the late nineteenth century had demonstrated a deep sense of commitment to a conciliatory strategy of mobilization of diverse groups by respecting their plural identities (McLane, 1977). An institutional process of learning by organizing such patterns of coherence among multiple groups helped impress a sense of how group identities gradually evolve, change, reform and regroup in changing political contexts among leaders over many decades.

The implication of this premium on conciliative procedure was important for the process of incorporating those who perceived themselves as being in the periphery into an evolving compound expressed as the national entity. The position of the central core within this compound entity was supposed to depend upon a *changing coalition* of forces within or across political parties. The partners of this coalition were supposed to represent their constituent units in accordance with democratic elective procedures. Given this democratic requirement of representation, the leaders had the option of seeking either exclusively particularistic mandates based on region, religion, language, caste or other divisive markers or to cultivate common elements of support cutting across multiple social affinities.

In any event, political competition in this context implied that there were few fixed sets of sub-national entities equipped with self-evident spokesmen who were endowed with monopoly charters to speak for them. The newly emerging public space, in fact, offered competing groups an incentive for seeking a set of definitions based on ethnic markers and identifications. Why some definitions of collectivity proved to be more persuasive than others for people and leaders seeking certain values was more often a matter of strategic political choice than one of a natural inheritance. Fortunately too, these choices admitted periodic change and the identifications were subject to reconstructions (Dasgupta, 1995; Pandey, 1990) with changing issue configurations.

The developmental dynamics of choice and change of ethnic identification in the context of shifting perceptions of collective advantage and assurance has been missed in the literature on federalism and national development because of some unfortunate presumptions. The idea of a strong state has somehow been associated with a strong centre. Centralized bureaucratic unities have been consistently admired in the theories of modernity and modernization as being the most important sources of national coherence and capability (Migdal, 1988). Societies with multiple ethnic divisions have been regarded as weak and vulnerable bases for strong states. The historical identification of dominant, or better still of homogeneous, ethnic groups enjoying a commanding lead over other groups, with strong states has been frequently invoked to post repeated notes of warning regarding the inherent weakness of multi-ethnic states.

It has been difficult to entertain the idea that ethnic divisions need not turn into political divisions. The tragic failure of the so called strong states in eastern Europe should at least henceforth make it easier to appreciate that the equation between a dominant ethnic group and a durable strong centre may not necessarily work. Besides, the political use of identific markers of most ethnic or regional groups may change from time to time in a manner that may allow for different coalitions for dominance or opposition. Thus, in undivided India, a Muslim individual or group in Bengal could switch from religious, to language-based and then further to class-related identific markers. In fact, just a few years before the partition of 1947, the reality of these political shifts showed how primordial labels can serve as poor predictors of coalitions that can make or break nations or national capabilities[6] (Hashmi, 1992). Thus Bengali identific affinity in this case was used in the same setting either to oppose or to support sepa-

[6] The reference here is to the popular Muslim leadership represented by Fazlul Huq and its alliance once with Muslim League leadership and then with the Hindu Mahasabha and soon again the loss of leadership to the Muslim League within the span of the brief period of 1941-1946! See Hashmi (1992), pp. 220 ff.

ratism with equal vehemence in moments of history that were not very far apart! Also, if the Gandhian leadership made extensive use of religion to build bridges within and across religious groups in the sense of weaving together caste groups within Hindu society and linking Hindus with other religious communities, other leadership at the same time fragmently used religion to promote divisive politics.

Thus it is the institutional enterprise of constructing, mediating and utilizing social divisions in the field of public action that tends to determine the texture of strength and capability of a national political system. The important question is how institutional modes can generate a sense of assurance among diverse groups of various strength - numerical or otherwise - to make them willing partners eager to let the system work. This calls for more than a mere mechanism of balancing well-formed societal interests in a formal democratic structure. In fact, it requires an understanding of the creative role of a *simultaneous* system of institutional processing of *emerging demands* from contending and cooperative groups as well as institutional cultivation of *mobilized support* for pursuing positive programs for enhancing the quality of collective functioning of the national society. The collective program, however, needs to be seen both in terms of the quality of the unity and its constituent units. The importance of including the perspective of the units, of course, makes the democratic compulsion of negotiated national construction so crucial as well as strategic.

IV

It is reasonable to assume that the emergence and practice of developmental federalism in India since independence can be explained from the point of view of an institutional enterprise seeking to offer a system of simultaneous action to politically process societal demand and to generate strategic support for collective avenues of development. The nature of the units constituting the initial federation was more contingent than final. These units were not sovereign in status before the construction of the federal institution. They derived their relative autonomy from an agreement among the founders regarding a pattern of division of powers between the general and the component governments that were supposed to be consistent with the goals of national development. The actual content of division of powers was left flexible through a complex set of conditions attached to the original provisions. As one study of the constitution-making process in India has noted, the most significant feature of the founding deliberations related to the federal provisions 'was the relative absence of conflict between the 'centralizers' and the 'provincialists' (Austin, 1966, p. 186).

The use of the term 'provincialist' is an interesting reminder that the federal process in India grew out of a colonial history of convenient territorial demarcation and a nationalist movement to challenge those alien terms of administrative expediency. Federal sentiments among the regional constituents of the nationalist movement did not have a fixed territorially demarcated referent except for a general sense of areas associated with major language groups. A case for reorganization of provinces on language basis was conceded by the nationalists long before independence but there was no scope then for building a federal state on the foundation of a prior mutual agreement of language-based States. The members of the Constituent Assembly were drawn from 12 provinces of uneven size - ranging from 55 members from the United Provinces, to 1 from Coorg, for instance - and from 29 state units. The state units, in this context, refer to princely states of the colonial era, large ones like Mysore or smaller ones clustered in groups like Punjab States group, for example. Neither at the moment of the founding of the republic nor in its immediate aftermath was there any issue of creating a federation out of a voluntary agreement of well-formed units of any prior sovereign social or territorial standing. The federal form resulted from an eminently amicable sense of consensual division and sharing of authority for deliberately developing national coherence out of a plural base that itself was expected to change over time.

V

It was expected that sub-national affinities would grow *as a result of development* of literacy, mass communication, and economic opportunities particularly in the lower depths of regions. Social deepening of national development in a plural society was inconceivable without the benefit of mass education in regional languages and popular identification with proximate development projects and evocative cultural symbolism. Of course, such deepening of developmental processes was likely to impair some of the older notions or devices of imposed unity. On the other hand, new modes of consented or participative unity at the regional or even subregional levels were expected to be associated with popular incorporation into proximate and accessible institutions connected with federal authority and democratic governance.

The early years of consolidation of freedom and construction of the foundation of a developmental state, however, had seen considerable neglect of the basic issues of regional functioning of the new state. National leaders with international visions were reluctant to examine the particular concerns of the regional leaders. The nation-wide inheritance of a gigantic bureaucratic state led by a dominant party made it easier to emphasize upon collective aspirations to be guided by modernizing planners than to discern the specific terms of sharing authority developing at the regional levels. Regional movements were in a way reminders to these leaders of the importance of gaining the assent of publics who had good reasons to nurture a sense of disadvantage. The clumsy four part state systems of 1949 arranging 21 States and territories in packages that could be defended only by discretionary bureaucratic logic did not bring any credit to the democratic or distributive aspirations of the national system. Rather, the later success of the popular movements for linguistic reorganization of States offered a reassuring principle of legitimation of regional governance as ways of reducing the distance between the citizens and government.

The constructive implications of the regional movements for administrative reorganization of the country along language lines can be easily missed if we lend too much credence to the national rhetoric of the central leaders after 1947. Leaders like Nehru were never comfortable with the regional political processes. Mahatma Gandhi's death in 1948 made it easier to ignore the earlier nationalist concern for popular involvement in politics in idioms that are expressive of their autonomy, authenticity and regional concerns. Gandhi's federalizing concept of national development was reflected in the acceptance of the principle of linguistic reorganization of the country as early as 1920 by the Indian National Congress. A concrete embodiment of the principle was also reflected in the reorganization of the Congress into regional language-based provincial committees at this time. A few years later, this concept was also incorporated into a nationalist enterprise of drafting a constitution for post-colonial political framework.[7]

But the advent of freedom in a moment of widespread violence and disarray probably frightened the new leaders too severely to respect regional demands. Besides, many of them were ideologically inclined to favor large scale centralized organizations for political and economic development anyway. The national leaders did not even pause to recognize that their own central leadership, in fact, could be perceived by many regional movements as a disguised regional coalition monopolizing national power.

The idea of a virtuous or rational centre constantly battered by inferior parochial forces from the periphery was given a big play by the ideologues of statist modernization. The entire body of the discourse on national unity popularized by Nehru and his followers during the early decades of independence was informed by a sense of mission to realize the enlightened authority of a secular state to overpower the new forces of primordial persuasion. A fallacy of misplaced composition helped sustain an overvalued interventionism. The ruling party was equated with the modern state and since the dominant leadership enjoyed hegemonic command of the state, therefore any movement opposing the archaic administrative boundaries was to be rejected as anti-national or counter-developmental (Nehru, 1958, pp. 193-194).

[7] This is discussed in Dasgupta (1990), pp. 151 ff.

Fortunately, the public institutional space in India was not entirely monopolized by the Congress organization. The institutional failure of the Congress to express regional demands in the fifties put a premium on large scale political movements which resulted in radically altering the federal map of the country. Thanks to the flexible provisions in the constitution the force of popular movements succeeded in gaining a series of alterations of boundaries from 1956 onwards to a point when the number of States settled at 25 by 1987. This process of delayed responsiveness demonstrates a phase of the poverty of party-level institutionalization which is rarely noticed by observers when they mournfully assume a linear loss of institutionalization since the supposedly golden age of Nehru (Rudolph, 1990). A better way of looking at this phenomenon may be to recognize that there was a time lag in institutional learning that was partly overcome when the Congress organization remarkably succeeded in incorporating a large part of the popular movement after conceding the respective demands[8]. Above all, it is important to distinguish between the different phases of institutionalization and learning processes within a *party* and the institutional development across parties working through the constitutional process. Losses of degrees of institutionalization at one level need not be confused with that of the other. Even at the party level, losses of institutional health of one party need to be analysed in the context of its counterpart in other parties or their organizational substitutes.

VI

The proper functioning of developmental federalism requires a system of progressive incorporation of new aspirants for participation into an institutionalized structure of national assurance. From this perspective, the specific gains and losses of parties or leaders is less important than the *systemic gain of the structure.* The idea of systemic gain shifts our attention from specific *players* to *rules* of common importance for all players over longer periods of time than what is captured by short, though eventful, episodes. These rules, in their turn, can be conceived in formal or informal terms (North, 1990). They indicate certain enduring practices and accepted avenues of change and development. Enduring rules can also serve as indicators of developmental prospects of the political system. How has the Indian system worked so far in this respect?

If the system has proved to be fairly responsive to the demands for relatively autonomous statehood, does this incorporation make the union

[8] The loss of power in one election for a brief period of time either at national or at one or few States often offers temptation for premature theoretical conjectures regarding de-institutionalization, for example. See Rudolph (1990), and Diamond (1989).

more sustainable? How does the responsive ability of the system contribute to the quality of developmental functioning of the States? The opinion of the most exhaustive study prepared by the commission on centre-state relations published in 1988 is worth noting in this regard. Popularly known as the Sarkaria Commission report, this study concludes that the basic provisions of the constitution have served 'reasonably well' the functions of a 'heterogeneous society towards its development goals' (Commission, I, 1988, p. 554). But it also notes that the actual working of the basic rules leaves much to be desired. This report also includes detailed memoranda from the States including some that are highly critical of the existing operative structure. What can one make of these evaluations?

Despite many negative sentiments expressed occasionally, the basic issue of the legitimacy of the union has been widely accepted over five decades of the federal process.[9] Most States have eagerly cultivated the federal government for extracting maximum resources from the national pool. This has been true even for the States like Punjab and Jammu and Kashmir for most parts of post-1947 history, and in Punjab it has continued again since 1992. Such cultivation of central affection has not been limited to the States controlled by the central ruling party. It is interesting that party differences have not prevented close linkages between the rulers at two levels in most cases.

Several factors have facilitated the legitimating sentiments regarding the centre or the central authority. In the first place, even when the Congress party was the dominant party, the composition of the leading coalition inside the party did not remain constant. Although one state, i.e. Uttar Pradesh had supplied most of the Prime Ministers, the relative dominance[10] of this state within the central authority could be easily ex-

[9] Negative sentiments as, for example, in Punjab, especially between 1986 to 1991 and in Jammu and Kashmir since 1990 can be seen as some of the most recent events in a long chain of episodes that really began in the first decade of the federation in the Northeast, the South and spread elsewhere. Negotiated resolution within the constitutional frames has not been impossible in general. The special problem in Jammu and Kashmir - unlike other cases - is marked by an international complication beginning from an international war in 1947, later external intrusions including wars, a long period of continuity of constitutional process until 1990, followed by a crisis reflecting internal failure and external intrusion. It may be noted that even in the worst phase of dissidence in these two States, the best count of claimed support for separatism did not exceed a size of population constituting two per cent of the national total. If we add the total population of these states, the figure would not exceed three percent. For a good collection of readings from contending perspectives see Thomas (1993) on Jammu and Kashmir. See also Paul Wallace's contributions on Punjab in Frankel (ed.), II (1990), pp. 416-481; Gould (1993), pp. 138-158, 403-428; Dasgupta (1995), pp. 287-294.

[10] At the present moment (1996), the relative strength of states can give us some aid to judgment: Uttar Pradesh has a share of population of the order of 16 per cent, the Hindi speakers' total nationally constitutes about 38 per cent, by generous calculation, and they are far from politically homogeneous. Hindi States gave a rude shock to congress as early as 1967 when its national dominance was broken nationwide for the first time. Even in Nehru's life time - as early as the fifties -- he had a hard time dealing with other factions in his own state (Uttar Pradesh). By 1992 the congress party was out of power in five Hindi states! By 1994 it came

aggerated. Factional battles in this large state were alive and strong even in Nehru's life time and Uttar Pradesh or even the entire Hindi belt of States, never gained the commanding lead that, for example, Punjab in Pakistan enjoys in Pakistan's federation.

By 1967, about half of the Indian States went to the opposition. Party domination of the States has been fluid since then. Also the shift of national power from Congress in 1977 and 1989, the initial lack of its majority in parliament in 1991, and a precarious majority by 1994, simply shows that the dominance of the Congress party and the monopolization of power within itself by one State or a constant set of States have been exaggerated. The events following 1989, of course, reinforces the idea that shifting coalitions of State leaders can dominate the centre under different party flags - the Janata, Congress or whatever!

The fluidity of composition of the central leadership or the absence of an inflexible master-centre based on the commanding resources and internal cohesion of one dominant region or a rigidly exclusive coalition of regions may be some of the most assuring sources of legitimation of the federal system in India. A second type of source may be described as a structure of dependence which makes most of the States require resources from the centre to augment their own. This structure of dependence is partly the result of uneven distribution of financial power between the centre and the States as enshrined in the constitution, which allows the centre to collect the lion's share of the national revenue. In part also the structure of dependence is impressed by the wide inequality of the size, resource, willingness and ability to raise additional tax revenue, and the organizational capability to generate development among the States. The largest state in India, i.e. Uttar Pradesh with more than 140 million population (1991), also happened to be one of the poorest States in terms of per capita income (1987 = Rs. 2,146, at current prices). But it also ranked as the largest producer of food grains[11] in the country constituting more than 20 per cent of the national total. Punjab on the other hand with less than 17 million people enjoyed a corresponding per capita income of Rs. 4,719 and supplied nearly 11per cent of the nation's food grains. Endowed with a wide variety and levels of resources, the eagerness of States to seek central assistance or to share resources with other States have widely varied (Table 1). Central political authorities of all political persuasions and compositions have not shied away from making good use of this dependence, just as they all decry the disadvantage of poorer States when they lose access to central power!

---

back to power in two of them. In Pakistan, Punjab alone enjoys a single province majority in the country while the next largest population share of about 21 per cent belongs to Sindh.

[11] The population figures, unless specified differently, refer to 1981; the food grain share figures are for 1986 and the income figures refer to 1987. Source: Ninth Finance Commission, First Report 1988 (Ministry of Finance, Government of India, 1988).

Another source of legitimation and strengthening of the centre emerges from the internal disparity within the States. The perception of disadvantage by minorities, deprived districts or autonomous district councils, and opposition groups make the state leaders in power look about as evil as they often assume or accuse the centre to be. It then becomes easier for the centre to assume a role of protector or savior of substantial groups of population from their perceived oppressors in their own state! Muslims in north Indian States advocating official status for Urdu or protesting state-level discrimination, some hill tribes in Assam resenting the attitude of valley people in power, the depressed Telengana sub-region in Andhra Pradesh seeking better treatment in their own state, or the Jharkhand movement seeking autonomous political status for its community in Bihar have usually asked for central support in their struggle against regional authorities. The December communal riot of 1992 brought out the crucial protective role of the central government or national secular coalition for the minority groups. In a country like India dotted with a multiplicity of disadvantages and consequent resentments that cannot admit of a grand solution at any particular point of time, the role of the centre as the redresser of the last resort is not expected to make an easy exit from the political scene.

VII

The developmental significance of federalism in India can be appreciated in the context of the complex architecture of the state that has sustained a constitutional and political site of negotiated balance between the general, regional and sub-regional needs, sentiments, support and demands. Institutional maturation resulting from the ability of the system to cope with stresses and to provide sustainable modes of developmental cooperation in a coordinated manner in the fields of economy, security, education, social reorganization, welfare and justice promotion involving special efforts for affirmative action, has been reasonably impressed in the system over time and leadership changes through five decades.

If a retrospective glance makes one feel uncomfortable about the periodic oscillation of strength between the centre and the States, perhaps one is not asking the right questions. Most of the time when politicians and intellectuals look for some neat balance sheets they are probably using a distributive theory of power addressed to the simplified issue of who has power over whom. Developmental federalism requires an understanding, on the other hand, of a productive theory of power. This gives us an occasion to ask how can power be produced by collaborating agents who, in spite of their mutual problems, would be interested in expanding a common pool of capability[12] (Ball, 1988; Wartenberg, 1992). This constructive dimension is especially important for understanding the enabling effects of coordinated development that federalism has historically contributed in the Indian setting. The joint strengthening of two levels of governance may not necessarily imply equal sharing of initiative and authority.

A case for planned production of capability in the economy and polity on a national scale was almost consensually accepted in the visualization of development long before Independence. That this called for uneven location of initiative and decision in the earlier moments of historical transition was also readily conceded before and after independence. It is from this ground that a nationally popular case was built for the centralizing dimensions of federalism. The centre was accordingly invested with a clear advantage in powers, resources, control of the national administration, access to specialized coercive apparatus and, of course, planning in the realms of economy, education and culture. Many of the controversies and tensions in politics have been directed mostly to relative shares accruing from this planning for development rather than against the transitional compulsion of uneven authority and planned development. The most conspicuous case of blatant use of central power is, of course, manifested in the use of President's Rule that either suspends or dissolves elected legislatures. Between 1951 and 1995, this power has been used more than about 100 times.[13] These have evoked sharp reactions. On the other hand, whenever the critics of such abuse have come to national power, they have not hesitated to use these same powers to their own advantage! These or other kinds of central imposition have also been used by those leaders who have been effusively praised as the founding models of democratic tradition and institutionalization in independent India (Jeffrey, 1991).

Why do politicians of all colors accept such practices irrespective of what they say from opposition vantage points? Do they all accept these as traditional compulsions of a developmental federalism that are historically unavoidable in a country placed in India's situation? If specific States - those who are not adversely affected at a moment - lend support to this kind of federalism as a system rather than to a ruling group, what do they gain? Or is it more than a matter of calculation for individual gain? If we can set aside the issue of national solidarity for a moment, it may be worthwhile to look at how the system may have gained support by deliv-

[12] For different concepts of power, including some variants of productive notions but not necessarily the one used here, see Ball (1988), pp. 80-105. For another version of that discussion see Wartenberg (1991), pp. 14-31.

[13] For details see Commission, I, pp. 184-186 (Sarkaria Commission Report). Perhaps the most crucial central intervention in states was in December 1992 when the Uttar Pradesh state government failed to prevent the destruction of a mosque and the consequent communal violence that proved to be immensely costly in terms of human lives and inter-community trust. For a critique of the pattern of religion-based communal politics in the states that were targets of intervention in 1992, see Thakur (1993).

ering and enhancing material capabilities. All States have made significant improvements in their level of per capita income from the early decades to the present time. No doubt, some States have done better than others (see table 2). But some of the smallest and poorer States have, relatively, done better than their richer and bigger counterparts. The compound annual rate of increase of per capita income of States at current prices between 1960 and 1985 has varied in the case of major States from 10 to 8 percent and between 1970 to 1985 in the case of smaller States from 14 to 8 percent. The general pattern has been one of rising gain. Planned national outlay from 1951 to 1990 for these States has increased from an average of 38 rupees in 1951-56 to 1,026 rupees in 1985-90. For the latter period figures for specific States have varied from a small and poor state like Sikkim registering 5,750 to a large and poor state like Bihar registering 628 rupees. The Hindi States historically have not done very well despite their reputation of being the heartland. In fact, some of the best performers have been the States - large or small - that were carved as a result of popular movements for reorganization of boundaries.

Developmental gains of the States may raise questions that go beyond the normal confines of centre-state relations. To be sure, they do raise the issue of differential central aid contributing to variation in performance. The better performers have also been better supported by national resources disbursed by the federal government (Table 3). But it is hard to show much sustained ethnic bias inspite of the obvious political bias connected with the simple logic of attracting support from the stronger political bases. Punjab and Haryana have been equally favored despite their different religious composition - with Sikh and Hindu majority respectively. A Muslim majority State, Jammu and Kashmir, has consistently benefited more than most States with different religious composition.

What is more interesting is the issue of the attitude of States about other States. If federal questions are not reduced to a simple issue of relative decentralization but with good reason extended to raise complex problems of non-centralized systems (Elazar, 1987; Picard and Zariski, 1987) from a post-modern perspective (Elazar, 1991), then inter-state attitudes and relations would assume a special importance. The richer States of India, having gained most from the national pool of resources for planned development, have not shown much propensity to share with or transfer resources to the poorer States. Neither Punjab nor Haryana has given much thought about this side of the problem of federal equity. Certainly, the centre as a whole does not seem to fare that badly compared to the conspicuous self-orientation of the richest States. The poorer States, in their turn, blame more often on the biased logic of division of the national pool than seriously attending to their own quality of performance at home!

How much effort have they made to raise their own resources in a serious manner? Do they raise reasonable tax revenue from agriculture? The taxes on agriculture in 1987-88 as a proportion of total tax revenue of the States came to a mere 2.6 per cent for the country as a whole. The richest States like Punjab and Haryana were the worst performers in this regard (0.3 and 0.1% respectively) in terms of low current magnitude and historical decline from the earlier decades. Relatively poorer States like Assam and Orissa did much better in terms of recent comparison but not so in historical terms in their entire career in recent decades. West Bengal did well on both counts. A study of relative tax effort[14] of States shows that the best performers are the southern States with Tamilnadu remaining at the top position among all States in the early seventies and early eighties. The richest north Indian States trailed behind the southern set. But the worst performers in making relevant efforts were the poorer States like Assam, Bihar and Orissa. Jammu and Kashmir was not far behind.

The reluctance to dig deep into their own economy for resources, naturally, is not unconnected with a general sense of dependence on the national pool. Planned national development must be tempting for all these States and more so for the poorest States. No matter how the distribution of national affection is evaluated by them, the resources of the national authorities and the appropriate institutional complex appear to be continuously seductive.

VIII

Understandably, the rhetoric of the regional political discourse may be highly selective. At one level, its critical posture regarding the authority of the centre conceals its dependence on and continuous collaboration with the centre. Regional voices are also politically divided. They reveal a deep division of interests, social and economic advantages, and ideologies. Strategic silences in the regional discourse are also highly significant. The frequent failure of the state level government and ruling authority including the dominant groups in regional civil society to successfully pursue appropriate land reform, significant rural development to serve the poorest segments of the population, and protection of the disadvantaged groups based on minority religion or depressed social and economic status reveals a picture that is often better clarified in the critiques offered by the central and sub-regional discourses and practices. Dissonance among these discourses and practices is not easy either to unravel or to eradicate in a complex multi-national, multi-ethnic, and multi-class polity as it obtains in India.

14 Relative tax effort refers to a process of mobilizing more revenue 'as the economy expands and taxable capacity increases.' See M.A. Oommen, 'Relative Tax Effort of States', *Economic and Political Weekly*, 14 March 1987. The evidence cited is from p. 466.

To what extent does the failure of the regional authorities in matters of governance and social dominance to serve their own population strengthen the role of the national authorities in government and civil society in India? When in the early nineties a Hindu religion oriented organization like the Bharatiya Janata party ruled over four Hindi States covering a substantial part of the national population, the role of the Congress government at the centre was perceived by secularists and religious minority groups in a more positive perspective especially after the December communal riots of 1992. The Ayodhya dispute (Srivastava, 1991) once again served to highlight the dual impact of the centre; its earlier complicity and subsequent countervailing role in communal practice makes a simple search for villains and heroes rather ridiculous.[15] The difficult role of the Rao government in defusing the explosive possibilities and reducing the incidence of violence also brings to prominence the role and the dilemmas of the national judiciary in promoting balance and security processes among different communities and groups of people.

IX

The December riots of 1992, involving violence in several States and loss of many lives, once again demonstrated the importance of a nationally concerted leadership in generating collective assurance and national development. When communalization of politics pursued by the Bharatiya Janata Party, ostensibly to serve Hindu interests as defined by those leaders who chose to lock their vision to some sixteenth century episodes in one area of Uttar Pradesh, landed many parts of the country in a grave situation, the case for a nationally coordinated corrective action was unambiguously clear. It is interesting that this national moment of crisis called for not merely a prompt central intervention in Uttar Pradesh and three other States but also strong action by a number of States to curb the local communal forces.[16] In that sense it was much more than a test of strength of the

[15] The dispute regarding the Ayodhya site offers an interesting case to test the public labels of secularism, modernity, minority sensitivity, and fairness that have been used under the Rajiv Gandhi and the Narasimha Rao phases of Congress rule and by other political organizations. For a brief background see S. Gupta, 'The Gathering Storm', in M.M. Bouton and P. Oldenburg, (eds.), *India Briefing, 1990*, (Boulder: Westview, 1990), pp. 25-50. Also, P. R. Brass, *The Rise of the BJP and the Future of Party Politics in U.P.* (Gould, 1993); and Y. K. Malik and V. B. Singh, *Hindu Nationalism India* (New Delhi: Vistaar, 1994), pp. 59-178.

[16] The central government led by the Congress party (Prime Minister: P.V.N. Rao) promptly dismissed the BJP ruled governments in Uttar Pradesh, Himachal Pradesh, Madhya Pradesh, and Rajasthan following the mosque incident of December 1992. In November 1993, new elections in these states significantly reduced the power of the BJP when it lost power in three of the states and managed to regain power only in Rajasthan. The Congress party gained power in two (M.P. and H.P.) - a modest prize but certainly not any harsh punishment for dismissing

federal government taken alone. Rather, it was a test of the joint capability[17] of all three levels - central, state and local - of governance including at each level the respective strength of the forces of civil society in one of the most uncivil moments of the nation's history.

That the joint capacity of these levels of governance was readily forthcoming and fairly effective in dealing with the critical situation was indeed reassuring. This was more so because the central government was then ruled by a party that could assemble only a precarious majority! It was a minority government which won a majority status in 1993. Once again, one could see in this moment of coping with communalism a process of a nationally cooperative institutional enterprise that was composed of elements drawn from a number of different political parties. No matter how different their ideologies were or how deeply or weakly inducted their sense of secularism was, their willingness and ability to collaborate for a strategic action was a reminder that the federalized coordination system deserves as much, if not more, attention as the ruling authority at the level of federal government. But the secular convictions of the partners contributed only one element of strength in their struggle against the forces of politics that use communal appeal. The steady depletion of the political capital of the partners of the secular alliance through several decades due to factionalism, corruption, weak performance in the economic sphere, and poor leadership skills left a large room open for communal forces to recover and expand their strength. The striking success of the BJP and the Shiv-Sena-BJP alliance respectively in Gujarat and Maharashtra State elections in 1995 showed how anti-incumbent and anti-corruption campaigns can strongly contribute to the setback of secular forces without necessarily indicating any deep public enchantment with Hindu nationalism. That the Hindu nationalist forces are not free from the same weaknesses that led to the defeat of the secularists in those elections was also made clearly evident during the embarrassing post-election factional struggles in Gujarat and increasing cracks in the Shiv Sena-BJP alliance in Maharashtra (Thakkar, 1995).

Hindu party governments for Hindu communalism in a country of vast Hindu majority. Most of the Congress leaders were also Hindu! (Roy, 1994, pp. 204-205).

17 By 1995, besides the Congress party, the ruling parties at the state level include the Janata Dal, the Communist Party (Marxist), the AIADMK, the Telugu Desam, and the BJP and its ally, the Shiv Sena. Except for the latter, the cooperation of the other parties on the issues of preventing communal violence was not difficult to count on. Once, the course of action was decided upon, even the BJP ruled states had to follow.

X

However, the role of the ruling party at the federal level of government and its ability to quickly mobilize support from the state governments ruled by its own regional leaders and members cannot be overestimated. How such a national party deals with the regional leaders belonging to its own party or other competing or collaborative parties can make a difference in the pace and direction of federal action. The early years of Indian federalism, as we have noted before, were marked by organized coordination managed by Congress ruled governments at the federal and state levels. The Nehru years from 1947 to 1964 were supposed to be the period of hegemonic dominance. These were the years of laying the foundation of a newly independent and federalized state system. The Nehru style, unfortunately, was one of an ideological preacher and political instructor.[18] His letters to Chief Ministers written from the vantage point of the Prime Minister and party leader exemplified a style of a statesman keeping lesser leaders in line and leash. They were symbolic instances of the general style of offering directions that bordered on, and at times descended to, a level of dictation. How much did he or his generation of Chief Ministers belonging to his party really care for institutionalization based on mutuality, reciprocity, and equity?[19] The answer to this question needs to be considered in the context of the fact that the continuity of the Congress party as an institution enabled it to contain and conceal many authoritarian trends at the federal and state levels during the early decades.

When this party organizational continuity was rudely shaken in the late sixties, a new phase of less concealed authoritarian style of leadership took charge of developmental federalism. The uncertain interlude of the period of 1967-71 had reflected a sense of difficulty on the part of the Congress party to respect the rules of party-competition and to appreciate the merits of the wider party system as contrasted to the role of one dominant party[20] (Bose, 1987). When Indira Gandhi became a more confident Prime Minister and party leader after 1971, the case for a mode of institutionalization based on a negotiated partnership between competing leaders and parties scarcely got any stronger. The story of her attempts to rely on a centralized mode of disciplining the state by using authoritarian and manipulative action when permitted by law, and by emergency measures

18 See W.H. Morris-Jones, 'Shaping the Post-Imperial State: Nehru's letters to Chief Ministers', in Michael Twaddle (ed.), *Imperialism, the State and the Third World* (London: British Academic Press, 1992), pp. 225 ff.

19 Ibid., p. 239. W.H. Morris-Jones thinks that the tendency towards personal power was offset by Nehru's 'marked respect for the institutions within which he had to work.' For other versions see R. Jeffrey (1991).

20 See B. Arora, 'Party System and Federal Structures in India: Linkages and Issues', in T.C. Bose (ed.), (1987), pp. 174-186.

when denied by law, is covered in details by many accounts (Dasgupta, 1989, 1990, 1995; Kohli, 1990a, 1990b).

Even if we leave aside the emergency regime, the years of Indira Gandhi's leadership by moving the political process closer to a plebiscitarian pattern actually undermined the prospects of negotiated partnership in the federal system. The democratic process within the Congress party was weakened by evading electoral processes for about two decades. Regional leaders no longer had a voice in the national and regional system that could make them effectively deal with regional problems! Direct manipulation by the highest office of regional situations unnecessarily mixed and confused arenas that left little room for defusing explosive possibilities. Thus, during the early eighties the politics of short run gain of the central leadership led to long run systemic losses in dealing with the regional politics in Assam, Punjab, and Andhra Pradesh.[21] Explosive violence in Assam during this time could be avoided if the leadership was willing to negotiate with the leaders of a popular movement. When Rajiv Gandhi came to power, he showed a greater willingness to compromise and the Assam as well as the Punjab accords seemed to augur well for the system.

The Punjab accord (Singh, 1993), however, was violated by an attempt to link the regional issue with the central leadership's strategy to appease Hindu factions in Haryana and at the same time to score points in the Hindi States (Sen Gupta, 1989). If Indira Gandhi's assassination made the Congress leaders, including Rajiv Gandhi, to pause and reconsider the high cost of such manipulative craft, the effect certainly was not a durable one. Rajiv Gandhi was flexible enough to initiate ethnic accords but the upper leadership of the party even after the death of Indira Gandhi were so used to playing the game of palace politics that the new moves - except in the case of Assam - remained relatively ineffective. What one may identify as the Rajiv years including 1984-1989 as the Prime Minister - from the time he assumed *party* leadership - the basic pattern of undermining the legitimate right of the opposition parties to rule at the state level continued in a manner that gravely weakened the inter-party sense of collective assurance. The dismissal of the elected government of the Telugu Desam party in 1983 in Andhra Pradesh was a joint act crafted by a leadership group that included Rajiv Gandhi and P.V. Narasimha Rao. It was, again, not an isolated act. The political manipulations to discredit and dislodge non-Congress parties continued through the seventies down to the late eighties in Nagaland, Mizoram, Tripura, and in part in

[21] The cases of Jammu and Kashmir and those of the northeastern states are equally relevant. For examples of these cases see Teng (1985), Dua (1992), Bose (1987), Frankel and Rao (eds.), (1989, 1990), Thomas (1992), Singh (1993), Hazarika (1994).

West Bengal.[22] In all these cases, insurgent movements were openly courted and assisted when these processes promised or delivered dividends to the Congress Party (Dua, 1992; Bose, 1987; Hazarika, 1994).

XI

When the full story of such dangerous craft is revealed, the present partners of developmental federalism may be able to recognize that less blame lies with terrorism, insurgence, fundamentalism, or foreign hands in weakening the national democratic political system than what many custodians of the central government often urged them to believe! Fortunately, India's federal system has been ruled by many different groups at different levels. Political alternation of rulership roles among parties and among group within parties has contributed to an institutional capacity to learn, repair, and develop the democratic political system. A determined move on the part of the Telugu Desam party to call the central leadership's bluff led to the restoration of the party to power which they lost and regained in subsequent elections. The positive contribution of a number of non-Congress parties to restore the health and well-being of the federalizing processes needs to be noted despite some of the shortcomings of these organizations at the state and the federal levels.

A proper appreciation of developmental federalism and its indispensable linkage with democratic participation calls for an understanding of the immense difficulty of coordinating the central, regional and sub-regional levels of the state and civil society for simultaneously realizing unity, productivity and justice, political and social. The idea of seeking to realize all these goals at the same time may sound ridiculous. Unfortunately, this compulsion of simultaneity is very realistic (Hirschman, 1990). The luxury of attaining one thing at a time has given federalism in the Western world a rare advantage that cannot be repeated in large, multi-ethnic countries like India. This is what gives a distinctive quality to India's developmental federalism and its connection with the political including constitutional (Rawls, 1993) craft of democratic becoming.[23] Such an intriguingly innovative institutional enterprise is bound to evoke a sense

22 The reference is especially to the use made of the Gorkhaland movement by Rajiv Gandhi during his years as the Prime Minister, particularly in 1987-88 to discredit the West Bengal government led by the Communist Party (Marxist).

23 For an interesting discussion of the urgency and cruciality of 'practical agreement in judgment about the constitutional essentials' see Rawls (1993), pp. 227-230. The connection of this approach to the issues of justice makes it interesting for our constructive developmental view of federalism, constitutionalism and democracy. For the conventional notions of constitutionalism and its bearing on federalism and democracy see Friedrich (1963), Pennock (1979), and Elster (1988).

of despair among academic critics who continue to offer conventional judgments (Rudolph, 1987; Tummala, 1992; Horowitz, 1994).

XII

Exciting constitutional adventures lie ahead in many countries which in the course of consolidating their new democratic gains will need a durable architecture of authority elaborating basic rules of governance. Conventional constitutionalism celebrating the notions of balance, limits of designated authorities, and protection of the self against the interference of the ruling authorities, will need to be supplemented by deliberately designed measures of political, social, and economic coordination to enable political systems to respond to the challenge of simultaneous development. Our study of constitutionalism in India indicates that federal arrangements can be designed and pursued in a manner such that even a maddening array of social divisions and pluralities need not necessarily be counted as negative resources for constructive cooperation for national development. A crucial condition of making the system work is to assure the units - individuals, regions, constituent States and their component sub-units, - that they will have full participative rights and contributive functions so long as they adhere to the rules of reasonable respect for diversity, choice and dissent. This calls for an appreciation of a specifically political conception of justice among units, though I can leave its elaboration to others for the moment (Rawls, 1993, pp. 144 ff.).

The working of the federal arrangements in India shows how democratic constitutionalism, by combining representation, access to authority, and partnership in a system designed for developing the nation's resources at different levels, can offer multiple mediating institutional processes. But this implies more than simply a process of moderating rivalries or conciliating claims and counter claims. It also offers a positive system of common assurance and cooperative investment in the future of a nation and its components. The collective gain of the nation has a lot to offer to citizens who prize their membership in a gigantic state with a vast combination of opportunities implied in its national market of a continental scale. The processes of constructive cooperation have been historically encouraged by a steady flow of resources from the centre to regions and sub-regions. If the poorer States or regions have considerably improved their resources - material and human - as a result of these arrangements, why should they resent a centre that is stronger than what a conventional notion of a federal constitution would endorse? If the centre's privileged authority to raise resources from the States is resented by some better endowed ones, the resource-poor States may have other opinions. The redistributive implications of such federal enterprise should be evaluated in terms of its contribution to promote regional supports, national union and developmental partnership.

Our study suggests that democratic constitutionalism can enable the federal system to make such a combined contribution to cohesion, durability, and development of material resources and human functioning because it offers credible incentives to make participative partnership of the constituent units possible. As we have seen, changing coalitions of regions, groups, and orientations over almost five decades associated with central dominance have made it possible for visualizing the centre as an inclusionary authority promising the pursuit of a national purpose. The conventional concepts of federal government with its emphasis on even sharing of power is too preoccupied with the balance of power issue to appreciate the federalizing institutions of developmental partnership with variable balance that can produce power for national and regional use. Developmental federalism, in this sense, may offer a more productive understanding of the constructive possibilities of constitutionalism for many newly democratizing countries of our time.

TABLE 1
Selected indicators of difference among some Indian States

	Population		Per Capita Income		% Share of Food Grain Production
	1981	1991	1987 (*a*)	1971	1986
	(m)	(m)	(Rs)	(Rs)	
Richer States:					
Punjab	16.7	20.2 (2.4)	4,719	1,121	10.7
Haryana	12.9	16.3 (1.9)	3,925	960	4.9
Poorer States:					
Uttar Pradesh	110	140 (16.4)	2,146	497	20.2
Bihar	70	86 (10.2)	1,802	415	6.9

Note: Figure in parenthesis = per cent.

(a): More recent figures for the year 1990-1991 as reported in the Government of India, *Economic Survey, 1994-1995*, are Punjab, 8373; Haryana, 7502; UP, 3516; and Bihar, 265 Rupees. These are reported in a different source and in a different series of net state domestic product data at current prices (p. S-12) and hence we present them separately.

Source: Ninth Finance Commission, *First Report 1988* and *India, 1991.* Both published by Government of India.

TABLE 2
Comparable Estimates of per Capita Income of Selected States (at Current Prices) and Growth (Rupees)

	1960-61	1984-85	Compound Annual Increase rate, 1960-61 and 1984-85 (%)
Major States:			
Rich:			
Punjab	383	4,097	10.4
Maharashtra	419	3,493	9.2
Poor:			
Uttar Pradesh	244	1,508	8.2
Smaller States:			
Jammu and Kashmir	287	2,601	10.0
Manipur	408 (1970-71)	2,123	12.5 (1970-71 and 1984-85)
All States	308	2,355	8.9

Note: The data in column 2 here may not be comparable to those in column 3 of Table 1 because of different reporting sources and computations. Also, the CMIE's September 1994 report presents a slightly lower estimate for the growth rate presented in column 3 (Table 2) for the same reporting period. For our purpose the discrepancy is minor.

Source: Centre For Monitoring Indian Economy, September 1990.

TABLE 3
Per Capita Plan Allocation, Selected States for Examples:
1951-1990 (Rupees)

	I PLAN 1951-56	V PLAN 1974-79	VII PLAN 1985-90
MAJOR STATES:			
HIGH			
Haryana	*	481	1,871
Punjab	175	531	1,685
Maharashtra	37	372	1,434
LOW			
West Bengal	54	200	653
Bihar	25	155	626
SMALL STATES:			
Nagaland	*	1,359	4,000
Jammu and Kashmir	39	603	1,918
All States	38	262	1,026

Note : * Was not a State at that time.

Source: Centre for Monitoring Indian Economy, September 1990.

Local Politics, Violence and Panchayati Raj

T.V. SATHYAMURTHY

A macroscopic framework is vital to an analytic understanding of the dynamic of power relations in any concrete political situation. It is particularly important to work against the backcloth of such a view in order to appreciate the changes that have occurred in recent decades in India in the sphere of extending elected political representation to the three tiers of government below the national and State levels.[1] Such a framework must, of course, be neither rigidly behaviourial nor crudely reductionist. It should aim at making theoretical statements and hypotheses about the nature of politics with special reference to post-colonial India before defining the empirical remit of fieldwork.

Gung ho empiricism, casting about for categories and data for their own sake, examples of which abound in the social science literature on the sub-continent, is as counter-productive as simplistic or over-simplified theory. Theory should make room for analytic social scientific categories and for modes of explanation involving a flexible use of the ways in which different groups/classes see themselves or/and each other in the politico-social, cultural and economic areas.

The inter-weaving of the different dynamics simultaneously operating along vertical/hierarchical axes (e.g. inter-caste, inter-communal, inter-gender, etc.), and between horizontally/latitudinally (e.g. intra-class, inter-regional, inter-ethnic, etc.) divided segments[2] would constitute an essential analytic ingredient in the study of political phenomena specifically associated with the relations between the Centre and the States, and between these structures and the political structures of the *zilla, mandal* (or bloc), and the *panchayat* clusters.

I

The Indian Constitution was fashioned in an atmosphere in which the political *elite* was committed to a unitary view of the post-colonial state.

[1] Throughout this paper, the term 'State', (upper case 'S'), is used to refer to the States of the Indian Union or Federation, and the term 'state' (lower case 's') to the Indian state, the power of which at any given time is controlled by the government at the Centre.

[2] I. e. contradictions and conflicts that are elaborated in the course of power struggles and political competition, ranging from the fabrication of vote banks to the various political activities that take place in a variety of spheres (e.g. environment, displacement and enforced migration, pollution and dispossession of communal property, dispensation of customary justice located outside a narrowly defined politico-juridical arena).

The reason for this lay in a number of inter-weaving factors of which Partition was but one. Of equal importance to Partition in this regard was the significance attached by the framers of the Constitution in general, and the Congress Party in particular, to the emergence of a single cohesive over-arching and all encompassing nation state. The Indian national bourgeoisie and their supporters were of the view that the development of capitalist relations of production in India was bound up with the emergence of an ever expanding market, and, towards this end, at least in the medium run, with the establishment of a system of centrally planned production of the essential ingredients of a modern industrial economy. A power structure, in which the Centre would be disproportionately powerful, was crucial to the achievement of this goal.

The central government, for its part, and the Congress party that took control of it in 1946, strongly subscribed to the view that its role was to reflect and represent the interests of the Indian national bourgeoisie (equated with the industrial bourgeoisie during the first phase of India's post-colonial history), whilst acting as a controlling force in keeping the mass of the people (and, in particular, the working classes) in check. The homogeneity of the power wielding elite at the Centre and in the States (as well as its inter-changeability between the two foci of political power), during the first two decades of Independence, gave rise to the illusion that the Indian state could be controlled in a harmonious fashion by those in power at the Centre and in the State capitals at the head of the various State governments.

However, even the mildest tendency towards dissidence, let alone autonomy, was met with a disproportionate show of force by an intolerant Centre, always ready to interpret independence of thought as an unpatriotic and anti-national act. Thus, over five years *before* the Kerala State democratically returned a CPI-led government to power (1957), the PEPSU government, which had changed hands as a consequence of a minor democratic *bouleversement* in the Assembly, resulting in the Congress party losing its majority, was immediately brought to heel by the Centre. President's Rule was hastily invoked for the first time. The errant ministry was summarily dismissed as a prelude to political manoeuvres aimed at restoring the Congress party to power - an unusual augury of the political difficulties that were to be compounded in that sensitive area of the relationship between the different tiers of government.

Discussions of the tortured relationship between the Centre and the State in India often ignore the reluctance shown by State governments to devolve political power to the district and sub-district levels. The behaviour of most State governments, at least until the mid-80s, in this respect, has been of a piece. Although at one level, it is no more than a replication of the ideology of the Congress party towards the lower tiers of government, yet, at another level even a regional party such as the DMK/AIADMK has been known to be an adamant concentrator of power at its own headquarters (which, in this case, is the capital of the State concerned).

To some extent, this constitutes a reflection of the relatively low level of differentiation of the agrarian economy, whereby intra- and inter-class conflicts do not come into sharp and conflictual focus on the political arena. At the same time, the character of industrial development of the State - which depends upon the Centre's benevolence and on the rise of small and medium industry (for which the State government can act as a catalyst, and on occasion, even as a benefactor) - has been such as to pose no urban challenge to the ruling party at the State capital. For the rest, the lifeline of the regime stretches over its ability to deploy a brand of populism with the aim of mobilizing the *lumpen* elements in order to unleash anarchic violence against those who are critical of the government and demand a more democratic distribution of power.

In those regions (e.g. especially where the Green Revolution was introduced during the 60s) in which differentiation has been pronounced (and new class layers or strata of rich and middle peasantry as well as poor peasantry and agricultural labour have appeared), the State governments (and the Congress party) have been less able to resist persistent demands for greater devolution, democratization and local autonomy. The approaches adopted by different States have been shaped by appropriate local (i.e. regional) factors. Thus, even during the early years of Independence, the State of Bombay (subsequently, the States of Maharashtra and Gujarat) adopted a policy of devolving administrative responsibility through a system of modified *Panchayati Raj* (with the district administrative structure, under the Collector, as the fountain of power). This is not the appropriate place to consider the precise circumstances under which such changes take place, but it is worth pointing out that even in a State such as Maharashtra, with the accretion of the districts of Vidarbha (which had a radically different socio-economic background from, say, the relatively prosperous coastal districts of the former Bombay Presidency), the blueprint for the devolution of administrative responsibilities, as originally conceived, could not be followed uniformly throughout the State.

The decade of the 60s ended with the splits (of qualitatively different kinds) within the ruling party at two levels. At the Centre, the party split into the Congress(R), a major segment under Indira Gandhi's leadership, and the Congress(O), a minor segment under the control of the 'Syndicate'. At this level of the party, there was no difference in orientation between the two segments over the question of centralised unitary control of the power of the state.[3]

[3] Morarji Desai, as Prime Minister, was inflexible towards the Assam student movement and Sikh dissent in the Punjab which began as an agitation for greater autonomy for the State

At the State or regional level, however, the split was more complicated for two major reasons. First, the State Congress party suffered serious internal splits in those States in which new classes with specific interests came into being as a direct consequence of the Green Revolution (e.g. Punjab; Haryana, western Uttar Pradesh, and certain parts of Bihar). In the Punjab, this phenomenon was uniquely combined with the movement for regional autonomy of the Sikhs whose loyalties were divided between the Congress party and the Shiromani Akali Dal (SAD). In Uttar Pradesh, Haryana and Bihar, where there were no sizeable parties in opposition to the Congress, the Congress party itself underwent splits, the 'splittists' in these cases being, invariably, the political representatives of the newly emerging agrarian classes (especially the rich and middle peasantry), of which Chowdhury Charan Singh was the first pre-eminent inter-State leader.

At the level of the central party organization, the split between Indira Gandhi and the 'Syndicate' was hardly ideological on the dimension of the Centre *versus* the regions/States, and the former's donning the mantle of radical populism had nothing whatsoever to do with power-sharing between the Centre and the States, let alone increasing the democratic content of Indian politics. A specific thrust to local power, albeit power confined to representatives of the rich and middle peasant classes, was given by the political forces which developed along *Lok Dal* lines (and its subsequent transmogrifications and internal re-alignments). The competition for political power in these States, from the late '60s onwards, was between those who were seen by the rich and middle peasantry as more truly representative of their economic or class interests.

The premiss of the primacy of central power has never acquired the status of a hegemonic idea in India - not even in the halcyon days of the early phase of Nehru's Prime Ministership. The reason for this lies in the by no means negligible influence exercised by the ethos of decentralized, devolved or local power in the strands of political thinking associated with leaders such as Gandhi (and, since his death, in the *Sarvodaya* movement), Jaya Prakash Narayan, Ram Manohar Lohia, and socialists of various hues, all of whom resisted the temptation of office.

At a theoretical level, any discussion of the relations between central authority and local democracy that concentrates on the structures of power to the exclusion of movements of democratic resistance originating in a variety of forces of opposition - at the grassroots, in the regions, and in among the 'weaker sections' of society (e.g. *Dalits, Adivasis*, Scheduled Castes and [other] Backward Classes, poor peasantry, agricultural labour,

---

within the meaning of the *Anandpur Sahib Resolution*. Even Chowdhury Charan Singh (or, for that matter, Vishwanath Pratap Singh) was, relatively speaking, more 'centrist' or 'centralist' than 'federalist' in his political orientation. In this sense, all the Prime Ministers of India and their cabinets to date, have been uncompromisingly 'centralist'.

marginalized workers, and women) - can only throw partial light on the question of devolution of power, involving a double distortion. On the one hand, such accounts exaggerate the omnipotence and ubiquitousness of central power (and, by extension, power wielded in State capitals ruled by regional parties with equally centralizing tendencies); on the other, they underestimate the potential of the locality or periphery, as the case may be, to liberate itself from at least certain aspects of dominance by the Centre and to increase, to a corresponding degree, its democratic capability.

Regional parties in opposition to the Congress (e.g. DMK; AIADMK; Telugu Desam; and, to a limited degree, the SAD and the Asom Gana Parishad; and, latterly, the Yadav dominated Samajwadi party of Uttar Pradesh and Janata Dal of Bihar) have, in differing degrees, mounted struggles to supplant dominant higher castes and replace them with middle and lower middle castes (reminiscent of the struggles between tenants and zamindars in the latter part of the nineteenth century) in executive political control of State governments.

Exceptionally, in Bihar, this kind of struggle has, to a limited extent, taken on a slightly different colour mainly due to the initiative of Karpoori Thakur, who, as Chief Minister during the Janata interlude of the late 70s, did attempt to broaden the interpretation of the caste equation of power by reaching further down the caste hierarchy than any other regional party leader.[4] In the present decade, Laloo Prasad Yadav has added a somewhat variegated and successful caricature of the political experience bequeathed by the shortlived Karpoori Thakur regime.

I shall return to the question of democratic devolution of political power to the weakest sections of the population (at the grassroots level) towards the end of this essay. For the moment, I shall limit the discussion to the institutional aspects of the extension of democratically elected government by increasing the number of political tiers to five throughout the country (under the provisions of the 73rd and 74th Amendments to the Indian Constitution) - the Centre; the State; the *zilla*; the *samiti*; and the *panchayat* (or cluster of villages).

The characteristic features of the experiments in the devolution of power in India can be best understood against its historical background. It is well known that the first systematic blow in favour of power-sharing between the Centre and the States was struck by the multiple coalitions (and the DMK in Madras[5]) which defeated the Congress in eight States in

[4] Ram Manohar Lohia was the first socialist leader in India who advocated the primacy of the 'caste struggle' as differentiated from the 'class struggle'. During the last decade of his life he propagated the view that unless caste discrimination was removed there could be no future for India. Karpoori Thakur was the first politician in India's post-colonial history who attempted to put Lohia's idea into practice during his brief stint as Chief Minister of Bihar.

[5] Neither the DMK nor the AIADMK was serious about devolving power to sub-State structures, even though the former pioneered the agitation for more powers for the State down from the Centre by appointing a Committee which produced the celebrated *Rajamannar Report*

the general election of 1967. These coalitions embraced the whole of the political spectrum from the ultraconservative Swatantra party to the most radical left wing electoral party (namely the CPI-M).[6]

But it was not until 1977 that relatively stable opposition governments at the State level became a reality in several States. During the 80s and 90s, a majority of State governments have emerged which are ruled by parties or coalitions opposed to the Congress(I). During the last two decades, too, the hold of the Congress(I) on the Indian state has been challenged by a variety of political forces - in the form of coalitions which have included *both* parties with a highly centralizing orientation (and therefore in that respect not different from the Congress) towards political and state power (e.g. the BJP, and the Congress-O), and other splinters of the Congress party), *and* parties with a relatively decentralizing general orientation towards state power and a more or less strong commitment to autonomy at levels below the Centre and the State, often down to the village (e.g. the Socialist Party, the *Lok Dal, Janata Dal,* and parties that have split off from these).

In practice, however, even the party with the greatest de-centralising tendency among those opposed to the Congress (e.g. the lower caste political formations in Uttar Pradesh and Bihar such as the *Janata Dal, Samajwadi Janata Dal,* and *Bahujan Samaj*) has never shown a democratizing propensity beyond empowering the more wealthy and influential rural segments of the lower middle castes at the expense of those castes which, until recently, have been entrenched in local power. Moreover, its assumption of executive control of the State government is invariably accompanied by repressive violence being directed against the politically articulate segments of the lowest castes, mainly consisting of *Adivasis, Dalits,* Scheduled Castes, poor peasantry, agricultural labour, and especially their women.

II

The efforts to devolve political power and to suffuse the three lowest tiers of government with it must be viewed against the backcloth of an extremely complex process of socio-economic differentiation and contradiction. This has been taking place under conditions of acute and endemic scarcity, and within structures consisting of layer upon layer of encrusted and entrenched influence and power stoked up by corruption and venality

(Government of Tamil Nadu 1971). Thereby a start was made in the history of Centre-State relations which ended with the publication of the *Sarkaria Report* (Government of India 1988).

6 Since the late 70s, even some of the CPI(ML) factions have entered the parliamentary process, mainly at the level of the State legislature. The Indian Peoples Front (IPF), a front organization of the CPI(M-L) movement, takes part in elections at all levels.

which has reached monumental proportions during the last quarter of a century.[7]

Of all the attempts made by State governments to institutionalize democratically elected local government at the district level and below, those during the late 70s and early 80s by the CPI(M)-led Left Front coalition government in West Bengal and by the Janata administration in the State of Karnataka (under Ramakrishna Hegde as Chief Minister) represent the most far-reaching, serious and successful ones. In fact, so successful had the Janata experiment in local electoral democracy become that the Congress(I) ministry that was elected in the late-80s simply discontinued it, thus putting locally elected government in cold storage until forced by circumstance (i.e. the passing of the 73rd Amendment) to restore it.

It is important to note the sociological background of the party or coalition in power in each of these cases. At the heart of the political system of Karnataka over which the Janata Party presided during the early and mid-80s, the norms of the Congress culture continued to prevail. This was amply reflected in the corruption which quickly became as pervasive a feature of political life under the Janata administration as it had been under Devaraj Urs (a former Congress Chief Minister) or any of the other of Hegde's predecessors, and would be under his successors. However, even though the State leadership of the Janata Party quickly succumbed to the atmosphere of corruption prevailing in the State capital, its leadership (and, in particular, Abdul Nasir) did take seriously the party's commitment to establish electoral democracy at the three lowest levels of government.

The Janata regime's initiative in respect of *Panchayati Raj* was broadly consistent with its general orientation to devolution of power and to the spread of autonomy to the local level. The CPI(M)'s enthusiasm for democratically elected structures of local power is derived from a more complex world view. Unlike the Janata party, the CPI(M) carries out its political work through cadres. It has to its credit a long history of (partial) consciousness-raising political activity in the countryside. In Kerala, Tripura and West Bengal, the ruling communist party (even from before the 1964 split) has pursued reformist goals to a greater extent than any other political organization. The establishing of a strong democratically elected local government structure was seen as a strategic necessity for the realization of the social benefits and the general ethos of *Operation Barga*, in the long run, in the countryside. Thus, the Janata Party in Karnataka (and also the Telugu Desam, during the 80s, in Andhra

7 At the lower levels, this edifice of corruption and nepotism has been maintained intact mainly through collusion between the local elites on the one hand, and the all but omnipotent local bureaucracy on the other.

Pradesh) and the CPI(M) in West Bengal were motivated by different political considerations in their decision to introduce the three tiers of local administration on an elective basis. But, both were engaged in similar exercises of 'taking power to the people' (or, rather, 'taking power to the local elites').

The West Bengal and Karnataka experiments in establishing democratically elected and accountable local government structures, during the late 70s and early 80s, have provided the wherewithal for a blueprint applicable, with suitable modifications to take account of local/regional specificities, to the whole of India. Motivated in part by Congress(I)'s proverbial opportunism, and driven in part by necessity, the Centre itself sought, during the latter part of Rajiv Gandhi's Prime Ministership, to put forward an alternative approach to democratically elected local government bodies. This would have involved direct links between the Centre and the rural hinterland in different parts of the country (mediated through the District Collector), conveniently overlooking the intermediate 'federal' layer of the State government structure (which, in a large number of cases, has been ruled, from time to time, by regional and national parties of the opposition) in the process.

In actual fact, however, with the surfacing of new political pressures (extending far beyond conventional party politics and spilling over, literally, into areas of mass protests against the negative and anti-people policies of both the Centre and various State governments) on the one hand, and, on the other, the emergence of new coalitions or the recycling of existing coalitions involving different political parties, this particular intervention of the Centre never got off the ground. The only political alternative left to the central government with the dawning of the present decade, was to push through amendments to the Constitution requiring all States to carry out the task of establishing democratically elected local government at the three lowest levels (*zilla, samiti* and *panchayat*) as well as in all municipal centres. The initiative of the Left Front and Janata governments of well over a decade ago (followed by serious evaluations of their progress from time to time), can be said to have heralded the development of *Panchayati Raj* on an all-India basis. Before the end of this millennium, democratically elected *Panchayati Raj* will have been set in motion in all States.

We return to the difficult question of how political power can be democratically devolved to the weakest sections of the population. The magnitude of this problem can be comprehended by visualizing India as consisting of two halves - a smaller segment made up of those who, by virtue of their economic and social position, are able to benefit from the structures of power by exerting pressure of various kinds; and a major segment, consisting of the relatively undifferentiated poor, which is beyond the pale.

Whilst it is true that the exercises now under way in the sphere of decentralization of power and responsibilities (with, it may be added, no change in the pattern of central control over the purse strings) will produce a 'trickle down' effect from which the rural and local elites (e.g. small business, small retailers, etc., including members newly recruited from the lower castes as a consequence of power at the State level changing hands from the erstwhile dominant upper castes to middle and lower middle caste elites) will benefit, they will leave the poorest 40-50 per cent of the society untouched and, perhaps, even worse off (if that can be imagined!).

Therefore, there are two societies in India, one of which is poised to receive marginal benefits from the broadening of the institutional base of power that is being promoted under two recent Amendments to the Indian Constitution on the subject of decentralization and elected self-governing local authorities. The other is left to fend for itself under regional, national and international conditions more hostile than ever before experienced, at least in India's post-colonial history.

The future of the different segments of which it is composed can be charted only through political action, activism carrying a variety of impulses, and movements of resistance to institutional power in *all* its forms including the new *avatar* of decentralized power.

Entailed in the question raised above is the intellectual issue which can be formulated quite simply as follows: can one focus on 'decentralization' in a strait-jacketed framework of institutional power by adopting a method of approach which addresses 'conceptual' and 'programme-based' issues separately before linking them together? After reading the *Report* by Mukarji and Bandyopadhyay (1993), I was left with the impression that in view of the limitations built into the approach, no serious contribution can be made on the 'conceptual' side unless the basis of state power in India is challenged and a radical interpretation of it offered, which could act as a springboard on which alternative programmes may be hammered out with a view to generalizing, if not universalizing, the benefits of development. Questions of theory, conceptualization, methodology, and issues relating to the operational, functional and programmatic realms could thus be vigorously and *democratically* debated and fresh solutions aimed for. Here again, we need transfusion and suffusion of new intellectual blood imbued with an imaginative commitment to the goals of development.

III

In actual practice, the instruments of electoral democracy have taken a long time to appear on the horizon of local government and, even in 1995, their spread has been haltingly slow. The appreciation in 'higher' places (*viz.* the Centre and the States), to date, of the imperative need for devolution of political power and decentralization to lower levels, simultaneously in respect of the performance of administrative functions and in the exercise of primary fiscal control over resources allocated from above and (possibly) independently raised from the grassroots, continues to remain at the level of lip service (e.g. Mukarji and Bandyopadhyay, 1993).

However, certain tendencies have come to exercise a profound influence on the reality of socio-political life from one day to the next. The endemic character of violence as a common currency of politics has introduced a criminal culture into Indian political life at all levels (Kothari, 1981). To a large extent, Indian democracy has been persistently undermined by the process of criminalization to which electoral politics as well as the basic socio-economic activities of the mass of the Indian people have become subject.

Criminalization is pervasive. Along with corruption, it constitutes the pabulum of political power in India. Criminalization of politics is an enduring feature of social life which affects relations between different (religious and ethnic) communities; between regions; between castes (vertically, between higher and middle castes on the one hand and, on the other, lower and lowest castes, *Adivasis*, *Dalits*, and OBCs; and, horizontally, between different segments of the ruling castes in a given context - local or wider); between genders; and between classes and class segments (most notably, at the present conjuncture, between *lumpen* elements mobilized by populist parties such as the AIADMK and, say, workers in urban areas) (Sathyamurthy, 1994-95).

At the rural local (village, *panchayat*) level, criminal violence is rooted in the socio-economic and political domination of the land owning and rich-middle peasant castes, and in the resistance that those with no land but conscious of their civil and democratic rights are prepared to offer, in the last resort, in order to obtain a modest share of the public good and of the food in the production of which they are mainly instrumental. As has already been pointed out, there is also the violence that is built into the even more unequal relationship between the part of the society that has been able to hold itself above the poverty line, and its subterranean reaches where up to 40 per cent of the population barely survives under degrading conditions.

In order to place the growth of violence in perspective (Kothari, 1988; Sathyamurthy, 1991), it is useful to start with the role of the Congress administration under provincial autonomy (1937-39) in the large provinces of India. Its coming to power during the prelude to independence provided the Congress party with an ideal opportunity at least to declare itself in favour of the rights of the poor peasantry and landless labour as well as the need to release them from bonded debt and slavery. Not only did the

Congress fail to rise to the occasion, but it firmly nailed its colours to the mast of the rural rich.[8]

Congress politics conformed to the now familiar mould of electoral reliance on the social influence, economic clout and political support of the rich and middle peasantry (i.e. the upper and middle castes) for the mobilization of the vote bank of rural India. Typically, this meant that in a State such as Madras (the predecessor of Tamil Nadu) the landowning (former *mirasdars* included) rich and middle peasant castes ruled the countryside, whilst the Congress party, and the State bureaucracy and government provided the stamp of legitimacy for their dominance in the villages and blocs.

Over a period of time, the lower castes led a revolt of all the castes below against the dominant castes in which a number of demands were raised (among these were demands relating to language, opposition to Hindu religious practices associated with the higher or forward castes, and demands for a fairer distribution of land with appropriate ceilings as well as for a fairer agricultural wage structure in the place of the pre-capitalist and 'feudal' practices of bonded slavery that were still being followed in many areas) in order to shift the balance of political power around a new fulcrum represented by a share of local power for the lower (as differentiated from the lowest) castes.

Such was the underlying dynamic of the apparently sudden (and permanent) loss of power suffered by the Congress party in Tamil Nadu in 1967. Nor, indeed, was such a transition accompanied by a lowering of the profile of violence in the politics of the State. Indeed, within 18 months of the DMK assuming power in Tamil Nadu, there were a number of instances of criminal violence being used by landowning castes against agricultural wage labour, of which the Kilavenmani bloodbath was a dramatic example. Other examples can be adduced from a number of States (e.g. Karamchedu in Andhra Pradesh, Bhagalpur in Bihar and Muzaffarnagar in UP). The intensity and frequency of criminal violence in the intercourse between the dominant and the oppressed castes have increased

[8] Imagine a situation in which the Congress party was indeed serious about its commitment to some form of social justice (similar to, say, the mainstream communist parties' commitment to a programme of land reform and ownership of land, extended as far down the social scale as the Indian Constitution would permit). The 1937-39 stint in provincial administration would have constituted an ideal opportunity for the Congress party to forge a vigorous propaganda in favour of rural social justice. Compare this with the UF governments of West Bengal (1967-70) in which the redoubtable Land Reform minister (Hare Krishna Konar) played a propagandistic role elaborating the nature of the land reform to which the CPI(M) stood committed. Konar's land reform policy made it possible for the majority administration under the LF to bring Operation Barga into legislation and to strike an important advance in the direction of extending political power to the panchayats. On the question of land reform, the Congress party and the Left Front have thus been poles apart despite their claims to favour more or less identical policies of ownership (ceiling) and cultivation.

manifold during the quarter of a century since the Internal Emergency (1975-77) (e.g. Das, 1992).

The picture of socio-political violence in contemporary India can be broadly characterized as follows:

1. There is a specific culture of violence that can be associated with the Congress party's role in politics at the national, regional and local levels. At the national level, corruption entered the roots of political life through the enormous importance attached to money as a building material for the garnering of power. Congress leaders (e.g. S K Patil, during Nehru's time, A R Antulay, Lalit Narayan Mishra, N D Tewari and many others during Indira Gandhi's tenure as Prime Minister/Congress President) played an important role in this process. This tendency encouraged a rapid spread of a black market economy, the linking of political violence with monetary corruption, and a systematic violation of bureaucratic norms accompanied by a politicization of the bureaucracy.

2. With the supplanting of the Congress in a number of States and its substitution by various coalitions, the tendency to violence continued to remain unabated. Violence became the coinage of inter-party relations. Gangs were recruited by rival political organizations in order that they could test each other's strength and intimidate the population at large. Over a period of time, powerful criminals, who had initially provided their services to politicians and acted as a sheet anchor to enable them to continue to wield legislative power through fraudulent elections, themselves directly aspired to power instead of remaining as intermediaries. As a consequence, almost all State Legislative Assemblies can now boast among their membership elected representatives against whom a number of criminal cases (murder being common among them) are still pending.

3. At the three lowest tiers of government, the interplay of political forces has been such as to raise social violence to an even higher pitch. Here, two interacting social contradictions need to be taken into account. First, the horrors of violence perpetrated by dominant castes against the low*est* castes,[9] the *Avarnas*, the *Adivasis* and against women have become more and more intensified and in-

[9] It is no longer possible to continue discourse based on divisions between high, middle and low castes. We need at least five (indeed more) qualitatively different categories - upper, middle, lower, and lowest and other backward castes, Dalits, Adivasis and the women of these latter four categories.

vasive of the few communal means of subsistence and livelihood upon which the latter have been dependent and which they have taken for granted from time immemorial. Second, the lower and lowest castes have been subject to intense pressure due to widespread marginalization, seasonalization, migration and displacement of rural labour. They have suffered massive destabilization and deprivation of traditional resources. At the same time, they are more politically conscious and less willing to accept oppression by powerful social forces. They offer resistance and are prepared to challenge the dominant elites of the countryside with the aid of political organizations and such movements as the Democractic Rights and Civil Liberties Unions.

The political awakening of the lowest tiers of society, including those which cannot even keep their heads above the poverty line, has resulted in struggles in which even the most elementary forms of resistance are crushed by recourse to a disproportionate amount of violence. It is not at all unlikely, given the calculus of power, that the institutionalization of elective politics with lower tiers of the state structure, would also have the effect of maintaining high levels of violence (of domination and oppression) in two respects:

1. In the intra-elite relationships which usually take the form of violence among different leading groups/fractions/factions in the same party or between leading groups belonging to rival parties.
2. The low living levels of the lowest rungs of the social hierarchy will, in all probability, continue under conditions of uneven development, increasing dependence on external assistance and acute scarcity of resources. This would mean that in order to maintain existing levels of appropriation of surplus, the ruling elites will tend to institutionalize oppression and use greater amounts of violence in order to achieve such ends. The political relationships in which the elites at all levels - national, regional, *zilla, mandal* and *panchayat* are enmeshed reek of violence and corruption to a degree that can only have the effect of deterring, not fostering, democracy.

Far from heralding representative political rule at lower levels of government, *Panchayati Raj* could equally well result in the institutionalization of political violence in civil society as a general phenomenon, stretching over the entire body politic of India's deeply and fundamentally flawed democracy. The spread of resistance to widespread oppression which, to date, is on the whole, non-violent, offers what little hope there is in India for the forms and ideas that inspire the conduct of politics according to the principles of democracy. Yet, the task of identifying, analysing and quantifying the factors involved in the power relationships engaged in the process of *panchayatization*, currently under way in India, is of paramount importance to students of the political theory of democracy (generally and with specific reference to this subject) as well as to the analysts of the instruments of democratic (or otherwise) and representative governance.

IV

To sum up: A pattern is clearly discernible, showing the acquisition of power by new caste groups (a sort of transfer of power from Forward Castes to Middle Castes to Lower Castes, one might say). In this pecking order, differentiation and contradiction develop along lines in which the aggressive potential for the oppression of castes below passes from one level of social hierarchy to the next rung.

However, this phenomenon must be viewed not only in the context of differentiation *between* castes or groups of castes but also in the context of differentiation *among* castes. Two related observations can be made:

1. The relations between castes or caste groups which have lost power and castes or caste groups which have recently gained power are usually matters of adjustment and re-adjustment. They seldom involve overtly violent conflict. The relations between (on the one hand) the castes and caste groups currently in dominance and (on the other) those occupying the lower rungs of the rural socio-economic order are invariably marked by violent oppression on the part of the ruling caste(s), whilst the resistance offered by the oppressed castes generally tends to be of a kind that varies between the non-violent and the counter-violent.

2. Differentiation cuts both ways in a largely poor rural society. On the one hand, the differentiation between dominant (powerful) and subordinate (oppressed) castes along vertical (and longitudinal) lines throws into relief the social contradictions engulfing the vast majority of the population. This larger picture of differentiation also includes a process of (downward) differentiation *within* the dominant caste; *between* the small and influential segments which acquire wealth and power (land and jobs) *and* the much larger ones which remain impoverished and dependent on the former.

   Under such conditions, the poor are *divided* between those who expect their poverty to be alleviated by their caste brethren and sisters enjoying local office, and the power and influence that go with it; *and* those who continue to experience oppressive violence with the transfer of political power from one caste or group of castes to another.

The poor are in no position to grasp the common thread of economic deprivation and political domination that binds them together and, therefore, to unite along lines of 'class solidarity' - genuine or even *manqué.* The different varieties of populism (Sathyamurthy, 1995a), that appear and disappear from time to time in different States, constitute a living testimony to the enormous difficulties involved in stimulating the emergence of conditions under which social power at the base can be 'democratically' (let alone, equitably) wielded.

History revisits familiar socio-economic pastures, not always in order to perpetrate a farce, but sometimes rather to reveal the new contours assumed by a ruling party (in this case, the Congress(I)) - ruling only in name, because it has squandered the hegemonic authority that it once (1947-67) wielded over all classes and in most regions of the country. Now (in the footsteps of its colonial predecessor), it is merely clinging to state power as an instrument for the continuation of 'dominance without hegemony' (Guha, 1989).

Conflicting Legitimacies in Pakistan: The Changing Role of the Objectives Resolution (1949) in the Constitution

DIETER CONRAD

Historical Setting

The Constitution of Pakistan in its present shape[1] has the unique feature of embodying a lengthy text twice at different places: the *Objectives Resolution* passed by the first Constituent Assembly on 12 March 1949, with minor variations forms the major part of the preamble and reappears *verbatim* in an *Annex* incorporated in the operative part of the Constitution by way of a reference provision (Art. 2A). Graphically it appears to be the opening and the end, the Alpha and Omega of the Constitution.

This happy symmetric arrangement, however, is not an artistic achievement. It is rather one of the scars of history marking the body of that maltreated organic law. The duplication, as we shall see, is inorganic and poses intricate problems of interpretation and reconciliation. In its ambivalence it betrays, as indeed does already the text of the Resolution itself, the deep cleavage in the perception of what the Pakistan polity legitimately ought to be: a cleavage which has accompanied the state from its very foundation till today.

It is well known that the group of politicians responsible for the foundation of Pakistan did not have in mind to create an Islamic State. The foundational document, the Lahore Resolution of 1940, does not mention Islam at all. Leading proponents of an Islamic state, notably Abul Ala Maududi and his *Jamaat-i-Islami* originally were opposed to the creation of Pakistan and doubted the Muslim League leadership's Islamic credentials.[2] The very name Pakistan, coined with an Islamistic tendency, was not originally elected by the Muslim League, but was rather thrust upon them as a polemical term by opponents, and was only reluctantly adopted.[3]

[1] The Constitution of the Islamic Republic of Pakistan, 1973 as amended by the Revival of the Constitution of 1973 Order, 1985 (P.O. 14 of 1985) read with Constitution (Eighth Amendment) Act, 1985 sec.19.

[2] *Report of the Court of Inquiry constituted under Punjab Act II of 1954 to enquire into the Punjab Disturbances of 1953* (henceforth: Munir-Report) (Lahore, 1954), pp. 243 ff.; L. Binder, *Religion and Politics in Pakistan* (Berkeley, 1961), pp. 90 ff.; Khalid B. Sayeed, *Pakistan. The Formative Phase 1857 - 1948* (Karachi, 2nd. ed. 1978), p. 199; K. K. Aziz, *A History of the Idea of Pakistan* (Lahore, 1987), p. 421; Mohammad Waseem, *Politics and the State in Pakistan* (Lahore, 1989), p. 81 f.

[3] Cf. Jinnah's presidential address to the All India Muslim League annual session, Delhi, 24 April 1943: 'You know perfectly well that Pakistan is a word which is really foisted upon us and fathered on us by some section of the Hindu press and also by the British press. Now our resolution was known for a long time as the Lahore resolution, popularly known as Pakistan Resolution. But how long are we to have this long phrase? Now I say to my Hindu and British

Its author, Rahmat Ali was kept at a distance by the League's leadership.[4] Jinnah himself warned his followers against speculations about an Islamic state,[5] and in his opening adress to the Constituent Assembly as Governor-General projected a vision of the future state which was secular all but in name.[6] What was really intended was a defensive position against Hindu dominance, a territorial bastion or homeland of the historically grown *Muslim culture* in India rather than a dogmatical religious construct.[7] In its political order it was to be organized on the lines of a modern national state perhaps like Turkey.[8] Today it is necessary occasionally to recall this opening position, in view of later developments and a continuous flow of subsequent twisted interpretations including some over-zealous contributions by Western scholars of Islam. The original consensus within the political elite was reaffirmed in 1956 by the then Prime Minister Chaudhry Muhammad Ali, in his speech on the Draft *Constitution of the Islamic Republic of Pakistan,* in the following terms: 'Sir, Pakistan came into existence as the result of a struggle by the Muslims of the sub-continent to win a homeland for themselves in which they would be free to live their own way of life and develop their own culture.'[9] This declaration on the

---

friends: We thank you for giving us one word.' [Quoted from K.K. Aziz, *Rahmat Ali. A Biography* (Stuttgart, 1987), p. 380, where the League leaders' original dislike for the word is discussed at some length, pp. 362 ff.]

4 See ibid. and pp. 148 ff. for an account of the extraordinary incident how Rahmat Ali was prevailed upon not to come to Punjab on his visit to India early in 1940 and thus kept from attending the Lahore session in March 1940.

5 Cf. Raja of Mahmudabad, 'Some Memoirs', in: C. H. Philips / M. D. Wainwright (eds.), *The Partition of India: Policies and Perspectives 1935 - 1947* (London, 1970), pp. 381-388.

6 Though it is not necessary to repeat extracts from that celebrated speech *in extenso,* two key sentences may be quoted here which show the essential secularist concept of distinguishing between the political and the religious spheres; using the example of England Jinnah explains: 'Today, you might say with justice that Roman Catholics and Protestants do not exist; what exists now is that everyman is a citizen, an equal citizen of Great Britain and they are all members of the Nation. Now, I think we should keep that in front of us as our ideal and you will find that in course of time Hindus would cease to be Hindus and Muslims would cease to be Muslims, not in the religious sense, because that is the personal faith of each individual, but in the political sense as citizens of the State.' [Quoted from G.W. Choudhury, *Documents and Speeches on the Constitution of Pakistan* (Dacca, 1967), p. 22.]

7 Muhammad Iqbal in his famous Allahabad Address to the All-India Muslim League 1930 clearly argues from this broad cultural conception, positing that 'the principle that the Indian Muslim is entitled to full and free development *on the lines of his own culture and tradition* in his own Indian homelands is recognized as the basis of a permanent communal settlement...' [L.A. Sherwani, *Speeches, Writings and Statements of Iqbal* (Lahore, 3rd. ed. 1977), pp. 3 ff., 8]. Iqbal's proposal for the formation of a single Muslim state in North-West India is based on the premise that '*the life of Islam as a cultural force* in this country very largely depends on its centralization in a specified territory' (ibid. p. 10, emph. add.).

8 On the original option for a national Muslim rather than an Islamic state and the subsequent development cf. generally Keith Gallard, *Pakistan. A Political Study* (London, 1957), pp. 200 ff.; Erwin I.J. Rosenthal, *Islam in the Modern National State* (Cambridge, 1965), pp. 181 ff.; Khalid B. Sayeed, n. 2, pp. 202 ff.; id. *Politics in Pakistan.The Nature and Direction of Change* (New York, 1980), pp. 8 ff.; Muhammad Munir, *From Jinnah to Zia* (Lahore, 2nd ed. 1980), pp. 19 ff.

9 Text of the speech in G.W. Choudhury (n.6), p. 298.

rationale of the State's foundation drew the spontaneous applause from the leader of the opposition, H. S. Suhrawardy.[10] It is significant that in this key statement again there was no explicit reference to Islam, let alone an Islamic state.[11] All that the Prime Minister permitted himself to say in this respect in the later course of his speech was a quotation of Jinnah's vague formula of 'principles of Islamic social justice' and the wish 'to find an atmosphere in which the spirit of Islam can flourish'.[12]

Nevertheless, it is also a fact that in order to generate mass support for the Pakistan demand the Muslim league leadership had at an early stage, and increasingly, taken recourse to religious propaganda. In the course of popular agitation the emphasis had been shifted from the envisaged Muslim national state and the preservation of Muslim culture to the more forceful rallying cry of saving Islam, and of ensuring its glorious future in the state to be founded. In this way the support of Mullahs and Pirs in the campaign could also be enlisted and the critical attitude of traditionalist *ulama* towards the Islamic modernism and nationalism of the Muslim league be overcome.[13] The ensuing kind of campaigning inevitably stirred up religious emotions as well as idealistic and utopian expectations, not only with the poorer segments of society, but also with parts of the educated middle class. In the event this produced a language of Islamic *rinascimento* which evoked many vague aspirations and projections of an ideal Islamic polity. At the same time it provided an opening for specialists of Islamic learning to formulate their more traditional and more stringent conceptions, and to initiate a debate on the Islamic State.

In sum, a potentially far-reaching, though little defined commitment had been entered, not without a measure of duplicity.[14] It could not openly

[10] Ibid.: 'Hear, hear. We agree.' In his own speech on the Constitution Suhrawardy took exception to the designation as 'Islamic Republic of Pakistan' because, in his view, this did not conform to the actual contents of the constitution; cf. ibid., p. 977.

[11] The general political background to this marked restraint, in the situation between 1954 and 1956, and in particular, foreign policy considerations weighing with the power elite, are analysed in Ayesha Jalal, *The State of Martial Rule* (Cambridge, 1990), pp. 184 ff.

[12] Ibid., p. 298. The quotation is from Jinnah's address to the Civil and Military Officers of Karachi on 19 October 1947 and in its context rather confirms the general picture: 'The idea was that we should have a State in which we could live and breathe as free men and which we could develop according to our own way of life and culture and wherein the principles of Islamic social justice could find free-play.'

[13] The spirit in which this was done is illustrated by the wellknown incident of the 'Mashaikh Committee' formed in the Punjab in order to bring together in the same body leaders of unquestionable religious standing, such as the Pir of Manki Sharif with some quite mundane politicians who had been assigned religious titles for the purpose, such as 'Pir of Mamdot Sharif' etc.; cf. *Munir-Report*, p. 255.

[14] See the summary appraisal by Khalid B. Sayeed, *Politics in Pakistan*, p. 28, n. 1: 'Muslim league leaders almost invariably presented the concept of Pakistan as an Islamic state to the Muslim masses, whereas the dominant group among these leaders planned and expected that it would be a Muslim state, the policies of which would be liberal and modern though influenced broadly by certain Islamic principles.'

be discounted, but in what manner, and by whom, it was to be honoured, was a deep-seated issue of contention between rivalling forces. The state of Pakistan, so to speak, was trapped in the semantics of its foundation. It is proposed here to document the resulting process of ideological elaboration, from the initial ambivalence to the progressive working out of fundamentalist tendencies, by the instance of a basic constitutional text and its unforeseen career. In focussing on one particular document the purpose also is to analyse the frequently underrated influence of legal language in its unobtrusive yet continuously formative operation on the minds, and the instrumental value of certain formulas - as interpreted and used by two different classes of legal experts.

Text and Analysis of Contents

The 'Objectives Resolution' was introduced in the Constituent Assembly of Pakistan on 7 March 1949 and after several days' debate was adopted on 12 March 1949.[15] As its title implies it is a statement of the general objectives of the Constitution to be made, an outline of the constitutional programme in its essential contours. The idea of such a solemn declaration of intent, and its designation, were perhaps taken from the earlier Indian Objectives Resolution which had been moved by J. Nehru on December 13, 1946 in the Constituent Assembly convened under the Cabinet Mission Plan for undivided India.[16] Some principles spelt out in this Resolution later became the essential part of the Preamble to the Indian Constitution. The Pakistani *Objectives Resolution* was passed comparatively late, a year and a half after inauguration of the Pakistan Constituent Assembly and half a year after Jinnah's death. It marked the beginning of actual work on the Constitution and was to serve as guideline for the Basic Principles Committee formed in March 1949. Later it was in its entirety incorporated as a Preamble in the Draft Constitution submitted by the Basic Principles Committee in 1952.[17] From then onwards it has, with minor modifications, been included as a Preamble in every constitutional draft or Constitution enacted in Pakistan. Since it will have to be considered in some detail the full text is reproduced here:[18]

15 For details of the historical context and debates in the Assembly cf. L. Binder, n. 2, Ch. 4, pp. 116 ff.; E.I.J. Rosenthal (n. 8), pp. 209 ff.

16 Text in B. Shiva Rao (ed.), *The Framing of India's Constitution. Selected Documents, Vol. II* (New Delhi, 1967), pp. 3 f.

17 See G.W. Choudhury, n. 6, p. 69. The decision to incorporate the *Objectives Resolution* in the form of a Preamble had already been taken in the *Interim Report of the Basic Principles Committee* submitted in 1950, cf. ibid., p. 34.

18 The text is given in the form in which it was originally moved and resolved in the Constituent Assembly, taken from an official, contemporaneous edition by the Government of

'In the name of Allah, the Benificent, the Merciful;

WHEREAS sovereignty over the entire universe belongs to God Almighty alone and the authority which He has delegated to the state of Pakistan through its people for being exercised within the limits prescribed by Him is a sacred trust;

This Constituent Assembly representing the people of Pakistan resolves to frame a constitution for the sovereign independent State of Pakistan;

WHEREIN the State shall exercise its powers and authority through the chosen representatives of the people;

WHEREIN the principles of democracy, freedom, equality, tolerance and social justice as enunciated by Islam shall be fully observed;

WHEREIN the Muslims shall be enabled to order their lives in the individual and collective spheres in accord with the teachings and requirements of Islam as set out in the Holy Quran and the Sunna;

WHEREIN adequate provision shall be made for the minorities freely to profess and practise their religions and develop their cultures;

WHEREBY the territories now included in or in accession with Pakistan and such other territories as may hereafter be included in or accede to Pakistan shall form a Federation wherein the units will be autonomous with such boundaries and limitations on their powers and authority as may be prescribed;

WHEREIN shall be guaranteed fundamental rights including equality of status, of opportunity and before the law, social, economic and political justice, and freedom of thought, expression, belief, faith, worship and association, subject to law and public morality;

Pakistan, Karachi, n.d.; cf. also the speech by the Prime Minister Liaquat Ali Khan moving the resolution, in: G.W. Choudhury, (n. 6), pp. 23 ff. This text is not accurately preserved, even apart from clerical changes, either in the Preamble to the present Constitution, nor in the Annex inserted by Art. 2A. For its use as a Preamble to the Constitution, its first paragraph had early been changed so as to omit the reference to delegation and replace it by the simpler formula 'and the authority to be exercised by the people of Pakistan' (cf. the speech by the Law Minister I.I. Chundrigar on the 4th Draft Constitution, 9 Jan 1956, in: G.W. Choudhury, n.6, p. 289). The word 'God' was changed to 'Allah' in the deliberations on the Report of the Basic Principles Committee on 28 Oct 1953 (cf. L. Binder) - an amendment which at the time may have estranged the Hindu minority. The second paragraph referring to the role of the Constitutent Assembly has been changed more than once, according to the historical situation; in the present Preamble it reads: 'And whereas it is the will of the people of Pakistan to establish an order...' The 'Annex' purporting to reproduce the original Resolution has restored the delegation clause and the reference to the first Constituent Assembly, but retained the designation 'Allah'. Furthermore, in the 6th paragraph, concerning the provisions to be made 'for the minorities freely to profess and practise their religions', the word 'freely' has been quietly dropped. This latter, surreptitious change must be considered as ominous.

WHEREIN adequate provision shall be made to safeguard the legitimate interests of minorities and backward and depressed classes;

WHEREIN the independence of the judiciary shall be fully secured;

WHEREIN the integrity of the territories of the Federation, its independence and all its rights including its sovereign rights on land, sea and air shall be safeguarded;

So that the people of Pakistan may prosper and attain their rightful and honoured place amongst the nations of the World and make their full contribution towards international peace and progress and happiness of humanity.'

This resolution, judged in the light of later events, and with the benefit of hindsight, today is considered a decisive first step from the ideal of a Muslim national state towards an Islamic state. It is praised as well as criticized on this account as a major departure in the constitutional development of Pakistan.[19] At the time it rather appeared as a document of compromise. Passed one and a half years after the inauguration of the Constituent Assembly, and half a year after Jinnah's death, it may have responded to a political need to proclaim unity of purpose. It achieved this by rhetorically bridging over the differences between Islamic traditionalists, fundamentalists and modernists of a more secular outlook (the latter being influenced, as a rule, by English legal training). Its virtue thus lay in a wording which has been characterised as 'carefully imprecise', providing agreed formulas which the orthodox as well as the modernist side could interpret their own way.[20] It represents what in German constitutional doctrine has been called a dilatory compromise formula - i.e. does not decide an issue but rather adjourns decision by using equivocal language. This will become clearer upon closer examination of the text. But it should not be overlooked that its harmonizing function was limited to integrating Muslim opinion in its various shades. It did not include, but inevitably rather excluded, the non-Muslim minorities, notably the Hindus - then still a sizable minority concentrated in East Bengal. The Hindu representatives in the Constituent Assembly vehemently argued against the Islamizing tendency of the Resolution. It was passed with all but one of the Muslim votes against the equally united opposition vote of the Hindu members.[21]

19 For approval, e.g. G.W. Choudhury, *Pakistan. Transition from Military to Civilian Rule* (Essex, 1988), p. 113: 'The first big step towards the concept of an Islamic state in Pakistan...'. For criticism: M. Munir, n. 8, pp. 29 ff.: 'Change of Ideology'.

20 L. Binder, n. 2, pp. 153, 181.

21 The speech by the East Bengal Hindu leader of the opposition, Sris Chandra Chattopadhyaya, against the Objectives Resolution (12 March 1949) is printed in G.W. Choudhury (n. 6), pp. 965 ff.

The Resolution has its own structural disposition which, for purposes of interpretation, ought to be taken note of. It begins with an explanatory *exordium* proclaiming, as motivating principles for all that is to follow ('whereas...'), God's sovereignty over the universe, the derivative nature of public authority as a delegated and limited 'trust', and the delegation of this trust to the State of Pakistan 'through its people'; the latter may be understood as a democratic principle in the sense that the direct recipient of the delegated authority is not the State nor a monarchical head of the State, but the people of Pakistan, i.e. the entire citizenry (presumably including the non-Muslim citizens).

This is followed by an 'operative' part stating first the Assembly's resolve as 'enacting' formula, and subsequently the actual contents of its determination, namely the objectives laid down as esssential features of the constitution to be framed (nine paragraphs introduced respectively by the word 'wherein' or 'whereby'...). The concluding statement expresses the aspiration of the Pakistan nation through its constitution to attain its rightful and honoured place as member of the international community. There is no reference to a closer unity or fraternity among Muslim nations, such as it is now emphasized in a Directive Principle of the Constitution.[22]

The objectives set down comprise a system of representative democracy, organized as a federation of autonomous units, with fundamental rights of the conventional occidental type, protection of the religious and cultural rights of minorities as well as of other legitimate interests of minorities including backward and depressed classes, independence of the judiciary as a guarantee of all these rights. There are two clauses specifically mentioning Islam:

(a) The principles listed in the second paragraph are qualified by the phrase 'as enunciated by Islam'. From the wording it is not clear whether the qualifying words refer to all the principles or only to the last mentioned 'social justice.' In view of the emphasis put on 'Islamic principles of social justice' by Muslim League leaders like M.A. Jinnah and Liaquat Ali Khan[23], an interpretation limiting the qualifying phrase to this specific meaning would not appear entirely out of place. The prevalent understanding, however, is to extend the Islamic reference to all the principles listed.

[22] Art. 40, the wording of which may be compared: 'The State shall endeavour to preserve and strengthen fraternal relations among Muslim countries based on Islamic unity, support the common interests of the peoples of Asia, Africa and Latin America, promote international peace and security, foster goodwill and friendly relations among all nations and encourage the settlement of international disputes by peaceful means.' A similar provision was already included in the Directive Principles of the 1956 Constitution (Art. 24).

[23] See the quotation from Jinnah's speech supra, n. 12; the formula was considered so important that it was later inserted in the introductory part of the Preamble (i.e. *Objectives Resolution*) of the Constitution 1956. For Liaquat Ali Khan and his catch word 'Islamic socialism' cf. Binder (n. 2), pp. 184 f.

This was clearly the view underlying the opening speech by Prime Minister Liaquat Ali Khan introducing the Resolution. But it might raise the question whether the Islamic qualification is to be read as a limitation, e.g. democracy, freedom, equality, tolerance only within the limits imposed by the *Shariah*. Such an interpretation was apprehended by the speakers of the Hindu minority.[24] It would correspond to the views of Islamists like Muhammad Asad or Maududi who, for instance, draws an antithetical distinction between 'Western Secular Democracy' and what he terms 'Democratic Khilafat'[25] and explains as vice-regency of the *community of believers* in the execution of the Divine law. On the other hand modernists like Jinnah and Liaquat Ali Khan tended to read the qualifying words rather as an assertion of historic priority and continuity of universal principles, i.e. democracy, freedom, equality etc. which have originally been enunciated by Islam.[26] The meaning of the principles thus 'further defined' is explained by Liaquat Ali Khan in his supporting speech as 'deeper and wider than the usual connotation of these words' but, by implication, not substantially different.[27]

(b) The 'enabling clause': providing for an opportunity for Muslims 'to order their lives in the individual and collective spheres in accord with the teachings and requirements of Islam' and specifying Quran and Sunnah as the authoritative source of such Islamic prescripts. The reference to 'the Holy Quran and Sunnah' has become the standard formula in the constitutional definition of 'injunctions of Islam'.[28] Its significance lies in the absence of a reference to *shariah* or *fiqh* - i.e. the implicit assertion that Quran and Sunnah are to be understood directly and in independent inter-

[24] See the speech by S.C. Chattopadhyaya (n. 21), p. 967: In this connection you say 'equal rights', but at the same time with limitations as enunciated by Islam. Is there any equal right in an Islamic country? '...*An honourable member*: 'There was in Islamic countries.' S.C. Chattopadhyaya: 'It was not between Muslims and non-Muslims.'

[25] Sayyid Abul Ala Maududi, *The Islamic Law and Constitution*, 2nd ed. (Lahore, 1960), p. 147: '...Islam has no trace of Western democracy. Islam, as already explained, altogether repudiates the philosophy of popular sovereignty and rears its polity on the foundations of the sovereignty of God and the vice-regency (*khilafat*) of man.' Cf. ibid., p. 235. Muhammad Asad, *The Principles of State and Government in Islam* (Berkeley and Los Angeles, 1961), pp. 18 f., holds similar views on the limitations of democracy and generally opposes the use of such Western concepts as misleading in the Islamic context.

[26] E.g. M.A. Jinnah, Broadcast talk to the people of the United States of America, February 1948, in: *Quaid-i-Azam Mahomed Ali Jinnah, Speeches as Governor-General of Pakistan 1947 - 1948* (Karachi, 1962), pp. 63 ff., 65: 'I do not know what the ultimate shape of this constitution is going to be, but I am sure that it will be of a democratic type, embodying the essential principles of Islam... Islam and its idealism have taught us democracy. It has taught equality of man, justice and fairplay to everybody.'

[27] See Liaquat's speech moving the resolution, n. 18 and 6, p. 26. Similarly I.H. Qureshi had explained that the principles of Islam do not conflict with the UN Charter's principles on human rights, 'only in Islam the meaning is richer and it is fuller' (quoted in L. Binder, p. 148).

[28] Art. 198 Constitution 1956, Art. 204 Constitution 1962 as amended by the 1st Amendment Act. 1964; Art. 227 Constitution 1973.

pretation (*ijtihad*) without deference (*taqlid*) to the interpretation and systematic elaboration by the classical schools of law.[29] Apart from this the enabling clause seems to be entirely prospective conjuring up the idea of Pakistan as a laboratory of Islam (Liaquat). The exact meaning, however, is again not very clear. While it was rightly said that 'no non-Muslim should have any objection if the Muslims are enabled to order their lives in accordance with the dictates of their religion' - as long, that is, as this remains a voluntary effort - it was also contended that the State was not 'to play the part of a neutral observer', but was 'to play a positive part in this effort', namely to 'create such conditions as are conducive to the building up of a truly Islamic society'.[30] The clause was meant to secure more than simply the free exercise of their religion by Muslims. What exactly this includes remained rather obscure, but it would not be unfair to surmise that the word 'order' and the active role of the State imply an element of compulsion at least with respect to Muslims[31] - with possible repercussions on the non-Muslim citizens.

Apart from these two 'Islamic' clauses the constitutional programme set forth in the resolution follows the pattern of a constitutional democracy on modern occidental lines. Federalism (autonomy of the federating units), fundamental rights and minority protection, rule of law (through the independence of the judiciary) are emphasized. In this part, judged by itself, the Resolution could as well figure as a constitutional plan for the secular state of India. This should not be surprising in view of the common traditions of legal culture in both countries. It even looks as if the latter paragraphs of the Resolution, beginning from the federal clause, were drafted under the direct influence of the Indian Objectives Resolution.[32] They seem to have been added *en bloc*, as it were, to the preceding paragraphs defining the religious status of the polity. This additive technique might help to explain the somewhat inorganic duplication of minority guarantees in two separate clauses.

29 An important concession to tradition is made, however, in the sphere of personal laws - for definition see sec.2 Muslim Personal Law (*Shariat*) Application Act, 1937 - where the interpretation of 'Quran and Sunnah' by any particular Muslim sect has been made binding for that sect; this may be interpreted as including a reference to the various classical schools of *fiqh*.

30 Liaquat Ali Khan, p. 26.

31 The necessity of such power of compulsion, and consequently of an Islamic State for the establishment of an Islamic society or way of life is expounded by Muhammad Asad (n. 25), pp. 3 *f*.

32 Apparently some of its phraseology has also served as a model; cf., e.g. with the corresponding passage in the Pakistan text, the passage on minority protection, No. 6 of the Indian resolution: '...(6)Wherein adequate safeguards shall be provided for minorities, backward and tribal areas, and depressed and other backward classes; ..."Similarly, the concluding sentence seems to have inspired the corresponding Pakistani version: " ..(8) this ancient land attains its rightful and honoured place in the world and makes its full and willing contribution to the promotion of world peace and the welfare of mankind.'

Be that as it may, one cannot fail to notice the lack of systematic integration as between the two major parts. Compatibility of the Islamic principles invoked in the first paragraphs with institutional guarantees as outlined in the latter half has simply been presupposed, without any overt attempt at reconciliation. There must have been doubts, however, well-known already to the authors of the Resolution, about possible contradictions between traditional Islamic principles and at least some fundamental rights, e.g. free exercise and propagation of non-Muslim religions, equality of sexes, equality of citizen status for non-Muslims etc. Such contradictions have since been noted by more than one observer,[33] and may be further substantiated by comparing a more recent document like the *Cairo Declaration on Human Rights in Islam*, with its many special as well as general reservations in favour of the *Shariah*.[34] The problems of consistent interpretation arising between the different parts of the Resolution are comparable to the difficulties encountered already within the narrower compass of the fourth paragraph or second objective (principles of democracy, etc., qualified by Islamic tenets in a general way). In view of such difficulties the apparent decision not to mention any needs of reconciliation may be interpreted as a bold assertion of modernist conviction. If the known differences of opinion among members of the Constituent Assembly, however, are taken into account, it is more realistic to assume that these difficulties were deliberately kept within a penumbra of ambiguity, each side playing for time.

Up to this day a systematic debate on the compatibility or harmonization of the various objectives stated in the Resolution has not taken place. It is the introductory sentence instead that has become, somewhat unexpectedly, the focus of attention and the politically sensitive clause. This potential does not seem to have been clearly realized by all participants at the time. While the declaration of God's overlordship over the universe appeared as an almost self-evident proposition, a truism,[35] there were profound differences of understanding with respect to the implications of using the term 'sovereignty' with its legal connotations. The essence of the concept of legal sovereignty is singularity: there can be only one sovereign

33 For an early critical analysis particularly of the aspects of citizenship, religious freedom and apostasy see *Munir Report* (n. 2), pp. 212 ff.

34 Cairo Declaration on Human Rights in Islam, by the Member States of the Organization of the Islamic Conference, Cairo, 14 Muharram 1411H (5 August 1990), publ. by UN General Assembly, A/Conf.157/PC/35, 9 April 1992. See especially Art. 24: 'All the rights and freedoms stipulated in this Declaration are subject to the Islamic Shari'ah.'

35 Cf. some of the statements reported in Binder (n. 2), pp.144-5, e.g. Sardar Abdur Rab Nishtar: 'it is a statement of fact, and whether we say it or not it is true', Mian Iftikharuddin: 'Sir, the authority, whether we say it or not, is derived from that Power. It does not lie in our power to change the law of nature or nature's God. In saying that we have not done anything very extraordinary.' (The quotations are from *Constituent Assembly Debates*, Vol.V, No. 4, 10 March 1949; unfortunately these debates are not here at hand.)

within one legal order. Yet after invoking God's sovereignty the Constituent Assembly resolved to frame a constitution for a second sovereign: 'the sovereign independent State of Pakistan'. One might attempt to rationalize this duplication by a distinction of perspective: Pakistan is to be regarded as a sovereign state in the context of the international comity of nations, that is it recognizes no superior earthly power like a former suzerain or colonial ruler. It is not sovereign in its relationship to God, because in this relationship God alone is the Sovereign, and the state's power can only be a derivative *authority*, delegated, and circumscribed by the qualification that it is to be exercised 'within the limits prescribed by Him'.[36]

The question: What are these limits? then becomes the crucial question for practical purposes. Are they legal restrictions, in a constitutive sense defining the extent of delegated authority so as to render transgressions invalid, technically speaking *ultra vires*? Or are they moral precepts, admonitions to man's conscience directing him towards responsible use of a comprehensive authority delegated? Liberals and modernists within the Assembly all along expounded the latter interpretation, though in often vague and flowery language. In a broad perspective of the need for 'God-consciousness'[37] the 'limits prescribed by Him' were interpreted to mean 'ethical standards' or moral precepts, modifying the 'Machiavellian' Western concepts of sovereignty (Liaquat Ali Khan[38]) and bringing back morality to the political sphere (Mahmud Hussain[39]). In comparison the orthodox side seemed to have a more clearly defined, if narrow, conception. In their view the 'limits' were of a legal nature, i.e. limits of Divine law. The formula had been used by Maududi as translation of the arabic term *Hudud-Allah*:[40] God's legal commandments. In the perception of minds trained in traditional learning the conclusion was natural that 'limits prescribed by Him' meant the law of the *Shariah* as interpreted by the *ulama*. By adopting Maududi's language of God's sovereignty and the divine limits imposed on the state's power the Constituent Assembly could be understood to have adopted the orthodox major premise: the denial of popular sovereignty and the principle of the non-sovereign Islamic state as expounded by Maududi and Muhammad Asad. This point of view was clearly expressed by speakers from the *ulama* side in the Constituent Assembly

36 Cf. a similar explanation in Muhammad Munir, *Constitution of the Islamic Republic of Pakistan* (Lahore, 1976), p. 67: 'The word "sovereignty" is used in paragraph (1) in a religious and not in a political or legal sense... Internationally, however, Pakistan is a politically sovereign state.'

37 I. H. Qureshi, qoted in Binder (n. 2), p. 144; Liaquat's speech (n. 18), p. 25.

38 Ibid.

39 In Constituent Assembly Debates 12 March 1949, as reported in Binder (n. 2), p. 145; in a similar vein I.H. Qureshi and Zafrullah Khan.

40 (n. 25), p. 147.

(Maulana Shabbir Ahmad Usmani and Dr. Omar Hayat Malik).[41] Nevertheless, it remained a partisan view. The word *shariah* was not used, and ambivalence is further restored by the reference to state sovereignty in the next paragraph. State sovereignty, if the 'limits' were interpreted to be legal limitations, would be limited in the international sphere as well. The state would perhaps be powerless to enter into certain international commitments, e.g. accede to the UN Covenant on Civil and Political Rights without reservations. There is nothing to suggest that the liberal and modernist majority in the Constituent Assembly understood Pakistan's sovereign international status in such a limited sense.[42]

In the face of such ambiguities the question as to the correct interpretation really resolves into the question: Who shall have the power of interpretation? This question was asked with clarity in the speech by the Hindu member S.C. Chattopadhyaya: 'What are those limits, who will interpret them? Dr. Qureshi or my respected Maulana Shabbir Ahmad Usmani?'[43] On a more general plane the query is echoed in the speech on the Constitution of 1956 by the then opposition leader H.S. Suhrawardy: 'Then we have to see who will decide what is Islam and what is not. In accordance with what principles you propose to decide it? Who are going to be the interpreters of it?'[44]

Original Constitutional Position

At the time when Suhrawardy reiterated this fundamental question the Constituent Assembly had in effect taken a decision on the power of interpretation, and this decision has remained the common basic structure of all constitutions of Pakistan before the military intervention of 1977. The power to determine the requirements of Islam in the context of a modern democratic constitution, and to bring all legislation in accordance with the 'injunctions of Islam', was vested in Parliament as the final interpreting authority. The Objectives Resolution was *en bloc* incorporated in the Constitution as a Preamble, *i.e.* it remained what it had been from the outset: a purely programmatic statement. All its ambiguity and uncertain balance of promises was left to be clarified and decided, one way or the other, by the constitution making Assembly through selective

41 Cf. L. Binder (n. 2), pp. 146, 149.

42 Pakistan has not yet ratified the Human Rights Covenant - a fact which has not enhanced Pakistan's stature vis-a-vis India in complaining about Indian human rights' violations in Kashmir. But it is quite a different matter to contend, on the basis of the *Objectives Resolution*, that Pakistan lacks legal capacity to unreserved ratification.

43 (n. 21), p. 966.

44 In G.W. Choudhury, *Documents* (n. 6), p. 977.

translation into the operative provisions of the Constitution. The preamble to a statute (i.e. in this case: the Constitution), according to settled doctrine, is not an independent source of legal rules. It is a statement of intent setting out the main objects of legislation, but is not itself the legislation. Where there is a discrepancy between the preamble and the enacted provisions the latter prevail and the preamble is, to that extent, superseded. It is only in cases where the statute (i.e. the operative provisions of the Constitution) is ambiguous and permits of more than one interpretation that the intention of the legislature as stated in the preamble may be referred to as an aid to construction.[45]

The incorporation as Preamble to the Constitution thus represented a deliberate decision not to allow its provisions to be used as applicable rules. This decision had already been taken when the first Draft constitution was submitted to the Assembly in the Report of the Basic Principles Committee;[46] at an earlier stage it had been contemplated to incorporate the resolution as a 'Directive Principle', subject, significantly, to the provision 'that this will not prejudice the incorporation of Fundamental Rights in the Constitution.'[47] The Objectives Resolution was to be reckoned among the 'dignified parts' of the Constitution, but was to remain innocuous and certainly did not belong to the 'efficient parts'.[48]

This is further borne out by the fundamental scheme of the operative parts which has remained unchanged in the enacted Constitutions of 1956, 1962 (as amended by the first Amendment Act, 1964), 1972 and 1973. They uniformly proceeded upon the principle that the evolution of Islamic elements and their concretization in the shape of legal rules was a matter for future, and for the legislature. In its task it might be assisted by advisory institutions, such as the Islamic Research Institute or the Council of Islamic Ideology. But the final determination of what the 'injunctions of Islam' meant under the political and social conditions of modern Pakistan remained the domain of the legislature. The Islamic provisions were, therefore, couched in prospective terms and technically appeared as directive principles. Thus the 'enabling clause' of the Objectives Resolution was translated into a directive principle under the headings 'Promotion of Islamic Principles' or 'Islamic Way of Life'.[49] The elimination of *riba* 'as

[45] A.K. Brohi, *Fundamental Law of Pakistan* (Karachi, 1958), p. 571; M. Munir, *Constitution of the Islamic Republic of Pakistan* (Lahore, 1976), p. 65 f.; Maxwell on the *Interpretation of Statutes*, 12. ed. by P.St.J. Langan, Bombay 2nd impr. 1976, pp. 6 ff.; House of Lords, in *Attorney-General v. H.R.H. Prince Ernest Augustus of Hanover* [1957], A.C. 436.

[46] On 22 December1952, see the Report in: G.W. Choudhury, *Documents* (n. 6), p. 69.

[47] In the Interim Report of the Basic Principles Committee, presented to the Constituent Assembly on 7 September 1950; cf. G.W. Choudhury, *Documents* (n. 6), p. 34.

[48] W. Bagehot, *The English Constitution*, quoted from Oxford edition, 1963, p. 4.

[49] Art. 25 Constitution 1956; Art. 1 A Constitution 1962 (1963); Art. 31 Constitution 1973.

early as possible' was mentioned as a special directive.[50] The task of bringing existing and future legislation in accordance with the injunctions of Islam was not technically included in the chapters on Directive Principles, but was, in an analogous manner, reserved for the determination by Parliament.[51] The essential point in all this was the exclusion of judicial review. No court - neither ordinary court nor any special board of *ulama*- was to have jurisdiction to decide on the actual repugnancy of laws to the injunctions of Islam and to strike down laws in case of inconsistency. This arrangement served to keep the power of final interpretation with the politicians and the legislature. It ensured that general principles, like the ones spelt out in the Objectives Resolution, could not be directly applied as legal rules without being filtered, as it were, by the law-making responsibility of Parliament. Such a role of Parliament doubtless could be related to modernist reasoning about the collective exercise of the power of *ijtihad* by a Muslim legislative assembly, as modern form of *ijma*.[52] But there was good practical sense also in opting for a systematic and methodical handling of these complex questions in preference to the rather haphazard process of piecemeal adjudication, as particular issues happened to turn up in individual cases before the courts. The general disposition thus was to treat the Islamic principles as a matter of the future and to entrust their realization to the overall political responsibility of the legislature. While the modern democratic parts of the Constitution, notably fundamental rights, were immediately enforceable by the courts, enforceability of Islamic provisions by judicial review was excluded. All this would tend to show that the Objectives Resolution was not meant to be a storehouse for legal rules to be applied by the courts.

It remains to be said that by ranking among the dignified parts of the Constitution the Objectives Resolution is not rendered irrelevant. In referring back to Bagehot's classical distinction we should be mindful of his further reflection that the dignified parts may serve an important function in *gaining* authority and legitimacy for the Constitution.[53] The difficulty with the Objectives Resolution as a source of legitimation is its unintegrated agglomeration of conflicting principles rooted in differing orders of ideas. It has been harshly criticized on that account by the authors of the *Munir-Report*. Against one-sided claims advanced by the *ulama* that the Resolution represented a deliberate option for the Islamic state and had rendered Jinnah's earlier conception of a modern national state obsolete, the *Munir-Report* had this to say: '...it has been freely admitted that this

[50] Art. 29 (f) Constitution 1956; Art. 38 (f) Constitution 1973.

[51] 1956: Art. 198; 1973: Art. 227; in the Constitution of 1962 there is no corresponding directive, but only a function of the Advisory Council of Islamic Ideology to give recommendations in such matters, Art. 204.

[52] Muhammad Iqbal, *The Reconstruction of Religious Thought in Islam*, ch. VI (pp. 146 ff.).

[53] '...every constitution must first *gain* authority, and then *use* authority...' ibid.

Resolution, though grandiloquent in words, phrases and clauses, is nothing but a hoax and that not only does it not contain even a semblance of the embryo of an Islamic State but its provisions, particularly those relating to fundamental rights, are directly opposed to the principles of an Islamic State'.[54]

On a cautious interpretation of the Resolution, perhaps, a less uncharitable view seems possible. What the *Objectives Resolution* did was to place an ambitious task on the political agenda of the nation. The task was not, as the *ulama* side would have it, the evolution of an Islamic state,[55] but rather the *reconciliation* of Islamic and modern constitutional principles. In projecting this ideal the Objectives Resolution had a role to play precisely because it laid no claim to immediate effective status and represented a compromise in formulas which could be interpreted by either side in their own way. On account of its very ambivalence it could figure, substantially unaltered, as a preamble to so many different constitutions. It could thus acquire enhanced status by sheer continuity in the face of recurring constitutional upheavals, while its authority remained persuasive and exhortatory rather than a peremptory command.

The Spell of Words: Obiter Dicta and the 'Grundnorm'

From its position of unquestioned, if only programmatic authority the Resolution has been shifted, by the intervention of the military, into the arena of actual constitutional controversy. By this operation it has changed from its original character of compromise into an arsenal of supporting grounds for contradictory contentions. Its very relation to the Constitution of which it has been made an operative part, has become problematical. The change, however, even if effected by a rather sudden exercise of Martial Law powers, did not entirely come as a bolt from the blue. It had a prehistory of repeated attempts to vindicate an enhanced and even transcendental normative status to the Resolution.

Its new career starts with a rather esoteric legal discourse. In the famous case of State *v.* Dosso,[56] when the Supreme Court upheld the *coup d'etat* of 7 October 1958 staged by President Iskander Mirza and General

[54] Munir-Report (n. 2), p. 203. The derogatory word 'hoax' had been used by some *ulama* (cit. Binder, n. 2, p. 343) as well as by the Hindu member S.C. Chattopadhyaya in his speech (cf. G.W. Choudhury, *Documents*, n. 21, p. 967.

[55] Cf. the 'Views of the Board of Talimmat-e-Islamia' as submitted to the Subcommittee on Federal and Provincial Constitutions of the Constituent Assembly in 1950, printed in L. Binder (n. 2), pp. 383 ff., 385: 'The decisions taken by the Constituent Assembly in the form of the 'Objectives Resolution' go to give Pakistan the character of an Islamic State, i.e., an ideological State as distinct from a National State...'.

[56] PLD 1958 SC 533.

Ayub Khan, the Chief Justice Muhammad Munir writing the leading opinion drew heavily on the theories expounded by a renowned international lawyer, Hans Kelsen, in order to establish the proposition that a successful revolution is a law creating fact.[57] Since this judgment was referred to in a number of cases in other Commonwealth countries, notably in the Rhodesian Madzimbamuto case by the Appellate Division of the High Court of Rhodesia and by the Privy Council,[58] this sparked off a jurisprudential discusssion, in Pakistan and also in legal circles of the Commonwealth, about the interpretation of Kelsen and his description of revolution as a change in the 'Grundnorm' (or basic norm) of a legal order. The concept of 'Grundnorm' itself - that very peculiar construct of Kelsen's system and 'outlandish word'[59] - had not been mentioned at all in the *Dosso* judgment, but figured prominently in English analytical writings on the Rhodesian case and in the judgment of the Rhodesian appeal court itself.[60] In Pakistan the learned discussions about the nature of the 'Grundnorm'- not all of them relevant for the practicalities of Pakistan's situation - were resumed at the bar in the later case of Asma Jilani v. Government of the Punjab, in 1972.[61] In this case the Supreme Court struck down the Martial Law proclaimed by Yahya Khan in 1969 as unconstitutional, overruling the decision in State v. Dosso and its doctrine. The then Chief Justice, Hamoodur Rahman, in his judgment extensively dealt with the interpretation of Kelsen, concluding that the Court in *Dosso* erroneously had applied a descriptive theory about law as an actual, prescriptive legal rule, but apart from this had also fallen into error in thinking that Kelsen's doctrine was a generally accepted doctrine of modern jurisprudence.[62] Having

57 A lengthy quotation from Kelsen's book *General Theory of Law and State*, translated by Anders Wehberg and Hans Kelsen (Cambridge, Mass. 1949) is inserted in the judgment.

58 Madzimbamuto *v.* Lardner-Burke, Appellate Division of the High Court of Rhodesia: 1968 [2] SALR 248, 457; Privy Council: [1969] 1 AC 645. For fuller reference on the influence of the *Dosso*-case see L. Wolf-Phillips, *Constitutional Legitimacy: a study of the doctrine of necessity* (London, 1979); for analysis of the *Dosso* case: D. Conrad, 'In Defence of the Continuity of Law: Pakistan's Courts in Crises of State', in: W.P. Zingel (ed.), *Pakistan in its Fourth Decade* (Hamburg, 1983), pp. 64 ff.

59 Muhammad Munir in his commentary on the Constitution (n. 36), p. 66.

60 See e.g. J. M. Eekelaar, 'Splitting the Grundnorm', in *Modern Law Review* 30/2 (1967) p. 156; R. W. M. Dias, 'The UDI Case: The *Grundnorm* in Travail', *Cambridge Law Journal* 25/5 (1967); id., 'Legal Politics: Norms behind the *Grundnorm*', *Cambridge Law Journal* 26/233 (1968). The Madzimbamuto case is often referred to as 'Grundnorm case' - a description which may be illustrated by the following quotation from the judgment by the Rhodesian Chief Justice, Sir Hugh Beadle: 'The present Government has effectively usurped all the governmental powers under the old *Grundnorm*, but has not yet succeeded in setting up a new *Grundnorm* in its place... until the present Government has achieved the status of a *de jure* government, and the revolutionary *Grundnorm* becomes the new *Grundnorm*, it must govern in terms of the old *Grundnorm*...' (Quoted from Wolf-Phillips (n. 58), p. 54).

61 PLD 1972 SC 139 (20 April 1972).

62 Asma Jilani *v.* Government of the Punjab, PLD 1972 SC 139 ff., p. 181.

thus disposed of Kelsen and the doctrine of successful revolution the Chief Justice, rather unnecessarily, went on to add the following observation:

> 'In any event, if a grund-norm is necessary for us I do not have to look to the Western legal theorists to discover one. Our own grund-norm is enshrined in our own doctrine that the legal sovereignty over the entire universe belongs to Almighty Allah alone, and the authority exercisable by the people within the limits prescribed by Him is a sacred trust. This is an immutable and unalterable norm which was clearly accepted in the Objectives Resolution passed by the Constituent Assembly of Pakistan on the 7th of March 1949...'.[63]

This remark, though an *obiter dictum* and clearly hypothetical ('...*if* a grundnorm is necessary for us...'), was not lost upon attentive lawyers who soon thereafter tried to build new cases on its suggestive language. Kelsen's term 'Grundnorm' which had been rather accidentally brought in by an excursion into Western jurisprudential writing, was expanded beyond its original analytical function and, partly by misunderstanding, helped to evoke ideas of a substantive basic law, or Higher Law background to Pakistan's constitution. Such ideas cristallized in the ready-made, solemn text of the Objectives Resolution which by this process grew to almost mythical stature. The Lahore High Court assuming that the Objectives Resolution had been held to be the grund norm of Pakistan in *Asma Jilani* defined *grund norm* as 'an ideology, aim and the final object of the country and a nation.'[64] Later on President Zia-ul-Haq in his *Enforcement of Shari'ah Ordinance, 1988* was to enact a section providing that 'Shari'ah shall be the supreme source of law in Pakistan and *Grund Norm* for guidance for policy making by the State...'.[65] The issue in the cases of 1972/73,[66] however, was quite different and still related to the validity of revolutionary usurpation. The challenge was to the re-validation of Martial Law - which had just been declared illegal and invalid by the judgment in the *Asma Jilani* case - through Art. 281 of the Interim Constitution, 1972, and more specifically, the validation thereby of certain judgments by Military Courts passed under Martial Law Regulations as late as in spring 1972. It was argued that Martial Law itself, and consequently such validation of Martial Law by a constitutional blanket provision was un-Islamic and violated the Objectives Resolution as the 'Grundnorm' of Pakistan. The argu-

63 Ibid. p. 182. With these observations the Chief Justice was taking up arguments advanced by the counsel for the appellant, M. Anwar (cf. p. 171).

64 Hussain Naqi *v.* District Magistrate, Lahore, 23 Aug. 1972, PLD 1973 Lahore 164, at 174 (*per* Sardar Muhammad Iqbal, J.).

65 Enforcement of Shari'ah Ordinance, 1988 (I/1988 dtd. 15 June 1988).

66 Ziaur Rehman *v.* State, decided by the High Court Lahore on 6 July 1972; Hussain Naqi v. District Magistrate, Lahore (cf. n. 63); State *v.* Zia-ur-Rahman, PLD 1973 SC 49 ff., 8 Jan 1973.

ment implied that a provision of the Constitution itself could be 'unconstitutional', and possibly, that the 'Grundnorm' - equated with the Objectives Resolution - had transcendent authority controlling the Constitution itself. This extraordinary proposition was not accepted by a majority in any of the cases; but it had found favour with one of the judges of the High Court (later to become Chief Justice of Pakistan) who in an elaborate minority opinion developed the conception that

> 'The Objectives Resolution is Supra-Constitutional Instrument which is unalterable and immutable and the present National Assembly has no power to enact any Constitution or law which either directly or indirectly contravenes any of the provisions of the said Resolution... . The Constitution of Pakistan must be in accord with the Objectives Resolution. If it does not, the Courts would not, rather would have no jurisdiction to, recognize it as a Constitution.'[67]

Though in the result all the judges including the minority upheld the validity of Art. 281 subject to restrictive interpretation the Government considered some of the reasoning in the case sufficiently alarming to seek clarification of the theoretical issues in an appeal to the Supreme Court.[68]

The Supreme Court unanimously negatived the proposition that the Objectives Resolution could be applied by the courts as a supra-constitutional norm whereby the validity of constitutional provisions might be judged; once a constitution had been lawfully adopted by a competetent body and generally accepted by the people the courts created by that constitution had no jurisdiction to declare any of its provisions *ultra vires* or invalid. The Court, speaking again through its Chief Justice Hamoodur Rahman, took care to clarify that in mentioning the *grundnorm* in the *Asma Jilani* case it had not equated the *grundnorm* of Pakistan with the Objectives Resolution; rather it had referred to the principle of Allah's sovereignty which was spelt out in the Objectives Resolution but was something even above that text.[69] Having thus explained the *ratio decidendi*,

67 *Per* Afzal Zullah, J. (as he then was) in Ziaur Rehman *v*. State. It is an interesting detail that the full judgment was not reported in 1973 together with the Supreme Court decision in the case. Headnotes appeared in the PLD 1974 Headnotes 4 (note 3), but a full report was published only much later, in 1986 (PLD 1986 Lahore 428), i.e. after a significant change of the political climate and after the incorporation of the Objectives Resolution in the operative part of the Constitution as Art. 2A; the passages quoted are to be found on pp. 628 f. of this report.

68 Statement of the Attorney-General appearing in the case, PLD 1973 SC 65. The reference presumably is not only to the opinion by Afzal Zullah, J. quoted in the text, but also to the opinion by another Judge, Ataullah Sajjad who held certain principles enunciated in the Objectives Resolution binding on any Constitution-making body, but concluded that these principles had not been violated by the enactment of the Interim Constitution, 1972.

69 Ibid. p. 73. It may be added, with respect, that not all the judges in the *Asma Jilani* case had been equally clear on this point. In the opinion by Sajjad Ahmad, J., e.g. it is stated that the unchangeable 'grund-norms' of Pakistan 'are epitomised in the Objectives Resolution... and were

however, the Chief Justice again added some incautious and unnecessary remarks (italicized in the following quotation):

> 'Therefore, in my view, however solemn or sacrosanct a document, *if it is not incorporated in the Constitution or does not form a part thereof it cannot control the Constitution.* At any rate, the Courts created under the Constitution will not have the power to declare any provision of the constitution itself as being in violation of such a document.... It follows from this that under our own system too the Objectives Resolution of 1949, even though it is a document which has been generally accepted and has never been repealed or renounced, will not have the same status or authority as the Constitution itself *until it is incorporated within it or made part of it.* If it appears only as a preamble to the Constitution, then it will serve the same purpose as any other preamble serves, namely, that in the case of any doubt as to the intent of the law-maker, it may be looked at to ascertain the true intent, but *it cannot control the substantive provisions thereof.*'[70]

One might well ask how one constitutional provision, even if incorporated in the operative part of the constitution, may control its other substantive provisions, and how a court could have jurisdiction to declare a constitutional provision invalid on account of inconsistency with another 'controlling' constitutional article.

These words, however, gave the hint and a handle for orthodox demands. In 1983, when Zia-ul-Haq ventilated ideas to introduce an Islamic Constitution replacing or substantially amending the suspended Constitution of 1973, he commissioned various bodies and institutions[71] to work out guidelines for such an Islamic system. He finally appointed a 17-member Commission consisting mostly of *ulama* and scholars of Islam, under the chairmanship of Maulana Muhammad Zafar Ahmad Ansari,[72] with the mandate to undertake 'indepth examination' of the various existing recommendations', 'and to submit to him viable proposals in this behalf keeping in view the conditions of the country and the interests of the

---

incorporated in the first Constitution of the Islamic Republic of Pakistan of 1956 and repeated again in the Constitution of 1962', (p. 258 of the report).

70 Ibid. p. 71.

71 The bodies which had undertaken preparatory work were (1) a Cabinet Sub-committee; (2) a Special Committee of Majlis-e-Shura (the designation of Parliament introduced by Zia), and (3) the Council of Islamic Ideology; cf. *Ansari Commission's Report on Form of Government* 24 Shawal 1403 - 4 August 1983, p. iii. A summary of the recommendations submitted by the other commissions and institutions may be found in G.W. Choudhury, *Pakistan. Transition from Military to Civilian Rule* (Backhurst Hill, 1988), pp. 135 ff.

72 Maulana Ansari was an old Muslim Leaguer from the times of Jinnah; after 1945 he had served as Office Secretary of the Muslim League and helped to establish contact with Maududi and to organize the *Jamiat-ul-Ulama-i-Islam* in support of the Muslim League.

Millat so that he could present to the nation *by 14th August, 1983*, the framework of the future political set up of the country as promised by him'.[73] The time allotted for this ambitious task was 15 days which seems short and perhaps is indicative more of the working of a military mind than of the intricacy of the subject matter; the recommendations of the Report published on 4th August 1983 were dubbed an 'instant framework' on that account in a newspaper comment.[74] The Report *inter alia* recommended an Islamic consultative system of government under an *Amir-e-Mumlakat* (Head of State), the consultative parliament (*majlis-e-shura*) to be elected on a non-party basis. In a special section on 'Islamic Provisions and Islamic Institutions', the Report contained the following recommendation:

> 'The Objectives Resolution shall be included in the text as an operative portion of the Constitution instead of as a mere Preamble so that it may become enforceable through the courts and may provide a guarantee that all the laws of the land, *including the constitutional laws*, shall be governed by the injunctions of the Quran and the Sunnah, and the principles laid down in that Resolution and only that interpretation of the provisions of the constitution and law shall be valid which accords with the principles of the Objectives Resolution, and all laws in conflict with those principles shall be deemed to be void.'[75]

The irony of the situation, and of this particular recommendation, ought not to be overlooked. In the discussions on a transcendental authority of the Objectives Resolution, as highlighted by the judicial pronouncements quoted, the 'Grundnorm' had always been invoked against the pretensions of Martial Law, military justice and dictatorship by 'successful revolution'. The immutable principle insisted upon on the basis of the Resolution's opening paragraph was democracy as trust under God's sovereignty. Yet here was a military dictator arrogating to himself the power to effect fundamental changes in the Constitution, fulfilling uncalled-for 'pledges' and 'promises' 'to present to the nation ... a positive outline of a real Islamic State'.[76] The Commission was recommending incorporation of a text which, rightly understood, nullified all these constitution-making pretensions by a single individual, because as stated in Ziaur Rahman's case, 'under the *grund norm* ... the trust for discharge of sovereign functions has been reposed in the people. They have to exercise their choice in free and fair elections for a Constituent Assembly to frame

[73] Ibid.

[74] *Viewpoint* (Lahore, 11 August 1983), p. 14.

[75] Ibid., p. 73 (in the 'Summary of the Recommendations'), emph. add.

[76] Political Plan Announced by President General Muhammad Zia-ul-Haq on 12 August 1983, printed in: Hamid Khan, *Eighth Amendment. Constitutional and Political Crisis in Pakistan* (Lahore, 1994), pp. 171 ff.

the Constitution and thus the main purpose of the *grund norm* is served.'[77] This reflection, at any rate, does not appear to have occurred to the President who adopted the recommendation on the Objectives Resolution in his announcement of a political plan on 12 August, 1983.[78] Eventually the Resolution was incorporated in the Constitution by the *Revival of the Constitution of 1973 Order, 1985.* [79] The insertion was confirmed by the Constitution (Eighth Amendment) Act, 1985.[80]

Confusion Institutionalized

In order to fully appreciate the impact of the incorporation one has to take into account the fact that a far reaching change in the operative part of the Constitution had already been brought about by earlier Martial Law decrees. For the first time judicial review with respect to the Islamic provisions had been introduced by the creation of *Shariat* Courts and, in particular, the *Federal Shariat Court* in 1979/80.[81] This implied a fundamental alteration in the original constitutional disposition according to which the Islamization of laws had been kept reserved to Parliamentary legislation, whereas constitutionality of laws with respect to fundamental rights was safeguarded by judicial review. Under Martial Law, on the contrary, Parliament and fundamental rights were suspended and their reintroduction left to future legislative changes, while Islamic provisions became directly enforceable through the operation of specialized superior courts. Whether a particular law was in accordance with the injunctions of Islam could now be inquired into by Court proceedings without paying heed to the compatibility with fundamental rights - which were suspended under Martial Law. This was a revolutionary change running counter to a long standing constitutional consensus. The jurisdiction of the Shariat Courts, to be sure, was strangely limited, and remained exclusive of Constitutional law (including Martial Law), Muslim personal law (!) and laws concerning the financial system.[82] But the fact remained that piecemeal adjudication of Islamization issues had been introduced albeit on a limited scale.

77 PLD 1986 Lahore 486 (*per* A. R. Sheikh, J.).

78 Hamid Khan (n. 74), p. 181.

79 P.O. 14 of 1985 dtd. 2 March 1985, Art. 2 and Sched. No. 2.

80 Act 18/1985 of 9 November 1985.

81 The President's Constitution (Amendment) Order, 1979 (P.O. 3/1979) had inserted a Chapter 3A on *Shariat Benches of Superior Courts* (i.e. High Courts); this had been replaced by creation of a single *Federal Shariat Court* in 1980, Constitution (Amendment) Order 1980 (P.O. 1/1980).

82 Art. 203 B (c) definition of 'law'; the exclusion of financial laws comprised 'any fiscal law or any law relating to the levy and collection of taxes and fees or banking, or insurance practice and procedure; ...' .

An obnoxious trait of the new dispensation was the lack of personal independence on the part of the judges of the Federal Shariat Court. The judges were to be appointed for a term of three years by the President; the President could reappoint them for further terms, but could also

> 'at any time, by order in writing, -
> (a) modify the term of appointment of a Judge;
> (b) assign to a Judge any other office; and
> (c) require a Judge to perform such other functions as the President may deem fit;
> and pass such other order as he may consider appropriate.'[83]

The insecurity of the Court's position *vis-à-vis* executive interference was not a mere academic proposition. This is evidenced by the scandalous affair of the *rajam*-case. On petition of a citizen[84] the *Federal Shariat Court* had held the punishment of stoning to death for the offence of adultery among Muslims[85] to be un-Quranic and, therefore, repugnant to the injunctions of Islam.[86] By this judgment the Court incurred the displeasure of the President who forthwith proceeded to reconstitute the Court, appointing a number of new judges and, with retrospective effect, introducing a power of the Court to review any decision made by it.[87] On a review petition by the Government the reconstituted Court reviewed its earlier judgment and, predictably, reached the politically desired result that the punishment of stoning to death were in conformity with the Injunctions of Islam.[88] The issue in both cases turned on the question whether a clear Quranic injunction could be supplemented, or modified, by a later *hadith*. The decision in the later judgment was reached, significantly, not so much on grounds of pure Islamic methodology, but on the positive constitutional mandate to follow (both) the Holy Quran *and* Sunnah.[89] Quite apart from the political ma-

83 Art. 203 C (4) and (5).

84 The Federal Shariat Court may examine a question of repugnancy to the injunctions of Islam 'either of its own motion or on the petition of a citizen of Pakistan or the Federal Government or a Provincial Government', Art. 203 D.

85 As provided in the *Offence of Zina (Enforcement of Hudood) Ordinance, 1979* (7/1979), sec. 5 (2) (a).

86 Hazoor Baksh *v.* Federation of Pakistan, PLD 1981 FSC 145 (dtd. 21 March 1981).

87 Constitution (Amendment) Order, 1981 (P.O. 5/1981) sec. 3 and Constitution (Second Amendment) Order, 1981 (P.O. 7/1981) sec. 2.

88 Federation of Pakistan *v.* Hazoor Baksh, PLD 1983 FSC 255 (dtd. 20 June 1982).

89 p. 257: 'The Constitution-makers had already decided that *both Qur'an and Sunnah* [are] in a primary position by making them both as the touchstones for examining the validity of any law.... Jurisdiction of Court is restricted to find repugnancy of a law with Qur'an *and* Sunnah ... it is not open to the Court to say that although this law is not repugnant to Sunnah but it is repugnant to Qur'an, therefore declare it invalid. Doing so will be making unjustified distinction between Qur'an and Sunnah. Such distinction is not justified in view of the numerous Qur'anic Injunctions themselves. *But even apart from the Qur'anic Injunctions* such

nipulation this is an instance of the hybrid mixture of Islamic jurisprudence and modern state law which is characteristic of the present set-up.

It is this mixture which has been incorporated in the Constitution by the Eighth Amendment and which has been made a permanent part of the Constitution including all the objectionable features described. With the revival of the other parts of the Constitution and particularly the fundamental rights, however, latent contradictions have come to the foreground and are posing manifest operative dilemmas. There are two sets of Superior Courts applying two different and even heterogenous standards of judicial review: first, the *Federal Shariat Court* and the *Shariat Appellate Bench* of the *Supreme Court* adjudicating according to the injunctions of Islam; second, the *High Courts* and *Supreme Court* enforcing fundamental rights and other constitutional provisions. There is no preestablished harmony between the two standards, and contradictions are, indeed, not difficult to foresee. It is not clear what happens in cases of conflict, e.g. between fundamental rights and Islamic principles.

The addition of the *Objectives Resolution* as an operative provision can only add to the confusion. After Islamic judicial review has become, contrary to the former constitutional framework, a feature of constitutional adjudication, some courts have tended to view the incorporated text of the Resolution as a further source of Islamic review, outside the parameters of the chapter on *Shariat* courts. Thus the ordinary courts could now, for instance, test the Muslim personal law on the touchstone of Islamic injunctions. Strangely, the significance of the Objectives Resolution in the new context is almost exclusively seen as centering on its introductory sentence and the clause that all worldly authority is to be 'exercised within the limits prescribed by Him'. These limits are usually simply equated with the Shariah or even the *fiqh*. It is often overlooked that the Resolution contains references to other constitutional principles as well, and thus duplicates the conflict or tension between various parts of the Constitution in its present shape. Thus in the sphere of Muslim personal law the Objectives Resolution referring to 'fundamental rights, including equality of status' might demand equality of the sexes in matters like unilateral divorce or polygamy - but this might lead to a conflict with the 'limits' clause if the latter is construed as a reference to the traditional *fiqh*.

Direct application in the field of Muslim personal law has indeed been made by the High Court Karachi in a case involving the *Muslim Family Laws Ordinance, 1961.* [90] This is a reforming law hated by orthodox opinion, since it imposes some restraints on the unilateral male rights of polygamy and extra-judicial divorce (*talaq*); for that very reason it has

---

distinction is not visualised in our Constitutiton.' (*per* Zahoorul Haq, J.; unanimous opinion of the Court, emph. add.).

[90] Qamar Raza *v.* Tahira Begum, PLD 1988 Karachi 169.

always been specifically protected against judicial review under the fundamental rights chapters of the Constitution.[91] The exclusion of 'Muslim personal law' from the jurisdiction of the *Federal Shariat Court* probably also served this main purpose. Islamic review under the Objectives Resolution now opened a new line of attack. The Court, speaking through the single judge Tanzil-ur-Rahman[92] struck down sec. 7 (concerning *talaq*) as violative of Islamic Injunctions under Art. 2A. In doing so it equated the 'limits prescribed by Him' not only with the *Shariah* in general, but with the subtle differences of the various schools of *fiqh*.[93]

Earlier the Court had already indicated this approach in a case involving payment of interest and the Islamic prohibition of *riba*.[94] Other courts, however, did not follow suit and either stated a different opinion[95] or at least took a more cautious line of approach. The Objectives Resolution was considered and cited in many cases,[96] but was often merely applied as an additional argument and a help to construction. This was not materially different from the position obtaining when the Resolution was only incorporated as a Preamble. It is significant, too, that the more indirect and general application has tended to emphasize other aspects of the Objectives Resolution. Thus in 1993 the *Supreme Court* invoked the Resolution to give a progressive interpretation to Art. 247 (6): reforms in the Tribal Areas directed towards establishing governance by representative institutions and separating judicial from executive functions (i.e. reforms in the direction envisaged by the Objectives Resolution) could not be revoked without giving special reasons for such retrograde step.[97] Similarly in the *Sharif Faridi* case the 8th Objective envisaging guaranteed independence of the judiciary was relied upon in order to invigorate

91 Art. 8 (3) (b) i read with 1st Schedule Part II, III 3 Constitution 1973; similarly Art.6 (3) ii read with 4th Sched. III 6 Constitution 1962. Apparently the Ordinance was to be protected against challenges under the fundamental right guaranteeing free exercise of religion.

92 Tanzil-ur-Rahman had previously been Chairman of the *Council of Islamic Ideology*, later he was to become President of the *Federal Shariat Court*.

93 The court also relied on the two other 'Islamic provisions' of the Objectives Resolution, namely cl. 2 - principles of social justice as enunciated by Islam - and cl. 3 - enabling the Muslims to order their lives in accordance with teaching and requirements of Islam.

94 Bank of Oman Ltd. *v.* East Trading Co. Ltd., PLD 1987 Karachi 404. See also Habib Bank Ltd. *v.* Muhammad Hussain, PLD 1987 Karachi 612.

95 Sharaf Faridi *v.* Islamic Republic of Pakistan, PLD 1989 Kar. 404; Habib Bank Ltd. v. Messrs. Waheed Textile Mills Ltd., PLD 1989 Kar. 371; Kaniz Fatimah *v.* Wali Muhammad, PLD 1989 Lahore 490 (ss. 7 & 8 Muslim Family Laws Ordinance).

96 The cases dealing with the Objectives Resolution and Art. 2A are carefully listed in the opinion by Shafiur Rahman, J. in Hakim Khan *v.* Government of Pakistan, PLD 1992 SC 595, at 630 fq.

97 Govt. of NWFP *v.* Muhammad Irshad, PLD 1995 SC 281 (dt. 13-12-1993) concerning the *Provincially Administered Tribal Areas Criminal Law (Special Provisions) Regulations, 1975* and *1976*.

the constitutional mandate to bring about separation of the judiciary from the executive (Art. 175 cl. 3).[98]

Concerning the Islamic provisions in the Objectives Resolution the position was sometimes taken that the inserted new Art. 2A, and direct application of Islamic principles by the courts derived from it, could not overrule the express constitutional provisions of Art. 30 (2), 203 G, 227 (2)[99] which had established a certain methodology for the Islamization of laws.[100] In other words: The original disposition in the Constitution had been the reservation of the task of Islamization of laws to the determination by Parliament; an inroad into this structure had been made by the insertion of the chapter on *Shariat* Courts which according to its express terms had overriding effect so far as it went (Art. 203 A). But a further extension of the principle of Islamic judicial review, by implication from Art. 2A, was hardly permissible in view of these express constitutional provisions.

Such reliance on the constitutional framework, however, had to meet a still more radical and potentially disruptive argument arising, once more, from the intrinsic logic of transcendental language. If the 'limits' clause of the Objectives Resolution is given the orthodox meaning that all authority on earth is to be exercised within the limits of the *Shariah* as interpreted by the *ulama*, it is hard to see how this transcendental claim derived from the sovereignty of Allah can be confined to sub-constitutional law. On what authority could the Constitution be based in order to be above the limits prescribed by God? As we have seen, an argument had early been derived from this intrinsic logic to the effect that the Objectives Resolution was a supra-constitutional instrument which could serve as a yardstick to measure the validity of the Constitution by means of judicial review. The argument had found early judicial recognition, but had been repelled by the *Supreme Court*, with the superadded observation that the Objectives

[98] Govt. of Sindh *v.* Sharif Faridi, PLD 1994 SC 105.

[99] Art. 30 (2): 'The validity of an action or of a law shall not be called in question on the ground that it is not in accordance with the Principles of Policy' - which means that there is no jurisdiction of the courts to decide on such matters; the relevance for the present context lies with Art. 31 (*Islamic Way of Life*) which translates the 'enabling' clause of the Objectives Resolution into a Principle of Policy.

Art. 203 G: 'Save as provided in Article 203 F [*i.e.* appeal to the Shariat Appellate Bench of the Supreme Court against a decision by the Federal Shariat Court] no court or tribunal, including the Supreme Court and a High Court, shall entertain any proceedings or exercise any power or jurisdiction in respect of any matter within the power or jurisdiction of the [Federal Shariat] Court.'

Art. 227 (2) states the original principle discussed above in No. 3 of this article that Islamization of laws shall be the final responsibility of Parliament.

[100] This view was tentatively advanced by Afzal Zullah, J. in Sardar Ali *v.* Muhammad Ali, PLD 1988 SC 287; it was followed in Habib Bank Ltd. *v.* Waheed Textile Mills Ltd., PLD 1989 Kar. 371 (*per* Mamoon Kazi, J.). It is also set forth in an incisive article by Asif Saeed Khan Khosa, 'The Ineffectiveness of Art. 2-A Constitution of Pakistan', in: PLD 1990 Journal 50.

Resolution had not even been incorporated in (the operative part of) the Constitution.[101] After the incorporation through Art. 2A the argument was bound to be resurrected. It appeared in judicially considered *dicta* in the above mentioned decisions by the High Court Karachi. In Qamar Raza *v.* Tahira Begum[102] it was said that the incorporation of the Resolution made it 'evident that all laws prevailing in Pakistan are firstly to conform to the Constitution whereas the Constitution and all such laws are then amenable to be tested on the touchstone of the Qur'an and Sunnah...'.[103] In Farhat Jaleel *v.* Province of Sindh a division bench, speaking again through Tanzil-ur-Rahman (Acting Chief Justice, as he then was) condensed the doctrinal genesis in the following words:

> '... the Constitution is the Grundnorm for the other legislation and the Objectives Resolution made substantive part of the Constitution is the Grundnorm of the Constitution itself.'[104]

The decisive step was finally taken by a constitution bench of the Lahore High Court[105] when it held the President's pardoning power under Art. 45 'unconstitutional' because violative of Art. 2A insofar as in its wide wording it included cases of *quisas* imposed as *hadd* punishment under the classical criminal law of Islam - where the victim alone or the victim's relatives (in cases of homicide) can pardon or accept blood money in lieu of punishment. The Court does not explicitly use the term supra-constitutional instrument, but states that the Objectives Resolution was held to be the *grundnorm* of Pakistan in the *Asma Jilani* case, and after its incorporation was 'in control of the Constitution'; a Court denying this would have 'violated the Constitution'.[106]

It is intriguing that the logical difficulties inherent in this approach should have been so little discussed by the learned judges, though the question was clearly posed: 'Can one Article of the Constitution be superior to another?'[107] If the principle of Allah's sovereignty is of a transcendental nature, as explained by C. J. Hamoodur Rahman in Ziaur Rehman's case, it can be perceived to be 'in control' of all man-made law under a Higher Law doctrine. But if it owes its binding force to its being incorporated in the Constitution on a par with the other provisions, its superior ranking is difficult to explain. The Court went as far as to approvingly quote observa-

101 See the discussion of *Ziaur Rehman's* case, supra note 4.
102 See supra note 90 .
103 Ibid., p. 201.
104 PLD 1990 Karachi 342, p. 358.
105 Sakina Bibi *v.* Federation, PLD 1992 Lah. 99.
106 Ibid., pp. 113, 114.
107 Ibid., p. 114.

tions from an earlier High Court case, to the effect that even if a provision like Art. 270A was found to be beyond the limits of principles of the Objectives Resolution, it could be held to be without lawful authority.[108] Art. 270A was inserted by the 8th Amendment and provides for the validation of *inter alia* all the legislative acts by the Martial Law regime 1977 to 1985, including, accordingly, the incorporation of Art. 2A and the Objectives Resolution by the Revival of the Constitution Order, 1985. As has been explained, the way the Objectives Resolution was incorporated by executive *fiat* was not compatible with the Resolution's own principles, according to which the authority delegated to the people of Pakistan was to be exercised through their chosen representatives; it bears repetition to remember that in this incorporation process the usurper-President had in fact altered the 'unalterable and immutable' supra-constitutional instrument by omitting the word 'freely' from the guarantee of the minorities' right to practise their religion. Consequently, if Art. 270A was found to be excessive on the touchstone of the Objectives Resolution, it would fall together with the touchstone, and the logical circle would be complete.

But apart from logical quibbles it is rather obvious that the doctrine of the *Sakina Bibi* judgment could be used to gradually destroy the constitution from within. There is hardly a major constitutional principle which might not be challenged by traditionalist Islamic interpretation of the opening clause. In the last analysis the existence of positive constitutional law itself might be questioned; for illustration the Islamic petitions by the former Judge of the Supreme Court, B. Z. Kaikaus, may be consulted.[109] On the other hand, modern constitutional principles are also spelt out in the Objectives Resolution and might be invoked for counter-challenges. Islamization of the legal system might be challenged as a violation of religious freedom promised in the Resolution; the structure of the *Federal Shariat Court* might be attacked as violating the guarantee of an independent judiciary, and so forth.

The *Supreme Court* clearly perceived the danger and came to the rescue, reversing the decision in Sakina Bibi in Hakim Khan *v.* Government of Pakistan.[110] In this case two major opinions have been written[111] in which the judges proceed on two different grounds:

108 Ibid., pp. 119, 120; the observations quoted are from a judgment by the Sindh High Court, reported as 1990 CLC 428 (*per* Wajih-ud-Din, J.).

109 See particularly B. Z. Kaikaus *v.* President of Pakistan, PLD 1980 SC 160; B. Z. Kaikaus *v.* Federal Government of Pakistan, PLD 1982 SC 409.

110 PLD 1992 SC 595. The destructive potential of the interpretation given to Art. 2A by the High Court is graphically described in the opinion by Nasim Hasan Shah, J. (as he then was), p. 617. The conclusion reached is that 'if this be its true status, then the above quoted clause [scil. Art. 2A] would require the framing of an entirely new Constitution.'

111 There is a third, short concurring opinion by Abdul Shakurul Salam, J. who makes the very pertinent observation that the punishments in the cases were not *hadd* but *tazir* punishments; the State therefore had an undoubted right to exercise clemency, and the whole discussion on

(a) In consequence of its formal position as an article of the Constitution Art. 2A the Objectives Resolution can only be treated as of equal status with other constitutional provisions; the transcendental content of some of the declarations therein does not render the Resolution a supra-constitutional norm. In cases of conflict with other provisions of the Constitution a harmonizing construction has to be evolved.[112]
(b) By incorporation in the Constitution the Objectives Resolution has not changed its fundamental textual character: it was a guide line for the Constitution making body and, after the Constitution has been framed, remains as a guide line for the National Assembly to amend possible discrepancies in the light of the broad principles stated; it is not 'self-executing' as a sufficiently precise rule for judicial application and does not establish a repugnancy test of compliance with the objectives stated.[113]

The two opinions converge in clearly rejecting the notion of a supra-constitutional status of the Objectives Resolution and in re-emphasizing the original texture and function of the Resolution; in both the conclusion is that final responsibility for the concretization of broad principles and for the resolution of contradictions has to be shifted back to the elected representatives of the people in Parliament. This is in line with the language as well as with the substantive contents of the Resolution. It is a wholesome reminder of the fact that the Resolution is designed as an outline for determinations to be made by a Parliament in its constituent function. To burden the courts with the task of directly applying its 'rather vague, general and flexible concepts'[114] and to resolve its many inherent difficulties is to put the courts in the position of a Constituent Assembly. This is contrary to their function as one branch of delegated and circumscribed authority under the Constitution. It would also mean a constant temptation for the courts to over-reach themselves. In applying and reconciling the many broad principles of the Resolution inevitably the personal convictions and predilections of the judges would have to play an inordinate role. The question: who shall judge, who is the judge? would then more and more become the decisive question. The winner in such a situation would be, in the longer run, the Executive who had the power to influence the course of interpretation by its policy of appointment.

The decision in Hakim Khan's case, therefore, deserves full praise and hopefully will put this controversy to rest. The word 'hopefully' is used

---

the nature of Art. 2A was, strictly speaking, unnecessary and *obiter*. This view is shared by Shafiur Rahman, J., p. 635.

112 Mainly opinion by Nasim Hasan Shah, J., pp. 605 ff.

113 Opinions by Shafiur Rahman, J., pp. 622 ff., and also by Nasim Hasan Shah, J. loc.cit.

114 Loc.cit., p. 620 (*per* Nasim Hasan Shah, J.).

here deliberately, for it is submitted, with great respect, that the emphasis in relying on that judgment should be on the second rather than the first line of argument (as restated above). The true ground for not applying the Resolution without the intermediate determination by Parliament is that by its intrinsic structure and its language it was never designed to be self-executing. To throw it into such a role retroactively is to do injustice to its Fathers who were, when passing it, more interested in formulating a convincingly broad and solemn declaration than in settling differences of detail. This was expressly stated many times in the deliberations of the Constituent Assembly: that the Resolution was but a kind of letter of intent, a preface to the operative chapters still to be written, that it was 'merely in the nature of a Preamble' and was 'neither the official legislation nor even the Constitution itself'.[115] In interpreting it this original texture ought to be constantly kept in mind. The famous introductory statement of God's sovereignty and the limitations of all human authority, in the context of the Resolution, is a kind of preamble itself ('whereas...'), as it were, the preamble to a preamble. This was often noted in judicial pronouncements on the Resolution.[116] But it ought to make one doubly wary of directly translating it into a rule of decision - contrary to the well established canons of interpreting a preamble.

All this is emphasized here in order to warn of a certain dangerous potential in the first line of argument pursued in the *Hakim Khan* judgments. Proposition (a) could be taken to mean that in cases of clear and unqualified assertion of principle the words of the Resolution may still be applied as operative rules on a par with, and perhaps overriding other constitutional provisions. The old strife would then stand revived. The danger is a real one in view of the presence of a school of thought which does not concede any lack of clarity or need for interpretation. In the perception of the *ulama* school of thought the 'limits prescribed by Him', the *hudood Allah*, are clearly revealed, and are accessible as elaborated in the classical body of *Shariah*law. They do not admit of modification nor even of elucidation and, according to their transcendental origin, must needs override all other principles stated within the body of the Objectives Resolution itself. This seems to be a seductive line of reasoning, so much so that only a short time after the decision in Hakim Khan's case the *Supreme Court* itself again followed it. In Zaheeruddin Khan *v.* State,[117] it was held by majority that Art. 2A had adopted the Injunctions of Islam as positive law and, consequently, the *Shariah* was a 'law' in the

115 Ch. Nazir Ahmad Khan, then a Minister of the government, quoted in *Hakim Khan* by Nasim Hasan Shah, J., PLD 1992 SC at p. 614; to the same effect Sardar Abdur Rab Nishtar, Deputy Leader of the House as quoted ibid.

116 The observation figures prominently already in the famous dissent by J. Afzal Zullah in the Ziaur Rehman case, PLD 1986 Lahore, at p. 630.

117 Supreme Court Monthly Review 1993, 1718, decided on 3 July 1993.

sense of Art. 20,[118] limiting free exercise and propagation of one's religion: 'Therefore, even the Fundamental Rights as given in the Constitution must not violate the norms of Islam.'[119] By way of this novel interpretation the Court practically wiped out the protection of religious freedom for the Ahmadiyya-sect which is held to be heretical. The ominous inference would be that the traditional law on apostasy is also adopted as a restriction on religious freedom - the consequences are already manifest for everyone to see. With respect, the interpretation is not only at variance with the reasoning in Hakim Khan's case - as is very cautiously indicated in the minority opinion written by Shafiur Rahman, J. - but also with the Objectives Resolution itself, even if taken to be a 'self-executing' provision. The Objectives Resolution cannot be reduced to an 'adoption of Islamic law', but states concurrent other principles on the same plane, *inter alia* fundamental rights and the rights of minorities to (freely) profess and practise their religions. On a pure textual analysis there is no hierarchy among these various principles stated, and no logical reason why the law of Islam should take precedence. This claim, in truth, is introduced by implicit reliance on the transcendental legitimation of Islamic law.

In conclusion, it is argued here that the rift is bound to reappear in one form or another, inspite of the hope of moderation held out by the Hakim Khan judgment. The reason is the underlying incommensurability of two kinds of legitimation. Art. 2A includes a transcendental claim of absolute legitimacy which does not accord with its formal position as a provision of the positive enacted Constitution, nor with the coexistence, in the same document, of legitimating principles of a different order. The conflict is sharpened by the presence of a specific school of traditional learning which tends to be uncompromising in its dogmatic assertions. Shifting the burden of this conflict from the courts to Parliament doubtless is a positive step offering a better chance of reasonable compromise and accomodation. But it does not, in itself, settle the problem which is potentially explosive and may engender civil strife. A durable solution of this metaphysical conflict is beyond the lawyer's province. It would require a major theological effort, in the nature of true *ijtihad*, to discover a legitimate space for the exercise of modern secular authority compatible with, but not suppressed by, the free exercise of religion.

118 Art. 20: 'Subject to law, public order and morality -
(a) every citizen shall have the right to profess, practise and propagate his religion;
(b)....'

119 Loc.cit. (n. 117), p. 1775, *per* Abdul Qadeer Chaudhry, J.

The Sacred and the Secular: A Crisis of Governance in Bangladesh

TAZEEN M. MURSHID

This chapter seeks to explore the nature of some of the internal challenges to governance and the quest for legitimacy in post-1971 Bangladesh. The country has been fraught with political crises and instability since its inception. The state was too divided over issues of ideology and national identity to enforce its authority impartially; the structures of state authority such as the police force, the intelligence branch and to an extent, the judiciary, had been weakened by political interference; and civilian institutions such as educational establishments had also been unable to withstand the intervention of unscrupulous politicians and their henchmen, - their interdependence upon one another for patronage in the form of licenses and muscle power in the streets and campuses ensured an atmosphere of unrest and political violence. The ensuing tensions have been exacerbated by the struggle between the forces of religious extremism and secular liberalism and have contributed to a crisis of governance.

The Heritage

A recent crisis has been on-going for several months. A parliamentary impasse was provoked by the mass resignation of all opposition Members of Parliament in December 1994 following a ten-month boycott. The loss of a safe seat by the leading opposition party, the Awami League, in the wake of a massive show of strength by officials in support of the ruling party, the Bangladesh Nationalist Party, during the Magura by-elections in March 1994, led to calls for a constitutional amendment whereby future elections were to be held under a neutral caretaker government.[1] The resignations reflect the inability of the political parties to come to a compromise. One major stumbling block was that the rules of engagement were variably interpreted by the political parties, thus, foreclosing the possibility of constructive dialogue among the leadership. Not only were the constitutional rights and privileges variously interpreted by the political parties, but also, the rules of democratic conduct were differently viewed and acted upon.

[1] Interviews with Prof. Rehman Sobhan, Director, Policy Institute, Dhaka, 5 January 1995; Dr. Moin Khan, Minister of State for Planning, Dhaka, 5 January 1995; Dr. S.M. Kibria, Advisor to the Opposition, 18 January 1995. See Shamsur Rahman, 'Magura BNPr Joi, Awami Leaguer Hartal', *Bichitra*, Vol. 22, No. 41, March 1994, pp. 19-21.

The parties were motivated by a range of considerations. At one level, they appear to be far more concerned with preserving their rights than meeting their obligations. The Jamaat-i-Islami Party hopes to maintain its position as a third force by influencing the national agenda.[2] The proposal to hold elections under a neutral caretaker government was first made by the Jamaat-i-Islami Party for the Twelfth Amendment to the Constitution in 1992.[3] At the time, the opposition parties, such as the Awami League did not heed it seriously. According to S.M. Kibria, Advisor to Sheikh Hasina, Leader of the Opposition and Chief of the Awami League, the party 'still believed in the system' and 'associated electoral riggings with authoritarian rule' as under Zia and Ershad.[4] However, the handling of the Magura by-elections by the ruling party, the Bangladesh Nationalist Party, convinced it that fair elections would not be possible under the sitting government. The ensuing movement inevitably contributed to anarchy and disorder.

While the immediate cause lay in a loss of confidence in the political process, longer term structural factors had weakened civil society culminating in an acute crisis of governability in the nineties. The democratically elected Bangladesh Nationalist Party which formed the government in 1991, has inherited weak institutions as well as a legacy of political disruption and authoritarianism. Long periods of military rule have led to the deinstitutionalization of civilian structures of political participation. Elections held frequently in an attempt to give a democratic facade to military dominated regimes, never really allowed the expression of a popular will: instead, these have contributed to a political culture marred by vote rigging and violence threatening the democratic process. The constitutional crisis has to be viewed in this context.

Inevitably, the primary arena of dissent shifted on to the streets instead of being located in parliament. Resistance took the form of agitation reminiscent of nationalist struggles against colonial regimes, such as demonstrations, *hartals* and strikes, but often enforced by coercive methods.

An incipient culture of violence became further institutionalized as the army under Zia and Ershad sought to civilianize its rule through establishing political parties and organizing youth and student wings to maintain territorial control over campuses, regarded as an essential indicator of political might. The death toll due to campus violence has continued to

2 The Jamaat-i-Islami Party was actively opposed to the liberation of Bangladesh in 1971. It was banned as a communal and fascist organization by Sheikh Mujibur Rahman, the Father of Bangladesh and Prime Minister of Bangladesh in 1972. The party was subsequently re-instated by General Ziaur Rahman in 1976.

3 Interview with Dr. Moin Khan, MP, and State Minister for Planning form the ruling Bangladesh Nationalist Party, Dhaka, 5 January 1995.

4 Interview with S.M. Kibria, Dhanmondi, Dhaka, 18 January 1995.

rise during the democratic phase of the nineties increasing to 25 a year compared to 7 per year in the eighties.[5]

The search of military regimes for new allies in the process of civilianization and demilitarization has created political space and given voice to those who were intrinsically opposed to the basis of the state, i.e. the once banned Jamaat-i-Islami Party and its supporters. The process, however, has threatened others with exclusion, viz., the Awami League which gave leadership in the struggle for the liberation of the country and segments of the secular literati.

The ensuing polarization of politics and ideology has opened up the debate on the nature of the state and national identity giving rise to an ideology conflict. Political elites have resorted to the manipulation of sacred and secular symbols to construct identities and nations which fit their particular ideological predispositions or conceptions of the state, - as Islamic based on *shariah* laws, or as endorsing religious neutrality. The ruling party, the Bangladesh Nationalist Party, is itself divided on these issues. The lack of consensus exacerbated further the weakness of the state in the nineties and compounded the problem of governability as parallel structures of authority were erected challenging the established judicial process. Ad-hoc *shariah* courts set up by *mullahs* in remote rural areas claimed divine sanction, while peoples' courts and citizens' committees sought temporal legitimacy in claiming to express the popular will.[6]

It may be argued that the resolution of the ideology conflict is far more fundamental to ensuring the future stability of the state than any other immediate political crisis, such as the parliamentary impasse, which is merely a symptom of the malady.[7] The conflict derives from variations in perceptions of identity and constructs of imagined nations and states, but is also a direct result of the legitimacy crises faced by successive regimes. The paper will now attempt to explore the nature of this conflict.

Ideology Conflict

The ideology conflict emerged in the context of the rise of the military in politics under whose auspices the religious right gained a political platform to challenge the liberal secular order that was encouraged by the elected government headed by the Awami League. It was focussed around differences in conceptions of national identity and the nature of the state in

[5] Statistics calculated from Ganoforum, *Eto Lash Rakhbo Kothai* (Dhaka, 1994), p. 30.

[6] This point is discussed in greater detail later. The facts have been widely reported in the local press since 1992, for example in *Bichitra, Jai Jai Din, Ajker Kagaj, Bhorer Kagaj, Sangbad*, etc.

[7] This point has been argued by Khurshida Begum, 'Bangladesh - Mul Dandya o Bibarjyasta Rajnitik Byabastha', *Sangbad*, (31 December 1994 - 3 January 1995).

Bangladesh: whether the national identity was to be Bengali or Bangladeshi, i.e. based on ethno-linguistic or religious markers of identity; and whether the state was to embrace sacred or secular laws.

The issues of national identity and the nature of the state remain contested in Bangladesh. Its national boundaries have been twice reconstituted within a quarter of a century: hence, political identity or citizenship changed from Indian to Pakistani in 1947 and to Bangladeshi in 1971. However, the people continued to share their Bengali 'nationality' and other social and cultural affinities with people in West Bengal across their national frontiers. But, elites have attempted to drive a wedge between the shared linguistic and cultural identities by contesting Bengali with Bangladeshi nationalism.[8] These developments indicate that the process of identity selection is not constant; the cultural markers adopted are not fixed. National and group identity have been constructed by 'elites in competition for political power and economic advantage'.[9] They have equally been motivated by the desire to gain legitimacy and broaden their support base.

Religion has periodically played a dominant role in this endeavour. It has been used as a cultural marker in the process of political mobilization alongside other markers such as language and has often been presented as a primordial bond of identity. But the experience of Bangladesh clearly suggests that there is nothing primordial or given about ethnic and national identity. As may be inferred from the argument above, these have been derived through social and political interaction.[10]

The history of Bangladesh and its search for a national identity is replete with tensions between religious orthodoxy and secular rationalism.[11] Certain Islamist political groups and parties claim to know the ultimate truth in matters pertaining to religion and demand the right to be the sole interpreters of Islamic law as experts in the field. Such groups declare certain principles of the faith to be uncontestable, such as the finality of the prophethood of Muhammad and the Quran as the supreme source of divine law. But it can be argued that there is no essentialized Islam in a world where its interpretation and practice has varied from place to place, where there are four major schools of Islamic jurisprudence, all with equal claim to legitimacy. There is, therefore, potential conflict at many levels, at the level of interpretation and the use of *ijtihad* (individual reasoning), as well as in relation to the position of religious minorities and the role of

8 T. M. Murshid, 'Bangladesh: The Challenge of Democracy - Language, Culture and Political Identity', *Contemporary South Asia*, Vol. 2, No. 1, 1993.

9 Paul R. Brass, *Ethnicity and Nationalism: Theory and Comparison* (New Delhi: Sage, 1991), p. 15.

10 J. D. Eller and R. M. Coughlan, 'The Poverty of Primordialism: The Demistification of Ethnic Attachments', *Ethnic and Racial Studies*, Vol. 16, No. 2, April 1993, pp. 195-196.

11 For a detailed study on the theme see T. M. Murshid, *The Sacred and the Secular: Bengal Muslim Discourses, 1871-1977* (New Delhi: Oxford University Press, 1995).

liberal intellectuals in determining the nature of the state. This becomes increasingly obvious by the nineties as the religious right gains in political strength and is able to challenge the legitimacy of secular institutions.

Perceptions of Identity: The Sacred and Secular Dimensions

It would be useful to examine the tensions which characterized the Bengali experience within a historical perspective in order to understand contemporary developments. These were largely due to clashes between elites about giving form to imagined nations. The sacred and secular were inevitably pitted against each other.

The emergence of Pakistan in 1947 was accompanied by a strong assertion of Muslim nationalism and an emphasis on Islam as the basis of identity and unity, binding together disparate groups. Indian Muslims felt deprived as Muslims *vis-à-vis* the Hindus and hence the emphasis on their religious and communal identity. The emergence of Bangladesh drew support from a rising Bengali ethnic consciousness. The Muslims of East Pakistan felt their relative deprivation as Bengalis *vis-à-vis* the non-Bengalis of West Pakistan who used religion to control Bengali aspirations. In both instances, the basic struggle was for economic emancipation, but the construction of ideology and identity served to mobilize support and provide legitimacy for that struggle. In both cases such construction achieved a fragile unity.

After the creation of the new nation-states, the fragile consensus on ideology and identity seemed to break down in both Pakistan and Bangladesh. Secular politicians had rallied Muslim support for Pakistan with slogans of 'Islam in danger'. In the new state, created ostensibly to guarantee that Muslims could live in their own way, there were several contenders for power challenging the authority (and ideology) of the ruling party, the Muslim League. Among these were the Awami Muslim League, a breakaway party (1951) which wished to open up its membership to all communities, irrespective of religion; the Jamaat-i-Islami which demanded an Islamic state ruled by *shariah* laws; and there was an underground communist movement which rejected the partition of India. Notably in the first provincial elections in East Bengal in 1954, the Muslim League was routed.

The emergence of Bangladesh in 1971, unlike that of Pakistan, was sudden - the inevitable aftermath of a genocide perpetrated by the West Pakistan dominated 'junta' in defence of its decision not to share power or resources with East Pakistan. The struggle of Bengalis in 1971 was one for sheer survival rather than a self-conscious attempt to build a secular polity, even though inspiration was sought in slogans like 'Jai Bangla' which had no religious connotations whatsoever. Yet, Bangladesh came to be associated with secular symbols and ideologies, until the state controlled reversals after the assassination of the first prime minister of Bangladesh, Sheikh Mujibur Rahman in 1975.

Independent Bangladesh came to be associated with a secular ideology, because the autonomy movement of the 1960s which was a sequel to the language movement of the 1950s addressed itself mainly to economic and political issues. The language movement had already created a secular cult and carried the message that culture should be allotted a neutral, non-religious and to that extent, a secular zone. Another reason was that the 1972 constitution enshrined secularism as one of the four pillars of the state.

However, there was no absolute national consensus about what secularism meant. Sheikh Mujib was at pains to explain that his message was one of religious neutrality on the part of the state, which was perfectly compatible with personal religiosity:

> Secularism does not mean the absence of religion.... No communal politics will be allowed in the country.[12]

But there was confusion even among educated intellectuals, not to mention the deeply religious masses. Some believed secularism to be a form of atheism, or absence of religion: they could not comprehend the prescription of religious tolerance in public life along with religiosity in personal life.[13] Yet in the 1973 elections, which was regarded by the ruling party as a referendum on the four principles of state policy - nationalism, socialism, democracy and secularism -, the Awami League won a massive victory. It secured 73.17 per cent of the votes cast and 292 of the 300 seats contested.[14]

Mujib faced strong opposition from two fronts: the fragmented left and the Islamic right. Neither recognized the basis of the new state. While the Islamic right had been banned, most of the pro-Chinese factions of the Communist Party had gone underground. The Islamic right had already challenged the foundation of Bangladesh at the very inception of the new state by the assassination of intellectuals, like Munir Chowdhury on 14 December 1971, two days before the Pakistan Army surrendered to the Combined Forces.[15] It may be assumed that the 'Islamic' parties still had

12 English translation of speech, Dacca, External Publicity Division, Ministry of Foreign Affairs, Government of the People's Republic of Bangladesh, 1972, pp. 16-17.

13 Ali Anwar (ed.), *Dharmanirapekshata (Secularism)* (Dacca, 1973), pp. 86-87.

14 *The Bangladesh Observer*, 8-10 March 1973.

15 *New York Times*, 26 December 1972, The Al-Badr, the action front of the Jamaat-i-Islami, was responsible for a mass murder in Muhammadpur. The only survivor, D. Hossain, recounted the events.

some support despite their anti-national role during the war of liberation.[16]

It was thus no wonder that a 'Muslim Bengal' movement emerged shortly after liberation. Kamal Hossain, the then foreign minister noted in a recent interview that the idea of Muslim Bangla came from a Radio Pakistan Broadcast on 17 December 1971, a day after Pakistan's defeat. In the broadcast, Pakistan welcomed the formation of Muslim Bangla and the restoration of the original spirit of the 1940 Lahore Resolution which envisaged Pakistan as a federation of independent states.[17] It is surprising, however, that this movement received support from some of the underground communist groups because of shared anti-Indian and anti-Awami League feelings. The East Pakistan Communist Party (Marxist-Leninist) claimed 'Muslim Bengal' as its ally in their underground paper Janayuddha.[18] Several factions of the pro-Chinese Communist Party - which either did not support the liberation war or fought a dual war against both the Pakistan Army and the Mukti Bahini - insisted that colonialism and exploitation persisted in Bangladesh, which was a client state of India and therefore there was continued need for struggle. They refused to recognize Bangladesh and described her as 'East Bengal' or 'East Pakistan'.[19]

The relative success of the movement to alter the identity of the new state is evident in the policies adopted since the assassination of the father of the nation, Bangabandhu, Sheikh Mujibur Rahman. That act was one in a series of events which led to the adoption of Islam as an instrument of state policy and rendered possible a return to the theocratic fold of Pakistan.

Bangladesh has inherited a tradition of state intervention in the process of identity construction from Pakistan, where the state subscribed to Islamic ideology, albeit superficially. With military intervention in politics, the new political elite was again actively engaged in forging new identities in the hope of gaining new allies and popular legitimacy. The outcome, however, was nationally divisive. Nationality, which was defined in terms of Bengali ethnic, linguistic and cultural identity since independence, was, since the 1975 coup, being redefined on the basis of political calculations. The new definition required that a distinction be made between the languages of East and West Bengal, where the former would be

16 Between the Jamaat-i-Islami, Pakistan Muslim League (Council), Pakistan Muslim League (Convention), the Pakistan Democratic Party and the Jamiat-ul-Ulama-i-Islam and Nizam-e-Islam parties, the Islamic right had won 12.72 per cent of the votes cast in the 1970 elections in East Bengal. Besides these, the Awami League too had non-secular elements among its members.

17 Author's interview with Dr. Kamal Hossain, 27 August 1994, Oxford.

18 *Janayuddha*, May-June 1973, p. 33, cited by Fazl Huq, p. 52.

19 For a detailed discussion of the role of the left in the Liberation war and in Bangladesh, see T. Maniruzzaman, *The Bangladesh Revolution and its Aftermath* (Dacca, 1980), pp. 141-153, 169-175, 175-179; Fazl Huq, pp. 49-55.

distinct from the Sanskritic Bengali of West Bengal. In 1978, under President Ziaur Rahman's military regime, citizens of Bangladesh were designated 'Bangladeshi', replacing the appellation of 'Bangalee' as stated in the Constitution of 1972. Bangladeshis, Zia implied, were different from the Bengalis of India and so were their culture and language: the latter had to be moulded 'in our own way'.[20] His speech to this effect recalls Jinnah's famous statement distinguishing the cultures and religions of Hindus and Muslims as two different social orders. Zia thus asserted the precedence of religio-political identity over the ethno-cultural. In ideological terms, this was something of a rejection of Mujib's secular stance. Although the preference for 'Bangladeshi' over 'Bangalee' had no strong religious connotation, 'secularism' was discarded as a principle of state policy through a constitutional amendment in 1977. Though Zia's political party, the Bangladesh Nationalist Party, asserted through its manifesto that Bangladeshis had freed themselves from 'the evils of communalism' because of the 'great teachings of Islam', Zia's actions nevertheless implied a reassertion of the distinct and separate identity of Bengali Muslims *vis-à-vis* the Bengali Hindus. To this extent, he acknowledged once again the concept of two-nations on which Pakistan had been founded and which had been rejected through the war of liberation in 1971. The basic complexities in the problem of culture and identity which existed during Pakistani rule thus persisted in Bangladesh.

The Quest for Legitimacy

Military rule in Bangladesh was inevitably concerned with gaining some degree of legitimacy at home and abroad as it had no popular mandate. Ziaur Rahman came to power after a series of coups, the first of which overthrew the popularly elected government of Sheikh Mujibur Rahman. In his search for a support base, he failed to win over Mujib's following. He was therefore compelled to seek allies from among the opponents of the Awami League which included the extreme left and the extreme right, neither of which had believed in Bangladesh.[21]

Zia resorted to policies aimed at giving an Islamic gloss to the state. Not only was he seeking to maintain the allegiance of his new allies but he also expected to obtain approval from the Arab bloc which had great sym-

20 Zia's speech in 1978, cited by Abul Fazl Huq, 'The Problem of National Identity in Bangladesh', *The Journal of Social Studies*, No. 24, April 1984, p. 58.

21 In April 1979, Shah Azizur Rahman was made Prime Minister of Bangladesh. He was a member of the counter vernacular intelligentsia who had resisted the movement to establish Bengali as one of the state languages of Pakistan. See *Eclipse of Secular Bangladesh. A Radical Asia Publication* (London, 1981), p. 17.

pathy for Pakistan and from which much money flowed. Among the Islamization policies were the enactment of Islamic Universities Act, 1980, and Islamic Education and Research Act, 1980.[22] Zia's decision to woo the Islamic world was informed by strong economic considerations. In exchange for a religious posture it would be possible to obtain Arab aid. Although the amount was not large in global terms, it was politically advantageous for it signified acceptance by the community of Islamic nations.

The Zia period has ushered in a new ruling ideology determined primarily by concerns for its own legitimacy rather than any ideological convictions. It was reflected in the usage of a new political and cultural vocabulary. The slogan of *Jai Bangla,* which is linguistically of Bengali origin was replaced by *Bangladesh Zindabad* where *Zindabad* is of Urdu and Persian derivation. The de-emphasization of Bengali language was carried further by referring to 'Bangladesh Betar' as 'Radio Bangladesh' and to the Bengali language as 'Bangladeshi language'.[23]

Undoubtedly, the rise of the military in politics provoked a legitimacy crisis. In its search for new support bases, the leadership adopted the measures discussed above which may be described as policies of inclusion and exclusion. Clearly, Islamists and the forces opposed to Bengali language and the liberation of the Bengali people from the control of Pakistan were included. Quite ironically, Zia, the freedom fighter, excluded the major force behind the liberation of the new nation state, the Awami League, which had also been the champion of secularism and inclined favorably towards India. By the same token he excluded Hindus and syncretists. Among the latter were people from literary circles, musicians, artists, dancers and painters - people who drew their inspiration from the common cultural heritage of Bengal.

Zia thus rejected Bengali nationalism without ever acknowledging the implications of the switch for national politics and international relations. Nationally, the formerly rejected right and left took his policies as signals inviting them to re-enter the political scene and stake their claims, a move facilitated by the 1976 Political Parties Resolution which lifted the ban on religion based politics. At the international level, a deteriorating relationship with India corresponded with growing overtures of friendship to Pakistan.[24] For example, Pakistani industrialists like the Dawoods and the Ispahanis who had lost their factories in the former East Pakistan as a result of the war were invited back to run these and paid compensation. Military rule in Bangladesh signalled a reversal in trends

22 On his Islamization policies, see Acts No. XXXI, XXXVII, *A Collection of Acts and Ordinances,* 1980, Ministry of Law and Parliamentary Affairs, Government of Bangladesh (Dacca, 1980).

23 *Eclipse of Secular Bangladesh*, p. 13.

24 Similarly, a deteriorating relationship with the USSR corresponded with improved links with the United States of America.

whereby the country was quietly headed towards becoming 'Muslim Bangla'.

Effectively, the foundations were laid during the Zia period for the rise of the Islamic right and the forces favorable to closer ties with Pakistan. At the time, however, no one suspected a potential threat to the forces of Bengali nationalism: The Bengali nation was complacent in the belief about its integrity, and united in its shared experience of Pakistani oppression in the name of religion. This complacency was shattered in the 1990s when it appeared as if the Bengali nationalists had lost the initiative while the Islamists were setting the political agenda and determining its tempo. The forces of liberalism and rationalism were caught unaware as those of totalitarianism and theocracy penetrated influential positions of government and emerged with a blueprint plus an armed cadre to enforce their vision of an Islamic state.

The rise of the Islamists was encouraged further after Ershad's succession to the Presidency, following the assassination of Zia in 1981, which signalled the end of the influence of freedom fighters in politics and ushered in repatriated officers from Pakistan into the helm of affairs. As a repatriated officer who had not contributed to the liberation struggle, Ershad had less credibility and popular appeal than Zia. In his quest for legitimacy, Ershad pursued Zia's Islamising policies but with less restraint. He identified the Islamic right as a potential ally, particularly the Jamaat-i-Islami which had successfully brought other religious groups such as the Wahabis within its fold and developed a broad front with the Nizam-e-Islam and Jamiat-ul-Ulama-i-Islam parties.

In order to woo them Ershad invoked sacred symbols with vigor, emphasized the Islamic character of the state, led Friday prayers, made periodic attempts to control the norms of social behavior, dress and manners, and more importantly, initiated policy changes which replicated constitutional measures adopted in Pakistan. Through the Eighth Amendment of the Constitution, Islam was given the status of state religion in 1988; even its wording is a carbon copy of the provision made for an Islamic state in the 1973 Constitution of Pakistan. No lessons had been learnt from Bhutto's predicament in Pakistan, who gave the country its first Islamic constitution in order to appease the Jamaat, but was nevertheless ousted and hanged by a Jamaat supporter. In his statement before the Supreme Court Bhutto said, 'I appointed a Chief of Army, belonging to the Jamaat and the result is before all of us'.[25] The moral of the tale, - that the forces of 'fundamentalism' will not be placated until they have control over political power-, was lost to Ershad. Eventually, the Jamaat was party to his fall from grace.

25 Afzal Iqbal, *Islamization in Pakistan* (Lahore: Vanguard, 1986), p. 106. In the years after partition, the political leadership took no chances and kept Maududi at arms length. While religious forces were allowed a social and educational role, they were barred from all political roles until the fall of Ayub Khan.

The Challenge from the Religious Right

The rise of the religious right is significant in that a new dimension was introduced into politics. Ideas and values derived from perceptions of the sacred were increasingly invoked to challenge secular ones. A simultaneous augmentation of violence, chaos and disorder seemed to favor the challengers in so far as these posed a threat to the uninhibited movement of women and the freedom of expression of the less-well organized secular society. In this context, it would be pertinent to examine further the factors which contributed to the rising influence of the religious right and the nature of its impact on political discourses.

The Eighth Amendment was a major gain for the Islamists, who were also making gains elsewhere, specially, in the areas of education and subtle forms of political decision-making. Their influence in the sphere of education was manifest in the number of *madrasahs* and recruitment of teachers and students (see Table 1 below). During the period of Ershad's rule there was more than a hundred fold increase in the number of government and affiliated *madrasahs* and nearly 300 percent increase in the number of staff and enrolment of students. Increased allocation from the education budget and financial assistance from Saudi Arabia, Kuwait, Libya and Pakistan have contributed to these developments. The curriculum of these institutions, kept secret until recently, contain a distorted history of the liberation of Bangladesh.[26] The graduates of these institutions along with those of the newly established Islamic universities began to receive specialized training and enter the professions. They have become doctors, lawyers, engineers, theologians of seminaries, imams of mosques, teachers of educational establishments and directors of Islamic missions and foundations. Inevitably, Bangladesh witnessed the emergence of two nations once again.

26 Interview with Dr. Kamal Hossain, Oxford, 27 August 1994.

Table 1
Number of Madrasahs with Teachers and Students
(1977/78 to 1991/92)

	1977/78	1981/82	1990/91	1991/92
Madrasahs (a)	1,976	2,864	5,959	6,025
Students	375,000	388,000	1.028,000	1.735,000
Teachers	21,579	29,608	83,761	94,961

(a) from secondary level and above - government and affiliated
Source: Bureau of Statistics, *Statistical Pocketbook of Bangladesh*, various issues, based on information obtained from the Madrasah Board.

After the elections of 1991, the Jamaat was catapulted into a position where it could influence state policy, another significant gain for the religious right. The election results showed that none of the major parties achieved an absolute majority: The Bangladesh National Party (BNP) won 140 seats, the Awami League led 8 party-alliance got 100, the Jatiya Party of Ershad had 35 while the Jamaat-i-Islami bagged 18 seats. [27] The BNP was unable to form a government with an alliance with the deposed Ershad's Jatiya Party as it held Ershad responsible for the assassination of Zia. Similarly, the Awami League held it responsible for the failure to arrest and try the self-confessed killers of Bangabandhu Sheikh Mujibur Rahman; in addition, the difference in their conceptions of state, nation and identity made an alliance with the Awami League impossible. Therefore, the BNP achieved a majority in Parliament with the support of the Jamaat.[28] In exchange, the Jamaat was allowed 2 of the 30 women's seats. While, other advantages have not been made public, it was widely speculated that it influenced key cabinet appointments, in the ministries of Education, Information and Home.[29] As a result, as unfolding events revealed, it could make an impact on policy in these areas, to determine the content of education curriculum, contain the dissemination of

27 BAMNA (Bangladesh Mukto Nirbachan Andolan) (ed.), *A Report on the Elections to the Elections to the Fifth National Parliament, 27 February 1991* (Dhaka: BAMNA, 1991), pp. 62-63. The Jamaat had obtained 12 percent of the votes cast.

28 The BNP obtained 28 of the 30 reserved seats for women with Jamaat support, thus achieving a majority in Parliament. Interview with Dr. Moin Khan, State Minister for Planning, Dhaka, 5 January 1995.

29 Interview with Syed Hassan Imam, 22 December 1994; *Khabarer Kagaj*, 28 June 1994; BNP sympathizers openly admit to this about the appointment of the Home Minister.

information and control security related decisions. The Information Minister has been charged in the press with spreading disinformation by attempting to rewrite the history of the liberation of Bangladesh and in particular, the role of Sheikh Mujib, the Awami League and the Jamaat-i-Islami.[30] The Home Minister was held responsible for the unchecked growth of training camps for the armed cadre of the Shibir. Thus, for the first time in the history of the new nation the Jamaat gained a formal role in government.

While its position in government was a recognition of its rehabilitation at the state level, the matter was far from resolved in the streets. The selection of Golam Azam as the *amir* of the Jamaat provoked a massive protest organized by the Nirmul Committee, which had been set up to counter the influence of the religious right and keep alive the threatened memory of the liberation war. Its membership included the secular literati, actors, musicians and journalists. The movement was spearheaded by its founder president, a woman called Jahanara Imam, who had lost her son in that war. Golam was accused of war crimes by secular liberal civilians who demanded that he be arrested and tried. Eventually, a people's court was constituted in 1992. This court found him guilty as charged and demanded that the state take action to mete out justice to the people of Bangladesh. Instead, the state declared this court unconstitutional and issued warrants for the arrest of 24 people involved with it. Subsequently, in order to divert attention, a trial was staged to determine the citizenship status of Golam Azam. In June 1994, the court declared his previous loss of citizenship during the Mujib period to have been unconstitutional: he was deemed a citizen by birth.

This outcome gave the Jamaat a new lease of life. It began a violent counter-offensive against the forces of secularism, rationalism and humanism: a process that had already been underway since the Nirmul Committee had begun its movement. Embarking on a concerted campaign for an Islamic state at many fronts it engaged in both institutional politics and street agitation, participating in Parliament and establishing youth wings which tended to be more radical as well as violent in the public domain. It pursued a strongly anti-feminist line believing female emancipation to be contrary to the divine plan. In the process it exacerbated the problem of governance.

The immediate concern was to divert attention away from Golam Azam. The feminist writer, Taslima Nasreen, offered them an emotive pretext, not only to do this, but also to increase the momentum of their campaign for the establishment of an Islamic state based on *shariah* laws. As a lone woman perceived to have stepped out of acceptable social bounds she became an easy target. Taslima was accused of subverting the cultural

30 *Janomot*, 19-25 August 1994.

and religious values of the state and hence was depicted as a traitor to the state and religion, *rashtradrohi* and *dharmadrohi*. A process of 'psychological manipulation' of the popular psyche was carefully orchestrated. Extracts from her works were presented out of context to portray her as one who insults Islam, hates men and is a woman of loose moral standards. In a leaflet, she is charged with accusing God to be a liar, of making fun of the Day of Judgement, of going against the dictates of religion by insinuating that the birth of a son or daughter has nothing to do with God's will but is determined by chromosomes.[31] The fact that this last point is part of a wider debate between scientists and theologians has been totally ignored.

Her feminist stance and concern for minorities were both suspect. She was deemed to be a traitor to her religion and her nation. Taslima advocates the freedom of women to determine the size of their families, which she provocatively describes as the 'freedom of the womb', *jarayur swadhinata*. In the campaign of calumny against her she is accused of campaigning for free sex, a charge she vehemently refutes.[32] Quotations from her book *Lajja* have been bandied about to prove that she deems Muslims to be unworthy of trust and the state to be communal and discriminatory to religious minorities.[33] This is a misreading of her essential message: Taslima, the social critic is shaming her country for failing its minorities and challenging it to show some nobility. *Lajja* depicts the insecurity of a Hindu family in Bangladesh caught in the reprisals against Hindus in retaliation for the destruction of the sixteenth century Babri Mosque in Ayodhya by Hindu extremists in 1992. The moral of her tale applies to minorities everywhere: they can not assimilate into the majority community however hard they try; an invisible line demarcates them even if there is no obvious visible distinction. Taslima shames a nation for betraying itself, - for she believes Hindus and Muslims to be one nation, - and challenges it to confront some unpalatable truths about itself.

Through such statements she places herself clearly in the camp of Bengali nationalists. This is further exemplified by her list of misdeeds by some militant or influential segments of the religious right. Her harshest critiques are levelled against *pirs, mullahs* and *razakaars*. In her columns she noted that the pir of Pabna abused girls, the pir of Shimulia had many wives, the pir of Sarsina opposed Bangladesh in the war of liberation, most pirs such as the pir of Sarsina engaged in politics, and the pir of Atroshi is reputed to make or break ministers. Then comes her scathing attack: 'The image of a pir is no longer that of a good and pure Muslim - pir

31 Leaflet, *Dharmadrohi o deshadrohi nastikder rukhe darao*, 26 June 1994 (Dhaka: Oitijhya Sangsad).

32 Taslima Nasreen, *Nashta Meyer, Nashta Gadya* (Dhaka, 1992, 1993), pp. 60-61.

33 Leaflet, *Dharmadrohi*, pp. 4-7. Taslima Nasreen, *Lajja* (Calcutta: Ananda, 1993), p. 31.

means evil, worthless and tremendously lustful men'.[34] It is thus no wonder that some of these men of religion wanted her dead invoking a *fatwa* to this effect.[35]

The Jamaat and its various front organizations took full advantage of the fact that Taslima's provocative message, language and style had alienated large segments of Bengali society.[36] Politically, her possible sources of support had been neutralized. The Awami League, her obvious champion as the proponent of a secular democratic state, gave her no overt backing. It was loath to jeopardize its 'undeclared alliance'[37] with the Jamaat in its joint struggle to force the BNP government to accept the demand for the establishment of a caretaker government. The government was hostile. Police protection after the first *fatwa* had to be obtained through a court injunction.[38] This was withdrawn and on 4 June 1994, the Home Ministry invoked a provision of Indo-Anglian law under colonial rule to obtain a warrant for her arrest on the grounds of hurting the feelings of Muslims. But, it took no action against those who caused incitement to murder, - a sharp contrast to its handling of the People's Court. The bias in the application of law to favor the religious right becomes obvious. Nationally, however, the state had played into the hands of *mullahs*.

Interpreting government and opposition roles as tacit support for their stand, the religious right believed that victory was within reach; they intensified their campaign for Islamic rule at various fronts. There were demands for the introduction of blasphemy laws as in Pakistan, for the execution of all atheists and apostates (*nastik* and *murtad*), for the ban on all publications by such people, for Ahmadis to be decreed non-Muslims etc. These were accompanied by massive demonstrations, meetings and the setting up of organizations such as the Sanmilita Sangram Parishad and branch committees with names such as Student Soldiers of Islam or Islami Chhatra Sena to spread the message into villages.[39] Through the repeated publication of lies the 'psychological manipulation' of a large segment of

34 Taslima Nasreen, *Nirbachita Column* (Dhaka: Vidyaprakash, 1991, 1992), pp. 27-28. All translations of extracts are by the author.

35 *Fatwas* were given in Sylhet in October 1993 and twice in June 1994 in Bogra and Khulna, Bangladesh. In Sylhet a price of Tk. 50,000 (approximately US $ 1,500) was put on her head.

36 Women accused her of 'derailing the feminist movement'. Politicians held her responsible for the bad press Bangladesh was receiving abroad. Religious bigots insinuated she was pandering to the West, India and the religious rightwing party, the Bharatiya Janata Party (BJP). Intellectuals implied that she was after cheap publicity. Literary competitors considered her work shallow. Others envied her success, while most men were annoyed at her audacity: In one of her poems she warns women to flee from men for they carried syphilis in the same way that one ran away from dogs which had rabies.

37 Barrister Sarah Hossain, interviewed for Newsnight, BBC 2, London, 4 August 1994.

38 Interview with Taslima's legal counsel, Dr. Kamal Hossain, Oxford, 27 August 1994.

39 *Inquilab*, Dhaka, 12 August 1994.

the population was effected. Taslima was even condemned by those who had not read her work. A mass hysteria was effectively created. Taslima had been transformed into a monster in the popular imagination and many 'were prepared to destroy that monster'.

The immediate background to this hysteria was a much publicized interview of Taslima in *The Statesman*, Calcutta, on 9 May 1994. In it she is quoted to have advocated a revision of the Quran. Her disclaimer to the effect that she referred only to *shariah* laws fell on deaf ears. The propaganda leaflets repeatedly quoted fragments of the *Statesman* interview but not her denial.

Although Taslima has not come to any physical harm, the fact that she is compelled to live in exile today is an indictment of the political process and internal security in Bangladesh. It is also a victory for the religious right. Taslima could emerge from hiding after two months only after her safe passage was negotiated through foreign intervention and bail assured at a higher court where she was more likely to obtain a fair hearing than at a lower court. [40] Barrister Kamal Hossain defended her with the opening statement: 'We have come to test whether the country has a constitution'; he was assured that it had. [41]

The controversy surrounding feminist literature and persona as embodied by Taslima Nasreen serves to illustrate the nature of the struggle between the forces of religious extremism and secular liberalism, which are both vying for the hearts and minds of the people in Bangladesh.

But there were many other victims of the vengeance of fanatical forces, some of whom perished because they neither achieved notoriety nationally nor fame internationally; who neither had access to defence lawyers nor citizen's committees. Among the less fortunate incidents of the recent past include the fact that one woman was stoned to death for alleged adultery whereas, in fact, the lustful gaze of a *mullah* had fallen on her. Another woman was forced to commit suicide to evade the shame of alleged *zina* crimes. A female Member of Parliament from the BNP also provoked the wrath of the *mullahs* when she called for a revision of family laws, and now faces the *fatwa* of death.

Several intellectuals and writers like the poet Shamsur Rahman and the scholar Ahmad Sharif also face death threats because they subscribe

40 She received support from various foreign governments including some of the European Union, Sweden, Norway and the United States. Some of these countries threatened to withdraw aid, while others thought it prudent to negotiate her safe conduct out of the country. Taslima went into hiding for she could not even present herself at court in safety. She emerged from hiding on the 4 August 1994, after assurances and armed protection was secured. She now lives in exile in Sweden while her case is being tried in absentia in Dhaka. Interview with Dr. Kamal Hossain, her legal advisor, and with Prof. K. S. Murshid who negotiated her safe conduct.

41 Interview with her defence lawyer Dr. Kamal Hossain, Oxford, 27August 1994.

to secular, rationalist, non-communal and democratic values. Fearing assassination, they often live in hiding. Religious extremists have described them as *deshadrohi, rashtradrohi* and *dharmadrohi,* traitors to the nation, state and religion.

A series of such provocative actions have virtually led to the establishment of a parallel structure of authority in remote areas far from the reaches of officialdom. Various front organizations of the Jamaat supported by their own armed cadre have begun to impart Islamic justice. They derive their authority from the *fatwas* given by local *mullahs* and not from any court, for these fatwas are treated as having divine sanction. Not only have thieves lost their limbs and 'adulterers' been stoned, but opposition newspapers have lost access to various distributors and their clients. Many rural women have been divorced by *fatwa* for practising birth control. Such a situation is novel in the history of the region. Women are also losing their marital status for taking bank loans for their small businesses. It is being argued that economic independence for women is undesirable because it can give them a status superior to men, which was not part of God's plan.[42] Non-government organizations like BRAC and their workers have been attacked by *madrasah* students for allegedly spreading Christianity. BRAC schools for girls have been burnt in protest against 'westernized' female education. Here coercion is a method of neutralizing the sources of alternative ideologies. Various women's groups and legal bodies have gathered evidence and successfully convicted some of the *fatwabaj mullahs*.[43] But the trend persists unabated while the police find themselves inadequately armed to face the challenge.[44]

The strategy of the religious right has been to pursue all means at its disposal, both constitutional and unconstitutional, to achieve its goal of establishing an Islamic state - whether it be through persuasion, intimidation or coercion. One of the constitutional methods resorted to has relied on its successful infiltration into the lower courts in small towns like Rangpur and Maulavibazaar. Its modus operandi followed a particular pattern which took advantage of the existing legal system. First, a *mullah* decreed a *fatwa*. Subsequently, one of the faithful filed a case in a lower court where the magistrate was a sympathizer or supporter of the Jamaat-Shibir. The magistrate immediately issued a warrant for the arrest of the accused without hearing his defence. Such warrants were issued against

42 *Inquilab*, 12 and 19 August 1994.

43 Ain-o-Shalish Kendra, 'Threats of violence and violations of human rights by imams of mosques and the religious right in Bangladesh' (a collection of cases compiled for the period 1992-94, unpublished), Dhaka, 1994.

44 In Chittagong, the police confessed their inability to control the Shibir-Yuva Command because their own weapons were inferior. There was evidence to suggest that arms were coming to specific Shibir members from Pakistan by post. See *Dainik Sangbad*, Dhaka, Friday, 12 August 1994, p. 6.

the editors of *Janakantha, Bhorer Kagaj, Ajker Kagaj* and *Jai Jai Din* who were accused of hurting the sentiments of Muslims.[45] For example, an issue of *Jai Jai Din* contained a cartoon involving the letter *alif* of the Arabic alphabet. The editor was compelled to obtain bail from three different courts for the same offence.[46] Such persistent harassment could hope to achieve conformity if not consensus.

These developments have been accompanied by provocative statements by some members of the religious right in key positions which raise serious questions about their commitment to democracy and the nature of the state, nation and religion envisaged. The Pir of Charmonai declared at a meeting on 29 July 1994, that 'all non-fundamentalists were of illegitimate birth'. At the same meeting, the Katib of the Baitul Mukarram Mosque, Maulana Ubaidul Huq, noted that Pakistan was divided in 1971 as a result of the *gaddari*, 'treachery', of certain western educated individuals' who were currently involved in similarly deceiving the people.[47] Later, in an interview on the 4th of August, he announced that 'the state should be run by a *fatwa* committee consisting of the *ulama*'[48] thus voicing the thoughts of Maududi for which Ayub Khan kept him behind bars for many years. The statements provoked an outraged protest from teachers, students, freedom fighters, political groups and a large section of the *ulama* numbering 227 of them, indicating that there were divisions in the ranks of the *ulama*. The Katib lost his lucrative job and a case was filed against him and the pir on the grounds of hurting the religious sentiments of crores of Muslims. Just when it seemed that religious extremists could no longer be contained, these measures acted as a check on their activism albeit temporarily.

It can be argued that the religious right and the secular intelligentsia have been engaged in the manipulation of sacred and secular symbols, appealing to religion, history and culture to mobilize support in order to secure the social and political order they desire. The main difference, however, is that the former is well organized, armed and carrying out a well thought plan of action much of which had already been tried out in Pakistan. The latter appears to be disorganized, unarmed and without a clear strategy whereby to challenge the onslought. Politically, the former has gained advantages over the latter through its various alliances. It has obtained the acquiescence of the state and a neutralized political opposi-

45 Anis Alamgir, 'Shafiq Rahman Ebong Bichaar', *Janomot*, 1-7 July 1994, p. 22. Apart from the editor of *Janakantha*, the others were released on bail.

46 Comment of the co-editor, Taleya Rahman, Saturday, London, 17 August 1994.

47 *Janomot*, London, 19-25 August 1994; *Saptahik Bichitra*, Dhaka, Vol. 23, No. 12, 12 August 1994, p. 27.

48 *Saptahik Bichitra*, ibid., pp. 27-33.

tion, while the latter appears to have no champion in the form of committed backing from a political party.

Implications for Democracy and the Role of the State

The developments identified so far portend ill for the future of a pluralist secular liberal democracy which enjoys legitimacy and good governance. A democratic system is essential for a country that has religious, ethnic and ideological diversity which must be accommodated if fratricidal tendencies and ethno-religious conflicts are to be avoided. Clearly, the state can play a role in determining the outcome of the tussle between the Islamists and the secular rationalists and in restoring a semblance of order in civil society. The history of Bangladesh shows that in the interest of legitimacy the state has been instrumental in constructing ideologies, identities and nations, and that it can enforce the rule of law if it sees fit. Essentially, the state must guarantee minimum human rights - to life, to property and to persuasion; it must challenge public violations of the legal system such as the authority of *fatwas;* and contain street violence in the interest of the public good. It must recognize diversity, help build a non-communal democratic ethos and propagate the values of civil society.

These have been difficult tasks not only because of the frequent crises besetting the government, as already noted at the outset, but also because the BNP government does not represent any ideological monolith. Like any centre party, whether of the Congress variety in India or the Liberal Democratic party of the United Kingdom, its support comes from both the right and the left - Islamists and secularists, pro-liberation and anti-liberation forces, Bangladeshi nationalists who are anti-Indian but not pro-Pakistani and those who are pro-Pakistani, those for whom the language martyrs day is meaningful and those for whom it is not. Naturally, these various opinions are reflected in key official appointments. Particularly controversial were the appointments to the Ministries of Information, Home and Education - Najmul Huda, Abdul Matin Chowdhury and Zamiruddin who have been identified as belonging to a strong pro-Pakistan lobby.[49]

The manipulation of history in school text books, in particular, the conspicuous absence of the name of Bangabandhu, the unchecked rampage by gun-toting members of the Jamaat-Shibir in campuses are attributed to these appointments.[50] No public investigations were carried out despite armed attacks on the BNP student wing in Chittagong. Here, they

49 View of Syed Hasan Imam, Secretary, Nirmul Committee, London, 25 August 1994.

50 *Khabarer Kagaj*, 28 June 1994; Yasif Akbar, 'Shiksha Pratishthane Santras: rajnitite ashani sanket', *Purnima*, Vol. 7, No. 6, 29 September 1993, p. 23.

protested alongside other student groups against Golam Azam who was holding a mass rally.[51] The inaction can be interpreted either as tacit approval or a failure of the state to govern.

While secularists accuse the government of pandering to the Jamaat, the latter charges it with not doing enough for Islam. Sections within the BNP hope to maintain Jamaat's support because the main objective of political parties today appear to be access to and the maintenance of power irrespective of the costs involved. The Awami League has entered the same game by forging alliances with the Jamaat and the Jatiya Party, thus obfuscating their ideological differences to some extent.[52] However, unlike the other parties, the Jamaat and the religious right have a very clear objective, the methods of achieving which has been tried and tested in Pakistan, - the establishment of an Islamic state based on their interpretation of *shariah* laws. If successful, it would lead to the emergence of a one-party theocratic state wherein all power would be vested in the men of religion and not in any representative body. If Maududi's dictum were followed to the letter, and some do aspire to it, then general elections would be dispensed with. This would pose a threat to the democratic aspirations of the majority, endanger minority rights and render the state 'irrelevant' to the needs of the people.[53]

Therefore, what is needed is a vigilant state that can rise above ideological differences, accommodate pluralistic structures and create a climate where democracy would have a chance to mature. Such a state cannot afford to pamper the forces of coercion, communalism or sectarian conflict. But there are only a limited number of options available to the state if it is to achieve these objectives. It can choose to exclude communal and fascist parties from the political process by banning them through constitutional measures as Mujib did after liberation. It can render such bodies ineffective by delineating the terms of reference within which these may operate, such as prohibiting the use of religion in politics, which too was once constitutionally guaranteed in 1972 but reversed under Zia. It can offer alternative ideologies and value structures based on humanist thought in order to maintain a climate favorable to democratic dialogue. It can enforce the existing laws of the land to ensure that fundamental human rights are not violated and by clearly delineating citizenship rights. But such measures may be possible only if the power elite itself is not compromised. Herein

51 *Sangbad*, 12 August 1994, p. 6.

52 While the Jamaat was held responsible for collaborating with the Pakistan army and killing Bengali nationalists, the Jatiya Party was accused of having links with the killers of Sheikh Mujib.

53 For a discussion of the idea of the irrelevant state see Julius O. Ihonvbere, 'The Irrelevant State, Ethnicity, and the Quest for Nationhood in Africa', *Ethnic and Racial Studies*, Vol. 17, No. 1, January, 1994, pp. 44-50.

lies the problem with the state of Bangladesh which is threatened with becoming irrelevant as the country becomes increasingly ungovernable. The state is unable to mediate between the various 'demand groups'[54] in the streets and outside these because the interests of the ruling elite are identified with specific segments of society and its actions are yet to rise above partisan interests.

54 The term 'demand groups' has been coined by the Rudolphs in Lloyd I. and Susanne H. Rudolph, *In Pursuit of Lakshmi: The Political Economy of the Indian State* (Chicago, 1987), pp. 15, 247, 252. For a discussion of the term also see T. J. Byres, 'A Chicago View of the Indian State: An Oriental Grin without an Oriental Cat and Political Economy without Classes', *The Journal of Commonwealth and Comparative Politics*, Vol. 26, No. 3, 1988, pp. 257-258.

Constitution-Making as a Political Resource: Crisis of Legitimacy in Sri Lanka

AMITA SHASTRI

After the tumultuous events that have taken place in Sri Lanka over the last decade and more, popular hopes were raised with the election of the new People's Alliance (PA) government in late 1994 after seventeen years of rule by the center-right United National Party (UNP). Chandrika Kumaratunge received an unprecedented 62.3per cent of the votes cast in the presidential election, highlighting the very high expectations of the people that she will solve the outstanding problems of her society which have contributed to a sharp decline in legitimacy of the Sri Lankan political system. The new President set to work immediately on the two most egregious political problems of the island society: the ethnic civil war with the separatist Liberation Tigers of Tamil Eelam (better known as the LTTE) controlling large parts of the North and East, and the high centralization of political power that had taken place in the position of the executive presidency under the UNP.

It would not be far-fetched to state that her success in reining in the Tigers and delivering a satisfactory constitutional package may well prove crucial for the survival of democracy itself in Sri Lanka. Indeed, these tasks may be looked at as a manifestation of the serious crisis of legitimacy that has built up across successive regimes in Sri Lanka. Looking at political developments on the island, the argument is made in this paper that, to a substantial degree, this crisis of legitimacy has its roots in the repeated inability of the ruling elites in Sri Lanka to promulgate a constitution and effect constitutional changes which were backed by a broad consensus incorporating the major sectors of the population. This failure has resulted in the fact that no regime in Sri Lanka has been able to successfully use constitution-making as a political resource to establish and consolidate a political system with broad acceptance in diverse segments of the population, and thereby win crucial support and legitimacy for itself as well. This is particularly true of the erstwhile UNP regime which was in power for seventeen years and enjoyed a four-fifths majority in Parliament for twelve of those years. It had the majority needed to effect any changes it deemed necessary and yet it presided over a period of crisis, largely of its own making, which was undeniably the worst in recent memory in Sri Lanka.

Before looking at the Sri Lankan case in greater detail, it is useful to briefly outline some of the theoretical perspectives informing this article. As the fundamental law of a democratic state, a constitution ideally embodies the agreement and consensus amongst different segments of the society regarding the political ideals, institutions, rules, and processes through which they are going to function to resolve issues relating to the acquisition, exercise, and distribution of political power. In the Lockean tradition, it represents the 'social contract' entered into by political actors who agree to constrain their individual actions to conform to an agreed set of rules and institutions, thereby generating order and predictability to their collective benefit. The making of a constitution and the amendment or reform of an existing one are thus political processes which provide a means as well as an opportunity to the political elite of a society to arrive at broadly accepted compromises and accomodations on contentious issues. And, as recent research on the processes of democratization highlights, such agreements need not have the unanimous approval of all sectors of the society, but should represent a strategically broad segment of the society (Friedman, pp. 21-23). If successfully carried out, these processes serve as a political resource to their sponsors, bestowing legitimacy on them as designers of the new or renewed order in society, and as laying the basis for better and improved governance in the future. As T. J. Pempel noted on nineteenth century crises of political mobilization in democratic Europe and in the USA, 'A party that forges a historical compromise among important socio-economic sectors in the crucible of crisis enjoys a halo effect for some period thereafter' (ibid., p. 23).

Legitimacy forms an elusive, but critical component of democracy and orderly governance. It denotes popular consent to the exercise of power in a manner perceived to be 'right' and 'good'. It leads to a willingness in the population to respect and obey the authorities. Issues of legitimacy may, however, arise in a variety of ways in a polity. They could be raised about the system as a whole by a group in the population which was excluded or whose assent was not attained at the time a particular constitutional 'consensus' was forged. Alternatively, issues of systemic legitimacy may be raised if explicit changes are made by power-holders to the established rules in a way which alters the basic compact on which the consensus between different groups rests. These above situations may be worsened by issues of regime legitimacy which are raised when power is exercised in a manner not in accordance with the established or declared political principles and procedures. This underlines the crucial role of the political process through which decisions are reached or implemented: they must be seen as being basically 'fair' and 'just' for legitimacy to be enjoyed by a given system and/or regime.

A decline in legitimacy of a democratic regime involves, as its logical corollary, a decline in the willingness of different segments of the populace to respect and obey the authorities. This results in a loss of power which a regime in a 'normal' situation draws on to carry out the process of effective governance. Such a loss of power caused by the decline in popular consent leaves a political vacuum which the weakened regime attempts to fill by the use of coercion. A decline in legitimacy thus propels a regime to increasingly rely on the Hobbesian solution of coercion to support its authority and implement its will. The degree to which this is an alternative option resorted to by the ruling elite will in part depend upon the degree of development and capacity of the armed forces in a particular society. It is possible a regime may partially succeed in regaining legitimacy on the basis of new initiatives. It is more likely, however, that popular legitimacy enjoyed by an established system or regime will ebb away towards its opponents who are acting to focus attention on the issues being neglected by the regime. Previous supporters of the regime often desert it to join the opposition. Despite its efforts to strengthen itself, a state based mainly on coercion remains a 'weak' state.

It is useful to differentiate between different segments of the opposition in order to understand the dynamics related to the growing crisis of legitimacy leading to the breakdown of democratic regimes. Many in the opposition may choose to continue to function as a 'loyal opposition', preferring to work within the instituted political structure to pressure or persuade the regime to follow what they perceive to be desirable or necessary policies. However, if the crisis of legitimacy is particularly severe, it is more likely that many of those who previously constituted the loyal opposition, will move over to becoming the 'semi-loyal' opposition and, perhaps, even the 'disloyal' opposition. As a semi-loyal opposition, they continue to function through non-violent means, but advocate an alternative regime and political structure of power. Members of the 'disloyal' opposition, on the other hand, choose to oppose the established framework and its accepted rules, and seek to overthrow it by force, if necessary. If large numbers or the majority of the population either join or develop sympathies with the semi-loyal and disloyal opposition, either of two outcomes are possible. The first, if the authorities persist in attempting to re-establish order and their dominance through coercion, is civil war. The second, more preferable outcome, is an opening up of negotiations between the significant competing groups in an effort to arrive at a new accomodation of interests which would embody a new consensus, on the basis of which a 'reequilibration' of the polity and its democracy could take place (Linz, p. 27-38).

It is my argument in this paper that the successful establishment of a constitutional consensus has not happened in Sri Lanka. An understanding of the crisis facing Sri Lanka can be gained by first looking at the degree to which the process of constitution-making itself has contributed to its long-term crisis of legitimacy. Following that, I will look at the amendments that were made by the UNP to the latest Constitution it promulgated in 1978. These changes coupled with a repeated manipulation of the proclaimed law and democratic norms, as well as the use of emergency provisions and organized violence, all contributed to a declining legitimacy of the political regime as well as the political system as a whole. It contributed to the growth of dissent, opposition, and violence by non-ruling groups within the society to the point that the ethnic problem became an 'unsolvable problem' for the UNP and remained as such through the eighties. Finally, I will look at the current situation facing Kumaratunge and assess her chances of success in overcoming the crisis.

The nature of the discussion is clearly an elite-oriented political-constitutional one. It holds the elites and power-holders of the society responsible for the current crisis in legitimacy. It is true that the major socio-economic changes that were taking place on the island during this period such as the chronic decline in the terms of trade on which Sri Lanka was so dependent, the growing population especially of unemployed educated youth, the dynamic processes of economic liberalization after the late seventies, were severe in their impact on the society. They served as important contextual factors which generated a climate of social disorder and propelled the elite to adopt questionable policies. However, it was the political calculations, decisions, and actions of the elites to gain or retain power which were critically important for the specific political outcomes that ensued. The discussion below serves to emphasize the realm of autonomy of the political. It reiterates the importance of political rules, processes, and institutions for the impact they have on the form that socio-political cleavages take, the coalitions that are forged, and how political conflict is managed.

Constitution-Making in Sri Lanka: The Growing Crisis of Legitimacy

Among comparativists, Sri Lanka has long been considered an exemplar of peaceful decolonization and constitutional change in the developing world. Its political evolution seemed to have resulted in a more egalitarian, socially-oriented and democratic pattern of political development and governance than was the fortune of perhaps any other developing country besides Costa Rica. Universal franchise was introduced in 1930 by the colonial authorities and Sri Lanka has had regular elections since then. Generous social welfare policies regarding food, health, education, and land were introduced within a decade or so of universal franchise and continue, more or less, till today. The constitution introduced at the time of its independence in 1948 was closely modelled after the British Westminster model with which the moderate Sri Lankan elite was most familiar. Within a decade of independence, a more radical nationalist opposition party, the Sri Lanka Freedom Party (SLFP), was voted to power. With the support of smaller parties, the two major parties alternated in power till the 1982 elections, a pattern of politics characteristic of the developed liberal democratic polities of the West and unique to the developing world. The politico-constitutional system introduced at independence thus clearly seemed to represent a broad political consensus shared by the major and minor parties who participated in the instituted 'rules of the game.'

I would like to focus on a different aspect of this process and argue in this section that the roots of the recent crisis in Sri Lanka lie in some of the shortfalls of its constitution-making process, the degree to which the exercise of the framing of each constitution was used as a partisan political resource which affected each post-independence constitution's very credibility and legitimacy.

The Soulbury Constitution of 1946, which became the Independence Constitution in 1948, was framed after restricted consultation between the departing colonial administrators and the moderate conservative elite represented by D. S. Senanayake and his Board of Ministers in the 1940s. The draft proposals for constitutional reform in 1944 were virtually drawn up by an all Sinhalese seven member Board of Ministers which had been formed in 1936 to ensure unanimity on constitutional issues.[1] The whole process of constitutional negotiations was dominated by one man, D.S. Senanayake, Chair of the Board, who did not invite the participation in the formulation of the proposals of any other body, not even the elected State Council whose leading representative he was, or the Ceylon National Congress, whose co-founder he had been.[2] Reflecting credit on Senanayake's political savvy, the constitutional document was passed with a vote of 51 in favor, 3 opposed, and 4 abstentions/absences. Amongst the members not in agreement, abstaining or absent at the time of vote were the 2 Hill-Country Tamils, the leading Sri Lanka Tamil (G. G. Ponnambalam), and all 3 radical members of the State Council (De Silva, ch. 9 and 10).

In comparative terms, such a restricted process was possible because there was no broadbased oppositional nationalist movement in Sri Lanka comparable, for instance, to that which had been built up through long-term mobilization against British rule in India. Efforts to broad-base the

[1] It was only at a very late stage in this process that D. B. Jayatilaka, who formed the 'duumvirate' along with D. S. Senanayake dominating Sri Lankan politics, retired from active politics at the end of 1943 and was replaced by the first Sri Lanka Tamil on the Board of Ministers, Arunachalam Mahadeva, son of Sir Ponnambalam Arunachalam, an early nationalist politician. De Silva, p. 102.

[2] He had never served as President of this leading nationalist political organization and he severed all links with it in 1943 to demonstrate his opposition to its new more independence-oriented stance at this time when Senanayake still preferred the goal of 'dominion status' within the empire, a status that had been conceded to the white settler colonies of Canada, Australia, and New Zealand. De Silva, pp. 124-125.

movement attempted at various junctures by the leftist parties, the petty-bourgeois Sinhala Maha Sabha, and the younger less conservative wing of the UNP, were effectively contained by the colonial authorities and the conservative UNP leadership. There were few constitutional debates on the numerous possible questions such as were witnessed in India at the time of and following independence. Few changes were made to the British Westminster-style unitary parliamentary cabinet model of government to accomodate the very different social environment of a pluralist developing society in which it was being instituted. The process of constitution-making, thus, did not invite participation by significant groups in the society nor a frank discussion of the issues important to different communities in the population.

However, the restricted nature of this process need not necessarily be viewed askance, since most democratic liberal constitutions have had restricted beginnings, if it had later been expanded to address the concerns of the neglected elements in the polity. Unfortunately, this was not done in Sri Lanka. The reluctant consensus that was belatedly achieved *vis-à-vis* the Sri Lankan Tamil community with the induction of G. G. Ponnambalam into the Cabinet in 1948, was rapidly undermined in the following period. The limited safeguards in the new Constitution that had been incorporated to protect the position of the ethnic minorities through Section 29(2) were eroded rapidly by the first actions of the independent regime passing the citizenship and election acts of 1948-49. These acts effectively disfranchised the Hill-Country Tamils who formed 12 per cent of the island's population and who were beginning to support the left parties posing the most potent challenge to the newly-formed rightist UNP. The new acts created a disproportionate weightage for the conservative rural Sinhalese vote and cumulatively served to undermine the political weightage of the minority communities as a whole in electoral terms. The Sinhalese majority, forming 70 per cent of the population, emerged by the late 1950s to control 80 per cent of the seats in the National Assembly. The acts also laid the basis for the eventual deportation of the majority of the Hill-Country Tamils to India after 1964.

The left's efforts to institutionalize a more inclusive version of democracy after independence was thus blocked and then redefined with the rise of the Sri Lanka Freedom Party (SLFP) in 1956 as an advocate of the interests of the Sinhalese majority. The SLFP's first act on coming to power was the passage of a law replacing the colonial language (English) with only one national official language, Sinhala, despite the objections of the Tamil representatives. This undermined the economic participation in the state services of the largest minority, the Sri Lanka Tamils, who formed 12 per cent of the population. Section 29(2) in the Constitution which had been included in the constitution to protect individual and minority rights provided little protection.[3] This Section explicitly forbade the passage of a measure which applied to and discriminated against any particular ethnic group. However, it soon became obvious that this prohibition could be bypassed if a legislative measure was framed in general terms to apply to all communities though in actual fact it might fall with undue impact on one or more of them.

The framing of the 1972 Constitution provided another opportunity when a broad-based consensus might have been reached by the major political groupings in the society and the increasing alienation within the Tamil minorities arrested. Unfortunately, this did not take place. The United Front (UF) coalition, dominated by the pro-Sinhalese SLFP and including the two smaller left parties, the Lanka Sama Samaja Pakshaya (LSSP) and the Communist Party (CP), who came to power with a two-thirds majority in Parliament in 1970 introduced a populist-socialist constitution. The proposed Constitution was passed with no guarantees for property rights despite the opposition of the other major party, the rightist UNP. The UF also did not concede the demands of the Tamil representatives related to a fair status for the Tamil language and regional autonomy for minority-dominated areas in the north-east.

Instead, the ruling coalition enshrined the changes that had been legislated in the post-independence period to favor the Sinhalese majority to a constitutional status, and strengthened the position of the Sinhalese yet further. Buddhism became the 'foremost religion.' Sinhala was declared the official language, while the use of Tamil was to be provided for by subordinate legislation later. The earlier provisions for electoral weightages continued. In addition, the judiciary was made subordinate to the will of the majority as expressed in the National Assembly in the new Constitution. This left the minorities with no avenues for the redress of their grievances. At the same time, the government introduced the controversial practice of standardization of marks by language for determining admissions to university. This new policy excluded a disproportionate number of Sri Lankan Tamil students from gaining admission to university. In a situation of high educated youth unemployment, it was strongly opposed by them, leading them to advocate secession from the existing state using violent means.

Despite the deteriorating situation, the framing of the 1978 Constitution followed a process that was even more partisan and restricted than had been the framing of the 1972 Constitution. With the four-fifths majority that the UNP won in the 1977 elections to the National Assembly, it single-handedly proceeded to entrench a political structure which central-

[3] It had been put in on the advice of Sir Ivor Jennings, D. S. Senanayake's British constitutional advisor, to replace the more comprehensive and justiciable Bill of Rights which had been proposed earlier by the Board of Ministers to address minority concerns.

ized power in the hands of a new Presidential executive and gave extensive protections to private and foreign capital. The leading opposition party, the SLFP, denounced the changes and declared that it had been hoodwinked and duped into participating in what had been proclaimed to be proceedings of a select committee of Parliament for the revision of the 1972 Constitution.

The Tamils, represented by the moderate Tamil United Liberation Front (TULF) in Parliament, were also deeply dissatisfied with the new Constitution because it did not take note of their grievances. The 1978 Constitution not only continued the unitary structure of government but centralized it further in the new executive presidency. It continued the status of Sinhala as the sole official language, giving Tamil a subordinate status as a 'national language'. The Buddha Sasana (Buddhist clerical order) was to be 'fostered' by the state. The new system of district ministers, appointed and controlled by the President, did not meet the Tamil demands for autonomy. Innovative features in the new Constitution which provided it with some saving grace for the Tamils were the provisions relating to elections. The introduction of the proportional representation system for election to Parliament would in all likelihood grant the Tamils an important role in the balance of power between the two major parties in view of the latter's traditionally evenly matched bases of support. Tamil support would, therefore, in all likelihood be critical for effective governance by a leading or ruling party in the future. The new rules for preferential election of the President would also make it imperative for aspiring presidential candidates of the two major parties to woo the support of the Tamil and other minority voters, who altogether constituted 25 per cent of the population. Antagonized by both the process and the outcome of this round of constitution-making, for separate (and to a degree opposed) reasons, the SLFP and the TULF boycotted the vote in Parliament for the passage of the 1978 Constitution into law. They also swore to legislate their own constitutions at an opportune time.

Thus, overall, the process of constitution-making which could have been used as a major political resource by successive Sri Lankan political elites in introducing and institutionalizing a process and structure of government which had a broad-based acceptance amongst them and their support bases, was expended through short-sighted attempts by the ruling group to ignore opposing views and interests. Critically, in each round of constitution-making, as outlined above, the interests that were ignored were not only those belonging to an ethnic minority group but included significant segments of the majority community as well: the left, the UNP, and the SLFP in the three constitutions respectively. This contributed to the growing crisis of legitimacy of the political system as a whole and posed the challenge of effective governance for the regime in power.

Constitutional Amendments under the UNP: A Partisan Exercise

The gaining and maintenance of legitimacy forms a particular problem for newly established political structures and constitutions. After the process by which a new consensus is arrived at, how far new rules are followed proves crucial for developing the legitimacy of newly established systems. Such legitimacy derives in large part from the benefits that flow to the different groups in the larger society from the newly established rules for collective behavior.

Not only was the process of constitution-making in Sri Lanka severely lacking in critical respects, but adherence to the newly proclaimed constitutional rules has been deficient as well. This tendency has been only too prevalent in the post-1970 regimes dominated respectively by both the SLFP (1970-77) and the UNP (1977-1988), each of which enjoyed absolute majorities in Parliament. Under each regime, the constitution promulgated by it was amended innumerable times in an arbitrary manner to serve the partisan will of the ruling majority in Parliament. This contributed to a further contraction in the legitimacy commanded by the ruling regime as well as the newly established system and exacerbated the crisis of governance posed by the growing opposition.

Focusing on the more recent regime, we find that the steamroller majority of four-fifths enjoyed by the UNP in Parliament was used in a capricious manner to pass several constitutional amendments for purely sectarian gain. The First Amendment freed presidential commissions from judicial controls, and thereby retroactively validated the actions of a commission of enquiry appointed by the President to investigate Sirimavo Bandaranaike, leader of the SLFP and the leading figure in the opposition, for 'abuse of power' during her term in office. Based on the commission's findings, Sirimavo Bandaranaike was deprived of her civic rights and banned from competing for political office for six years. The Second Amendment made it possible for opposition Members of Parliament to defect to the majority party but prevented an opposite flow of MPs, an arrangement to be allowed only for the tenure of the existing Parliament. A third amendment bill which did not come to fruition was a farcical one which would have allowed a ruling party MP whose election had been declared null and void by the Supreme Court to continue to hold his seat even after another representative had been elected to represent his constituency! The Third Amendment allowed the President to change and bring forward the date for his re-election in 1982 so that it took place before the parliamentary election, thereby giving him and the ruling party a tactical advantage in their bid for power. The Fourth Amendment allowed for the Parliament with its five-sixths UNP majority to continue in power for another six years after its term was over in 1982 through the device of a controversial referendum supporting the extension. The Sixth Amendment passed after the ethnic violence of 1983, banned the advocacy of separatism. This resulted in the largest opposition party contingent, consisting of the moderate TULF MPs who had been elected in 1977 on the mandate of struggling for a separate state, to withdraw from Parliament.

Not all constitutional changes in this period had a partisan character. The two most substantive amendments passed in the post-1978 period instituted the principles of pluralism and devolution into the Constitution in response to the demands of the Tamil minority, but did not serve to fully resolve the issues they were supposed to. The Thirteenth Amendment, legislated as a direct consequence of the Indo-Sri Lankan Accord of July 1987, introduced a new structure of provincial councils. The Councils institutionalized a certain measure of devolution on the island but fell short of the degree of regional autonomy desired by the Tamils. The Sixteenth Amendment made Tamil and English also official languages, but provisions for implementation were left till later.

The frequent constitutional changes were accompanied by numerous other changes in ordinary legislation which further undermined the quality of democracy and governance that had been promised by the political regime and its Constitution. Retroactive legislation and punishments were passed to fall adversely on leading members of the major opposition party, the SLFP. Guilt and penalties were determined on the findings of presidential commissions of inquiry without being aired and evaluated in an open court of law. In certain incidents, such as the one relating to a news photo caption mix-up in 1978, the Parliament asserted its right to sit as a jury of the whole and pronounce a judgement in a case in which the majority deemed themselves to be an injured party.

A large number of the most important (and often partisan) legislative bills and amendments were rushed through Parliament as 'urgent in the national interest' without allowing time for discussion and debate. Increasing use was made of emergency provisions to repress the opposition and dissent to the regime: to control and impose what amounted to censorship on the press, to ban strikes and trade union activities, to arbitrarily arrest or take action against anyone suspected by a member of the police or army to be engaged in anti-regime activities, typically at the time when elections were being held.

The actual practices of the regime were at sharp variance with its professed ideals. During the first tenure of President J. R. Jayawardene (1977-1982), the regime was flush with an unprecedented inflow of foreign aid and funds. Political offices and patronage were awarded to numerous individuals and factions in the ruling party to induce them to cooperate with the leadership. With the easy inflow of funds declining and the

UNP membership reportedly getting restive during and after 1982, their cooperation for the elections was secured by means of the controversial constitutional amendments mentioned above. These allowed the presidential election to take place before the parliamentary one in order to get the more popular figure of the President elected first. The presidential election took place under a state of emergency and amidst allegations of fraud and manipulation by the opposition. The main opposition leader Sirimavo Bandaranaike had already been arbitrarily deprived of her civic rights for six years and rendered ineligible to run on the basis of the recommendations of the controversial presidential commission of inquiry. The means of a referendum, conducted amidst conditions of intimidation and fraud, was used to extend the existing five-sixths majority of the UNP in Parliament on the basis of a positive vote by a mere one-third of the population. This result was at direct variance with the simple majority that would have been most likely to accrue to the UNP under the new proportional system of parliamentary elections which had been introduced by the UNP itself in the 1978 Constitution to prevent easy two-third majorities in future parliaments. In an unprecedented departure from democratic practice, the President acquired undated letters of resignation from his parliamentarians after his re-election in 1982 and before the amendment and the referendum seeking to extend the life of the sitting Parliament was initiated. These letters remained in the President's safekeeping through his second tenure making the massive majority of the UNP MPs captive to the will of the President.

Consequently, the Parliament could not perform its expected role in a democratic system of serving as a representative forum for competition and compromise between divergent views, seeking to resolve outstanding issues. The mammoth majority of the UNP in Parliament was kept in line with both material blandishments and the threat of expulsion by the ruling party leadership. The small contingent of opposition representatives, elected in 1977 and who continued after 1982, found themselves helpless to have any impact on policy-making. As a result, they were forced to resort to boycotts and withdrawals from the chamber to register their protest, and to join the opposition forces protesting in the streets outside. Comparatively speaking, Sri Lanka looked startlingly like an African one-party system in this period.

The gap between the professed ideals and the actual practices of the regime led to increasing opposition in the society. The gap was only too apparent to the general public within which distrust towards the regime and its promises grew apace. This general decline in the legitimacy of the regime was accelerated by the growing alienation and hostility of some of the most politicized and organized groups in the society, such as the active supporters of the major opposition parties, workers and trade unions, journalists, and the educated unemployed youth of both communities. The

UNP antagonized key leaders of the opposition parties by its draconian actions: Sirimavo Bandaranaike and her closest advisors within the SLFP after 1978, the TULF leadership after the failure of the District Development Councils experiment and fraudulent elections in Jaffna in 1981, and Rohana Wijeweera of the radical Sinhalese People's Liberation Front (JVP) after the presidential elections of 1982. The criticisms of the 1978 Constitution made by the SLFP and TULF at the time of its promulgation gained resonance and their promises to replace the existing system with a new one gained a new urgency and relevance. The two parties lost the ambivalence that seemed to characterize their behavior between 1977-1982 when despite their demands for a different system, they had functioned very much in the manner of a 'loyal' opposition. After 1982, they firmly became a part of what might be categorised as the 'semi-loyal' opposition. The JVP, with its base amongst the educated unemployed Sinhala youth in the Southwest of the island, failed to gain political power through open parliamentary elections in 1982. Faced with allegations regarding its democratic bonafides and repression following the 1983 violence, the JVP began to organize as a clandestine force once again, mobilizing the Sinhalese population against the regime and aiming to capture power through a violent coup d'etat. It swung from the ranks of the 'loyal' opposition to become once again a force in the ranks of the 'disloyal' opposition, like the LTTE and the other militant Tamil groups.

Protracted Violence and an 'Unsolvable Problem'

It is the tragedy of Sri Lanka in the eighties that its political leadership chose the strategy of repression as its central one to deal with its opposition. Following the 1983 ethnic violence, which leading figures in the government were implicated in sponsoring, the polity speedily descended into a state of civil war between the government forces and the militant Tamil youth groups fighting for a separate state. The challenge posed by the forces of the 'disloyal' opposition was exacerbated by a separate challenge posed by the JVP after 1986.

Increasing use was made of violence by the UNP to deal with these challenges resulting in a militarization of the society. Extraordinary legislation allowing arbitrary powers to the army and police forces were passed in an effort to maintain order and control. Increasing funds were channelled to equip and train more and better armed forces. The budget for the Sri Lankan armed forces rose in relative terms from around 3 percent in 1977 to a quarter of all government expenditure by 1990 (Lanka Guardian, 15 October 1990; Economist, 19 January 1991). This increase took place at a time when, in absolute terms, the total expenditure by the government rose from SL Rs. 9.7 billion in 1977 to Rs. 173 billion in 1993 (Central Bank of Sri

Lanka, Annual Report(s)), The number of men in the armed forces increased ten-fold from 12,000 in 1984 to a reported 120,000 by 1994.

The situation in the Northeast became increasingly complex over the eighties. The moderate Tamil leadership found itself increasingly marginalized after the 1983 riots with the initiative being seized by the militant youth groups. The ethnic conflict acquired an international dimension with Tamils fleeing to asylum in neighboring India and gaining support, funds, and training there. In the hostilities that followed between the armed forces and the Tamil militants, it is estimated that some 35,000 persons, includings civilian casualties, died by 1994 in the conflict in the north-east of the island.

Even as hostilities between the government forces and the Tamil militants escalated, there were successive rounds of talks between the government and the TULF (and even the militants) after 1983, often held at the urging of India. However, in my view, the recent actions of the UNP - the frequent and partisan manipulation of the Constitution, the controversial deprivation of the civic rights of Sirimavo Bandaranaike, and the manipulation and fraud in the 1982 presidential and parliamentary elections, prevented a peaceful resolution of the conflict. In the subsequent period, S. Bandaranaike and her party actively opposed any and all efforts by the UNP to reach any accomodation with the Tamils: as evident in her boycott and opposition of the DDC negotiations and elections in 1981, the 'All-Party Conference' held belatedly in 1984, the peace talks in 1985 and 1986, the Indo-Sri Lankan Accord in 1987, and the ensuing provincial council elections in 1987-1988. The threat of her playing the 'communal card' against any concessions made by the UNP regime to the Tamils made the regime wary of conceding anything substantial in that direction even if it had been of a mind to do so, making the problem relating to the ethnic issue an 'unsolvable' one for the UNP.

The narrow majority gained by President Premadasa in the Parliament, after he assumed the leadership of the UNP in 1988, denied him the luxury enjoyed by his predecessor, J. R. Jayawardene, of arbitrary constitutional amendments. Yet, the task of re-establishing legitimacy and good governance by the regime proved an elusive one. In certain respects, the situation worsened with the President using the more direct levers of control and coercion available to him as the chief executive in control of the government, the administration, the majority in Parliament, and the ruling party. Indeed, his position of chief of the security and armed forces acquired a new and sinister character, with the armed forces being used extensively or clandestinely intermixed with civilian goon squads loyal to the UNP to serve as secretive death squads to liquidate the clandestine JVP in the late 1980s. The brutal violence that became the norm in the society in this period can be gauged from the fact that, as estimated by human rights groups, some 66,000 deaths or disappearances carried out by both the JVP and government forces took place in the Southwest of the island between the years 1987-1990. And it is alleged that even after the insurgency was put down, the intelligence network remained under the President's direct command and continued to be used for the surveillance of and tapping the phones of politicians belonging to both the ruling party as well as the opposition.

Despite this, the actions of the President did gain him a limited amount of legitimacy through the results he produced. His success in crushing the JVP threat gained him support amongst the upper and middle classes, particularly those concentrated in the urban areas. His efforts to cease hostilities with the LTTE showed him to be receptive to discussions to resolve the ethnic issue and gained him a following amongst the ethnic minority groups.

However, although Sirimavo Bandaranaike's civic rights were restored to her for the 1988 presidential election in which she fought as the leading opposition presidential candidate against Premadasa, she alleged that there had been irregularities in the course of the election which was held under a state of emergency (to cope with the JVP onslaught). She and the SLFP remained antagonistic towards the ruling party and refused to cooperate on important initiatives such as the All Party Conference appointed by the President to consider amendments to the Constitution in an effort to resolve the ethnic problem.

The politics of violence reached a new phase in the late eighties and early nineties when assassinations of political figures began to take place with increasing frequency. While the LTTE killing of the SLFP-supported Mayor Durayappah in Jaffna in 1973 signalled the beginning of this trend, and internecine killings between the various Tamil youth groups were reported to have occurred with increasing frequency after the late 1970s, the killing of public figures more recently reached an unprecedented level even by world standards (and here one is taking into consideration groups with fearsome reputations such as the IRA, PLO, Shining Path, and even the Colombian drug mafia). To name only the most important incidents, the LTTE has commonly been held responsible for the assassinations of A. Amirthalingam, V. Yogeswaran and Sam Thambimuttu (all leading members of the moderate TULF), most of the leaders of rival Tamil militant youth groups (some of whom were cooperating with the government after 1987), the Minister of Defense Ranjan Wijeratne, the navy chief Clancy Fernando, a group of generals along with army chief General Denzil Kobbekaduwe, the former Minister of Security Lalith Athulathmudali, President Premadasa, and most recently in October 1994 one of the architects of the Indo-Sri Lankan Accord, Gamini Dissanayake. With the successive assassinations of leading political figures, most often in the heart of Colombo or having high security protection, the unmistakable message sent to all segments of the elite was that no one was immune to the attacks of the Tamil Tigers. Timed as the killings have often been to coincide with election campaigns, they were clearly intended to disrupt and damage the established constitutional and democratic political process by having a chilling effect on it, to expose the vulnerability of elections to a climate of fear, and to highlight the tenuousness of the power held by those in positions of dominance and leadership. In May 1991, the LTTE made world headlines with its assassination of the former Indian Prime Minister and sponsor of the Indo-Sri Lankan Accord, Rajiv Gandhi, in the course of his campaign for re-election. During its violent resurgence in 1987, the JVP targeted leading figures of the government, almost succeeding in bombing the whole Cabinet out of existence during a meeting in the old Parliament, injuring Rajiv Gandhi when he was receiving a guard of honor on signing the Indo-Sri Lankan Accord, assassinating the current President's popular and politically ascendant filmstar-husband Vijaya Kumaratunge for speaking out in favor of the Accord and the possibilities it offered for moving positively towards a resolution of the ethnic question.

The degree to which the political environment in Sri Lanka had been vitiated by the acute distrust and manipulation indulged in by the UNP power holders during their long tenure of seventeen years was only too evident in the allegations that circulated in the capital city of Colombo that the 'forces of darkness' allied to the ruling UNP were responsible for the assassination of Lalith Athulathmudali in the lead-up to the May 1993 provincial council elections and again for Gamini Dissanayake's assassination in the course of the presidential election campaign in October 1994. The publicly proclaimed version of the LTTE being responsible in each case was greeted with scepticism by significant and influential segments of the public belonging to both communities.

As a consequence of the political polarization and conflict in the society, previously quiescent groups, such as the Muslims on the East Coast, also started mobilizing in defence or in assertion of their rights, complicating an already tangled ethnic situation and the possibilities for its resolution. Hill-country Tamils have mobilized to unitedly back their leader, S. Thondaman, in reaping rewards for each act of cooperation extended to the UNP regime, the most crucial of these being the gaining of citizenship for significant numbers of them. But getting impatient and frustrated with the continued discrimination practized against them and their continued economic deprivation, a large number of estate Tamil youth have reportedly developed sympathies for militant Sri Lankan Tamil youth groups.

The political role of women has also expanded in a remarkable, even bizarre, manner as a consequence of the environment of war, violence, and assassinations in Sri Lanka. On the one side, many women and girls in the erstwhile highly patriarchal and orthodox Sri Lankan Tamil society have increasingly trained as fighters and commanders for the LTTE. Some of them form crack units of women ready to carry out suicide bomb attacks, as highlighted in the assassinations of R. Gandhi and Dissanayake. On the other side, wives of assassinated Sinhalese leaders have taken up, or offered themselves, as the political equivalences of their husbands: as evident in the cases of the widows of Kumaratunge, Athulathmudali, Premadasa, and Dissanayake. In this respect, they follow in the footsteps of Mrs. Bandaranaike who did the same three decades earlier. It could be hypothesized that the high class and caste position of the latter group of women (except notably Mrs. Premadasa) in a society deferential to traditional social status and hierarchy was used to minimize the damage done to the politico-social fabric by the assassinations.

Realizing the dangers inherent in this destructive trend of events, a senior SLFP MP Mangala Moonesinghe took the initiative to set up a bipartisan All-Party Select Committee in 1991-93, with the implicit backing of the SLFP and with the blessings of President Premadasa. The Committee invited proposals for resolving the ethnic issue, but because of the continued political manoevering and posturing by the major parties, it failed to get concrete submissions from the three leading parties in the drama: the UNP, the SLFP, and the LTTE. Also, no agreement could be reached with Tamil and other minority political groups on the critical issue of the merger of the Northern and Eastern Provinces and of the powers to be devolved to the provincial councils. The situation was complicated by the provision in the 1978 Constitution which requires that any change in the unitary character of the state to a federal system needs to be approved by a two-thirds majority in Parliament and a majority of the votes in a popular referendum.

The result of the partisan actions of the UNP to maintain itself in power, heedless of the norms of democratic behavior and politics, was a decline in legitimacy of the established system for significant segments of the opposition. This decline in legitimacy was sought to be filled by the increasing use of violence by the regime as well as its extremist opponents, exacerbating a decline in moderate politics and increasing the political polarization in the society. The efforts made by the ruling party to gain bipartisan support to make critically needed constitutional changes to the established political framework to overcome the deep ethnic divisions on the island, ended in failure since such cooperation was impossible for it to come by. The ethnic problem became an 'unsolvable problem' for the UNP, making its task of democratic governance virtually impossible. The option of using constitution-making as a political resource to resolve the issues at conflict proved an elusive one due to its abuse in the preceding period by the ruling party.

The Current Conjuncture and Hope of a Solution

Looking at the severity of the crisis of legitimacy in Sri Lanka in the eighties, it is surprising that democracy survived at all on the island. Yet, as a result of the elections in late 1994 and the presidential elections in November 1994, there is reason for hope again that the new regime may be able to resolve the political crisis and to establish a new and broadly accepted constitutional consensus.

Chandrika Kumaratunge led the SLFP-dominated People's Alliance in the two elections on the platform of solving the ethnic problem through negotiation to usher in peace once again as well as changing the executive presidential system of government back to a parliamentary one. The depth to which Kumaratunge's campaign promises resonated in the hearts of her people was only too evident in the unprecedented 62.3per cent vote that she won in the presidential election. The highest vote won previously had been by J. R. Jayawardene in the controversial presidential election of 1982 when he got 52.9 per cent of the vote. Moreover, she got this vote in an election held sixteen days after the assassination of Dissanayake and despite suspicions that the Tigers were the group most likely to have been responsible for the assassination. The costs in material and human terms of political manipulation, opportunism, and war had become only too clear; and there existed a weariness with war on the island and a deep, widely felt yearning for a peaceful settlement of the ethnic problem and for good governance.

The two issues focused on by Kumaratunge are clearly linked in that, among other things, a devolution of power in the direction of regional autonomy as a solution to the ethnic problem will also put limits on the executive and legislative powers currently concentrated at the center in the hands of the executive president. The introduction of a parliamentary system would make the chief executive, the prime minister, dependent on a majority in Parliament to remain in power. At present the President appoints and chairs the cabinet and is able to dissolve the legislature at will, but remains himself (or herself) virtually unaccountable to these institutions for the power he exercises through the administration and the armed forces for the full duration of his tenure. The provisions to impeach a president for ongoing or past wrongdoings are so demanding as to be virtually impossible to fulfill. Change of the political structure was, therefore, viewed as imperative to increase democratic accountability at the national level, while allowing for greater popular participation and autonomy at the regional level. Kumaratunge boldly promised a change to a parliamentary system by July 1995.

The smoothness with which President Kumaratunge will be able to implement her promises is not clear yet, though many of the signs have been favorable. After the August elections, she started with great imagination and political will to establish channels of communication with the LTTE without whose cooperation no solution to the ethnic problem other than a military one could be carried out. Without wasting any time, the new leader opened talks with the Tamil Tigers with the goal of resolving the major differences between the two sides before too long and appointed a committee to look into the changes that would be needed to revert the governmental structure back to a parliamentary one by the middle of 1995. After initially antagonizing the army by making critical remarks about it in a public interview, Kumaratunge included an army and navy commander in the committee formed for the second round of talks with the Tigers. Despite the setback to the peace process that Dissanayake's assassination constituted, the government went ahead with confidence-building measures and promises of relief and rehabilitation for the Tamil areas.

The political courage and skill the new President needs to negotiate the political minefields that surround her has already become evident in the short time that she has been in power. She opened negotiations with the LTTE, agreed to a ceasefire, and relaxed travel and transport restrictions *vis-à-vis* the LTTE and the Tamil population in the North, even while the results of investigations into past assassinations remain underway. She has appointed two commissions to investigate corruption and abuses of power under the UNP regime, even while she needs its cooperation to resolve the ethnic problem and effect the desired constitutional changes. She has risked the hostility of the army by publicly admonishing it and clipping its wings. The alleged powers and opportunities for material gain for strategically placed individuals in the armed forces were also diminished by the implementation of a ceasefire. The very size the military has grown to, its substantial share in the government budget, its key political role in executing the war, all highlight its increased importance in the island's politics. The dangerous, literally explosive, ground the President is treading on was dramatically emphasized in mid-January 1995 when 19 ounces of plastic explosives of the type used by the LTTE were found in the bags of three soldiers detailed to the personal security of the President and her family at her residence!

Most important of all, despite Kumaratunge's efforts, the Tigers proved unwilling to discuss the hard issues relating to the 'bargain' to be struck by the two sides. They probably felt threatened by the momentum the peace process was generating in favor of the government and launched an attack on 19 April 1995, on the armed forces to arrest the process, reverting to a situation of war again. At the time of writing in late July 1995, hopes of peace have been belied by the attack and the new constitutional package is still awaited. Concerned supporters and sympathizers of the regime have expressed a desire for the government to resolve the ethnic issue without any further delay while there is support in the public, both

Tamil and non-Tamil, for the peace process and her regime.[4] With Kumaratunge lacking an absolute majority in Parliament, she will need to get the support of the UNP to reach the two-thirds majority needed to effect any amendments to the Constitution. She will also need to get a positive majority vote in a popular referendum to change particular key provisions of the existing Constitution, such as those relating to the unitary state and the presidential structure of government. Whether the UNP will cooperate with the SLFP in effecting these changes, will depend on the political conjuncture and the agreements struck by its leadership about which little can be said a priori. Faced with non-cooperation from the UNP, as President under the existing 'Gaullist' Constitution, Kumaratunge can directly refer the issue to the people by dissolving the Parliament and asking the people to vote in a new one which will support her efforts to institute a new constitutional consensus. Before she can successfully do that, however, she has to mark out a stable political ground for herself. This involves not only subduing the Tigers to a subordinate position in the Northeast, but also crafting an acceptable consensus between her Sinhalese support base and the non-LTTE minority groups. The shape of the final agreement itself is difficult to predict at this point of time. Will it include a merger of the Northern and Eastern Province or, as is more likely, a partial merger with a redrawing of the boundaries of the Eastern Province, as espoused by the SLFP? Will it deliver a substantial devolution of powers in a formal structure akin to a federal one as is being rightly demanded by the Tamils based on their past experience, or will it do so only within a unitary framework? To forge a consensus will by no means be easy. What is clear is that if an agreement on a new political framework can be achieved without too much delay and controversy, and is backed by the relevant parties, it will be gladly accepted by the war-weary public in a referendum.

Conclusion

Thus the crisis of legitimacy and governance that has been faced recently in Sri Lanka has had both long-term and recent roots. Issues of systemic legitimacy were raised by significant sectors of the population in re-

4 That public opinion seems to be hardening on the question is indicated by the results of a recent poll of 2,260 individuals taken in 18 districts, excluding those in the Northern and Eastern provinces. It reports a decline in support for a political solution with the LTTE from 66 per cent of those polled in November 1994 to 32 per cent in June 1995. In contrast, those in favor of defeating the LTTE militarily and then negotiating with the other Tamil groups has risen from 21 per cent to 64 per cent in the same period. On the question of abolishing the executive presidency, given the current situation, between March and June of this year there was a 5 per cent decline to 47 per cent in those who favored its abolition versus the same number who favored retaining it in toto or merely modifying it. *Sunday Times*, 23 July 1995.

gard to the content and the process by which each of Sri Lanka's constitutions was passed. Within this the dissatisfaction of the Sri Lankan Tamil elite with the instituted arrangements was particularly made evident repeatedly, but neglected. The issues gained added depth in the wake of controversial and often highly questionable changes that were effected to the established rules and institutions by a ruling party or coalition. The most important of these such as the citizenship and franchise acts of 1948-49, Sinhala Only act of 1956, the predominance of the National Assembly in 1972, and the presidential system in 1978 critically changed the basic elements of the compact on which a particular consensus had existed. In recent decades, sharp gaps between regime pronouncements and practice to serve partisan and petty interests of the ruling party sharply undermined the regime's legitimacy. As seen in detail, this was only too true of the UNP's long tenure in power, with tragic results.

The decline in the consensus supporting the established 'rules of the game', when these rules were so frequently and arbitrarily changed, led to a decline in trust and consent as the basis of governance. The growing alienation and opposition to the UNP regime resulted in a decline in the moderate politics of a 'loyal' opposition, and the growing shift in support for the 'semi-loyal' and 'disloyal' opposition. In terms of the understanding of rational politics adopted by one of the co-editors in this volume, in Sri Lanka the alternatives to rule-bound behavior came to be seen as increasingly necessary because needed reforms by the 'managers of law and order' were not being undertaken. Ordinary people began to consider it more costly to obey the rules than to break them.[5]

The process of constitution-making has, therefore, not been successfully utilized as a political resource in Sri Lanka. Fateful in this process has been the unwillingness of the Sri Lankan ruling elite, in power at a particular moment, to forgo or give up some power and the advantages that accrue from it by constraining itself to play according to 'fair' and 'just' rules in order to maintain the longterm legitimacy of the political system. For this to happen, as the other co-editor of this volume puts it, 'Politicians must be statesmen in order to act accordingly, they must resist the temptation of equating their own position with legitimacy and all challenge to this position as fitna which must be suppressed'.[6] As seen in the article, starting with D. S. Senanayake, through the UF government and down to the UNP regime, it has been not only the Tamil minorities, but the leading opposition groups within the majority community which were sought to be marginalized in the constitution-making process each time. The danger of

5 See in this volume Subrata K. Mitra, 'Legitimacy, Governance and Political Institutions in India after Independence', pp. 17 ff.

6 See in this volume Dietmar Rothermund, 'Conflict as a Challenge to Legitimacy: A Historical Perspective', pp. 7 ff.

something similar happening in the course of the current efforts to restructure the political system, if cooperation between the UNP and the PA government breaks down, remains very high. However, if the constitutional package represents a reasonable set of rules incorporating a strategically broad consensus based on significant sections of the majority and minority communities of the island and is approved by the people at a referendum, it would constitute a major achievement. In such an eventuality, President Kumaratunge will have earned herself a place in history by her success in being able to 're-equilibrate' the democratic structures on the island and thereby re-establish their legitimacy.

Sri Lanka - Crisis in Legitimacy

CHRISTIAN WAGNER

Introduction

Looking at the present situation in Sri Lanka one faces a paradox. On the one hand Sri Lanka has one of the longest democratic traditions in Asia with reasonably fair elections, high voter turnout and regular change of government. The long democratic tradition since independence in 1948 seems to indicate a high degree of legitimacy of the political system. On the other hand Sri Lanka faces serious problems with regard to its political stability. Since 1983, more than 30.000 people lost their lives in the civil war between Tamil separatist groups and the Sri Lankan army which is tearing the country apart. The rebellion of armed Sinhalese youth groups under the banner of the *People's Liberation Front* (Janatha Vimukti Peramuna, JVP) in opposition to the *Indo-Sri Lankan Peace Accord* caused another 20.000 to 30.000 death from 1987 to 1989. The country is governed by emergency regulations which curtail civil liberties and seems to become a 'guided democracy'[1] like some Southeast-Asian countries. The internal conflicts caused a sharp increase of political violence and human rights violations, and questioned the legitimacy of the political system as a whole.

To shed some light on this paradox this paper will deal with the crisis of legitimacy in Sri Lanka. In the first part different western and indigenous conceptions of legitimacy will be examined. The second part will give a short overview of the reasons and different stages of the present conflict which finally led to civil war. The third part will take a look at possible solutions of the conflict. The last part will examine the change of government in 1994 in regard to a peaceful settlement.

Theoretical Background

Legitimacy belongs to the most important categories of the analysis of political systems. There exists, however, a wide range of possible definitions. Although Weber did not give an explicit definition of legitimacy, it was central to his concept of rule and power. On the one hand, the belief in legitimacy of power[2] denoted empirical, functional and structural aspects of legitimate rule and was closely connected with the performance and sta-

1 M. Moore, 'Guided Democracy' in Sri Lanka: The Electoral Dimension', *The Journal of Commonwealth and Comparative Politics*, Vol. 32, No. 1 (1994), pp. 1-30.

2 See M. Weber, *Wirtschaft und Gesellschaft* (Tübingen, 1972), p. 122.

bility of a political system. On the other hand, the various kinds of legitimacy were grouped into three ideal types of legitimate rule: traditional, charismatic and rational-legal.[3] Political analysts like Lipset, Linz, and Easton tried to explain legitimacy under the conditions of modern societies where legitimacy has to be build on democratic consensus and acceptance of power rather than on force. Lipset defined legitimacy as 'the capacity of the system to engender and maintain the belief that the existing political institutions are the most appropriate ones for the society'.[4] Moreover he discussed the relationship between legitimacy and effectiveness of the political system, which he defined as the 'extent to which the system satisfies the basic functions of government.'[5] For Linz legitimacy was 'the belief that in spite of shortcomings and failures, the political institutions are better than any others that might be established and therefore can demand obedience.'[6] He also pointed out, that 'no political system is legitimate for 100 percent'[7] and that legitimacy also 'implicitly involve(s) comparisons among alternatives (real or imaginary), and their absence assures a minimum of support even when an outside observer would assume a widespread lack of legitimacy.'[8] Easton introduced the difference between diffuse and specific forms of support for the political system. Whereas diffuse forms of support are regarded to be independent from the output, specific support is dependent on the output of the system.[9] Being a diffuse form of support, legitimacy of authorities and regimes can be derived by three sources - ideological and structural principles and personal qualities.[10]

Common to theoretical debates, whether legitimacy was on the decline in Western systems or not, was the problem how legitimacy could be operationalized. Often regarded as attitude of the people towards actors and institutions of the political system, legitimacy could be measured with the help of surveys giving a positive or negative feedback on the effectiveness of the system. But how can legitimacy be evaluated under the conditions of a developing society where similar surveys do not exist? Because of the lack of empirical data, an alternative approach would be to indicate various formal conditions for legitimate democratic rule, for example regular free and fair elections, a change of government and freedom

3 See M. Kopp, H.-P. Müller, *Herrschaft und Legitimität in modernen Industriegesellschaften. Eine Untersuchung der Ansätze von Max Weber, Niklas Luhmann, Claus Offe und Jürgen Habermas* (München, 1980), pp. 15-17.

4 S.M. Lipset, *Political Man, The Social Basis of Politics* (New York, 1959), p. 77.

5 S.M. Lipset, 1959, p. 77.

6 J.J. Linz, 'Legitimacy of Democracy and the Socioeconomic System', in: M. Dogan (ed.), *Comparing Pluralist Democracies: Strains on Legitimacy* (Boulder, 1988), p. 65.

7 J.J. Linz 1988, p. 66.

8 J.J. Linz 1988, p. 65.

9 D. Easton, *A Framework for Political Analysis* (Englewood Cliffs, 1965), pp. 124-126.

10 D. Easton, *A System Analysis of Political Life* (Chicago, 1979), pp. 286-287.

of expression. But, as the paradox of the Sri Lankan development showed, it is difficult to evaluate the positive content of such indicators. Despite regular elections and a change of government, and a comparatively high standard of living[11], the ongoing civil war in Sri Lanka shows the shortcomings of this approach. It seems easier, therefore, to measure the negative effects, like occurrence of riots, human rights violations, the number of coups d'états, and the absence of political rights and civil liberties, like for example freedom of expression and free and fair elections, to demonstrate the decline of legitimacy.[12]

Concepts of Legitimacy in Sri Lanka

The construction of legitimacy as a set of common principles within the population and as a functioning political system was one of the main tasks of 'nation-building' after independence. Sri Lanka seemed to have more favourable conditions than many other countries to be successful in this respect. The introduction of general suffrage with the *Donoughmore-Constitution* in 1931 opened the way for the first elections in 1931 and 1936. The newly created *State Council* almost completey handed over the internal affairs to the indigenous elite. The *Soulbury-Constitution* of 1947 gave the country a Westminster system of governance and a western concept of legitimacy which was supported by the westernized elite of Sinhalese, Tamil and Muslim politicians who founded the *United National Party* (UNP). Since 1947, ten parliamentary elections brought a regular change of government between the two major Sinhalese parties with one exception in 1989.[13]

Whereas the UNP could be regarded as the promoter of a secular state during the first years after independence, it was the *Sri Lanka Freedom Party* (SLFP) which took up Buddhist concepts of legitimacy and introduced them in the political arena. Taken from the background of Theravada-Buddhism these traditions were reinterpreted and adapted to the conditi-

[11] Looking at the *Human Development Index* of the UN, Sri Lanka is the country with the highest social development in South Asia, see UNDP, *Human Development Report* (Washington, 1994).

[12] The annual surveys of Freedom House give an overview on the development of democratic systems and civil liberties. Sri Lanka is regarded as a 'partly free' country, see Freedom House Survey Team, *Freedom in the World. The Annual Survey of Political Rights and Civil Liberties 1993-1994* (New York, 1994), p. 512.

[13] For the historical development of the conflict, see W.H. Wriggins, *Ceylon. Dilemmas of a New Nation* (New Delhi, 1960); R.N. Kearney, *Communalism and Language in the Politics of Ceylon* (Durham, 1967); S. Ponnambalam, *Sri Lanka. The National Question and the Tamil Liberation Struggle* (London, 1983); J. Manor (ed.), *Sri Lanka in Change and Crisis* (London, 1984); K.M. de Silva, *Managing Ethnic Tensions in Multi-Ethnic Societies: Sri Lanka 1880-1985* (Lanham, 1986); for a literary description of the events see W. McGowan, *Only Man is Vile. The Tragedy of Sri Lanka* (London, 1993).

ons of a modern democratic system by certain factions of the Buddhist reform movement.[14] One of the main points is the concept of the just ruler who 'as a universal monarch as described in canonical Buddhist texts ... is a "bodhisattva", i.e. a Buddha-to-be ... [and] the promoter and protector of Buddhism'.[15] The idea of monarchy was replaced by a democratic system, which should be controlled by the Buddhist majority. The state was regarded to have a special responsibility for religious institutions and was 'considered responsible for the material welfare of the people'[16] in order to create a just society. At the same time Sri Lanka was regarded as the holy island of Buddhism with the Sinhalese being the chosen people.

These ideas formed the core of a Buddhist nationalism which became one of the most important ideologies in the country. But there has been also a strong dissent among the Buddhist *sangha* on the involvement of monks in politics. The *All-Ceylon Buddhist Congress* (ACBC), the leading lay Buddhist organization, strongly criticized the attempts of monks to enter the political arena on religious grounds.[17] Many of the leaders of the so-called *political bhikkhus* (monks) had been to India and were inspired by the Indian nationalistic movement and by leftist ideas. Subsequently they supported marxist parties like the *Lanka Samasamaja Pakshaya* (LSSP) and the *Communist Party* (CP).[18] In 1946 they formed the *Lanka Eksath Bhikkhu Mandalaya* (LEBM, Ceylon Union of Bhikkhus) as their political platform which supported socialist ideas.[19] Their agitation was mainly directed against the rule of the UNP whose westernized, English speaking upper class still monopolized political power. English was still the dominant language in the administration and higher education thereby excluding large parts of the Sinhalese-educated intelligentsia. Therefore the *bhikkhus* tried to prevent the language settlement where Sinhalese and Tamil were regarded as national languages which should replace English. At the same time, this agitation was directed against the educational advantages enjoyed by the Tamil minority.[20]

In 1951, S.W.R.D. Bandaranaike split from the UNP and founded the SLFP which 'offered a home to those who rejected the concepts of a poly-

[14] For an overview of the development of the Buddhist reform movement, see K. Malalgoda, *Buddhism in Sinhalese Society, 1750-1900: A Study of Religious Revival and Change* (Berkeley, 1976).

[15] H. Bechert, 'S.W.R.D. Bandaranaike and the Legitimation of Power through Buddhist Ideals', in: B.C. Smith (ed.), *Religion and Legitimation of Power in Sri Lanka* (1978), p. 201.

[16] H. Bechert, 1978, p. 201.

[17] See K.M. de Silva, 'Buddhist Revivalism, Nationalism, and Politics in Modern Sri Lanka', in: J.W. Björkman (ed.), *Fundamentalism, Revivalists and Violence in South Asia* (New Delhi, 1988), p. 135.

[18] See U. Phadnis, *Religion and Politics in Sri Lanka* (London, 1976), p. 163.

[19] See S.J. Tambiah, *Buddhism Betrayed? Religion, Politics, and Violence in Sri Lanka* (Chicago, 1992), pp. 18-21.

[20] K.M. de Silva, 1988, p. 136.

ethnic polity, of a Sri Lankan nationalism, and of a secular state.'[21] In 1956 the leftist MEP (*Mahajana Eksath Peramuna*) coalition under the leadership of the SLFP won a landmark victory over the UNP with the slogan 'Sinhala Only'. With the help of *bhikkhu* activists which had formed the *Eksath Bhikkhu Peramuna* (EBP, United Front of the Monks) before the election, the MEP was able to mobilize substantial parts of the population on the language question especially in the rural areas.[22] It may be difficult today to share the optimistic view that the victory of the SLFP in 1956 was the 'most important single event in the history of the island since the British take-over of the Kandyan kingdom.'[23] But nevertheless, it can be regarded as a watershed election because Buddhist ideas of political participation and legitimacy had successfully entered the political arena. Under the conditions of democratic competition and the given majority of the Sinhalese[24] it became quite clear that both major political parties, UNP and SLFP, would have to use nationalist Buddhist propaganda in the future in order to win the majority of votes.

The influence of Buddhist ideas grew considerably from 1956 on. The constitution of 1972 under the SLFP government of Sirimavo Bandaranaike and the constitution of 1978 under the UNP government of J. R. Jayawardene assured state protection and promotion to Buddhism in accordance with Buddhist ideals. Yet, the claim of Buddhist superiority and state protection was not an acceptable idea of legitimacy for the other minorities. It seems to be ironic that the demand of Buddhist nationalists to preserve the unity of Sri Lanka as a Buddhist heritage paved the way for a civil war which promoted the further fragmentation of the island.

Apart from western and Buddhist concepts of legitimacy, a third concept was introduced in 1977. In reaction to the policy of sinhalization, various Tamil parties joined together to form the *Tamil United Liberation Front* (TULF) for the election in 1977. They claimed the right to self-determination for the Tamil speaking community and demanded a separate *Tamil Eelam* state. Although the structure of an independent Tamil state was and still is disputed even among the Tamils, it became obvious that the Tamil minority was no longer willing to accept the legitimacy of Sinhalese authority.[25] The demand for a separate state showed the deep

21 K.M. de Silva, 1988, p. 135.

22 See S.J. Tambiah, 1992, p. 43.

23 H. Bechert, 1978, p. 209.

24 According to the last census the proportion of the different ethnic groups is as follows: Sinhalese 74,0 per cent, Sri-Lanka Tamils 12,6 per cent, Moors 7,1% percent, Indian Tamils 5,5 percent, Others 0,8 per cent, see Central Bank of Sri Lanka, *Economic and Social Statistics of Sri Lanka 1991* (Colombo, 1992), p. 9.

25 For the development of Tamil nationalism and the role of language, see D. Hellmann-Rajanayagam, 'Tamilen, Tamilsprache und Tamilidentität = Tamilnationalismus?', in: D. Hellmann-Rajanayagam, D. Rothermund (eds.), *Nationalstaat und Sprachkonflikte in Süd- und Südostasien* (Stuttgart, 1992), pp. 127-156. For the different conceptions of Tamil Eelam by the

political contradictions between the Sinhalese and the Tamils[26] on various problems which felt the participants unable to solve in the various consultations since 1957. In the election of 1977 the TULF won all the seats in the Tamil areas therefore achieving a strong backing for its cause. At first, this demand seemed to be only another stage in the political conflict. But it turned out to be the prelude for a civil war which shaped the political development in the 1980s. The legitimacy of the political system was now challenged by the concept of a separate state and declined by a sharp increase of political violence and human rights violations even in the Sinhalese areas.[27]

From Political Conflict to Civil War

The landmark victory of the SLFP in 1956 caused considerable changes in the economic and political system.[28] High education standards and growing expectations for job opportunities did not match with the economic realities of a developing country. Nationalist Buddhist propaganda argued that the Sinhalese people were discriminated against in favour of the Tamils' employment in the public sector. These claims could be supported by statistics and that opened the door for a policy of sinhalization.[29] The idea of personal educational merit with regard to the entrance to certain careers was replaced by the idea that ethnic quotas were the right instrument to overcome the perceived disadvantages of the Sinhalese.

That affirmative action in favour of the Sinhalese had a well calculated political character was obvious from the beginning. Apart from Sinhalese, the Moors (Muslims) and the Indian Tamils were even more disadvantaged concerning their share in public sector employment and in the field of higher education. Yet, the preferential policy was not extended to improve the socio-economic position of other minorities according to their share of the total population. It remained strictly limited to the Sinhalese and served as a powerful instrument of patronage for the two major parties.[30] Sinhalization became closely connected with language,

---

separatist groups, see D. Hellmann-Rajanayagam, 'The Tamil Militants - Before the Accord and After', *Pacific Affairs*, Vol. 61, No. 4 (1988/89), pp. 612-613.

26 The term 'Tamil' will be used only for the Sri-Lanka Tamils, not for the Indian Tamil residents in Sri Lanka who were disenfranchized for the most part after Independence.

27 B. Olsen, Sri Lanka, in: P. Baehr, H. Hey, J. Smith, T. Swinehart (eds.), *Human Rights in Developing Countries Yearbook 1994* (Deventer, Boston, 1994), pp. 341-395; J. Rösel, *Sri Lanka. Die Entwicklungshilfe als Druckmittel zur Einhaltung von Menschenrechten* (Frankfurt a.M., 1993).

28 On the consequences of the election of 1956, see S.J. Tambiah, 1992, pp. 42-57.

29 On the politics of sinhalization, see A. Lamballe, *Le Problème Tamoul à Sri Lanka* (Paris, 1985), pp. 59-138.

30 It should be mentioned that the Sri Lanka Muslim Congress (SLMC) has repeated this kind of argument in favour of the Muslims. The SLMC demands a share of Muslims in public sector

education and employment policy, with land settlement policies and with the question of regional autonomy.[31]

The introduction of Sinhala as the national language after 1956 restricted the access of vernacular educated Tamil youth to the labour market. Especially in the public sector where in the past the Tamils had in certain areas a higher share compared to their share of the total population, their employment opportunities declined. A similar development could be observed in the field of higher education. The politics of the *United Front* (UF) government in the 1970s which introduced the system of standardization and district quotas for university admission restricted mainly Tamil students, and the education statistics show a decline of Tamil students in the following years. Especially these changes in the education system finally sparked off violent reactions by Tamil student organizations from which later evolved the *Liberation Tigers of Tamil Eelam* (LTTE) and other militant groups.

The question of land settlement became another matter of dispute. There are some indications that mainly Sinhalese settlers benefited from the state-sponsored land colonization schemes especially in the eastern province.[32] As a consequence the ratio of the local population changed in favour of the Sinhalese, for example in the Batticaloa/Amparai and Trincomalee districts, which were previously regarded as parts of the Tamil 'homelands'.[33]

The quest for greater regional autonomy sparked off great controversies between Sinhalese and Tamil parties. Since the mid-fifties the Tamil *Federal Party* demanded a federal constitution instead of the unitary state, giving the Tamil regions greater regional autonomy. The main problem concerning decentralization was that it was not merely viewed as a matter of administrative efficiency, but that it became politicized. From the viewpoint of Buddhist nationalism any federal concessions were regarded as the first step to an independent Tamil state which was incompatible with the Buddhist idea of Sri Lanka being a unitary state.

The resistance of Buddhist groups went hand in hand with the tactics of the Sinhalese oppositional parties to obstruct any compromise for a federal state structure. In 1957 the later president J. R. Jayawardene of the UNP initiated a march to the *Tooth Temple* in Kandy, the highest religious centre, in opposition to the *Bandaranaike-Chelvanayakam-Pact*

---

employment which is adequate to their share of 7 per cent of the total population, see C. Wagner, *Die Muslime Sri Lankas* (Freiburg, 1990), pp. 211-226.

31 See U. Phadnis, 'Sri Lanka: Crises of Legitimacy and Integration', in: L. Diamond, J.J. Linz, S.M. Lipset (eds.), *Democracy in Asia* (New Delhi, 1989), pp. 157-159.

32 See C. Manogaran, 'Colonization as Politics: Political Use of Space in Sri Lanka's Ethnic Conflict', in: C. Manogaran, B. Pfaffenberger (eds.), *The Sri Lanka Tamils. Ethnicity and Identity* (Boulder, 1994), pp. 84-125.

33 For statistics demonstrating this development, see Marga-Institute, *The Muslim Community of Sri Lanka* (Colombo, 1985), pp. 100-101.

which made concessions to the Tamils in the question of language and regional administration. In 1968 the UNP-government had to give up the *District Council* scheme for greater regional autonomy after protests and demonstrations of the SLFP and Buddhist groups.

The new constitution of 1972 of the *United Front* government under the leadership of the SLFP of Sirimavo Bandaranaike aggravated the problems between the ethnic groups. Buddhism was given state protection and promotion to the detriment of the other minorities. The Tamil parties could not even get concessions in regard to Tamil becoming an official language. The introduction of the *District Development Councils* (DDC) scheme as a institutional framework for decentralization failed because of the lack of financial ressources and its strong dependence on the center.

In 1983 the conflict entered a new phase. What for a long time had only been a political conflict turned now into open warfare between the Sri Lankan army and the LTTE after riots against Tamils in Colombo.[34] The consultations between the UNP which won the election in 1977 and the TULF on a devolution of power remained without success. Attempts to reach a peaceful solution like the *All-Party-Conference* in 1984 and the *Political Parties Conference* in 1986 failed. On part of the Sinhalese opposition, parties like the SLFP and Buddhist groups still refused any form of decentralization. On part of the Tamils, the LTTE, after ousting the TULF and other separatist groups by killing their political and military leaders, stuck to the goal of Tamil Eelam. The military conflict escalated in the following years and expanded into the Eastern Province which was claimed as a part of Tamil Eelam although it had a mixed population of Tamils, Sinhalese and Muslims.

Since the riots of 1983 the conflict was internationalized and the Indian government became more and more involved. Tamil refugees sought shelter in refugee camps in South India and the LTTE enjoyed considerable military, political and financial support in Tamil Nadu. Some cadres of the LTTE were even trained by the Indian secret service. At first the Indian government acted only as a mediator in peace talks and tried to put pressure on both sides to end the conflict. But India's involvement increased when the UNP-government sought assistance by Israeli and Pakistani military advisors to train the security forces and was asking for US-military support. This move was a threat to India's regional security doctrine according to which conflicts in the region should be solved only with the help of India and without interference of external powers.[35] It caused the Indian government to directly intervene in the conflict. After secret consultations the *Indo-Sri Lankan Peace Accord* was signed in 1987. The so-called *Indian*

[34] See J. Manor, 'Introduction', in: J. Manor (ed.), *Sri Lanka in Change and Crisis* (Beckenham, 1984), pp. 1-31.

[35] D.T. Hagerty, 'India's Regional Security Doctrine', *Asian Survey*, Vol. 31, No. 4 (1993), pp. 351-363.

Peace Keeping Forces (IPKF) were deployed in the North and East to disarm the LTTE.[36] What seemed to be the final chance to find a solution turned out to be only another stage in the escalation of the conflict. The policy to disarm the LTTE failed and the IPKF became involved in heavy fighting with the LTTE.[37]

But, at the same time, there was a strong resistance in the South against the *Accord*. Buddhist organizations like the *Mavbima Surakime Vyaparaya* (MSV, Movement for the Protection of the Motherland) felt threatened by the presence of Indian troops which for them was the first step towards the division of the island. For this reason they started their agitation, mainly by demonstrations and rallies, in order to prevent any federal solution and to maintain their notion of the unity and sovereignty of the country.[38] But the resistance against the *Accord* also became more violent. In opposition of the deployment of the IPKF, the Sinhalese *Janatha Vimukti Peramuna* (People's Liberation Front, JVP) declared war on all supporters of the *Accord*, mainly the rank and file of the UNP. It was the second time that the JVP launched a massive attack against the state. In 1971 the leftist *United Front* government under the leadership of the SLFP was surprised by the rebellion of the JVP and could only defeat it with the help of foreign military assistance.[39] In contrast to 1971, when the JVP cadres were influenced by marxist ideas, the rebellion from 1987 to 1989 was mainly influenced by Buddhist-nationalist ideas. The IPKF was regarded as a forefront of an Indian occupation of the island. As in 1971 the JVP cadres were mainly recruited from the educated youth of the South where poverty, unemployment and frustration had always been high.[40] The terror of the JVP was answered with death squads by the security forces. The human rights situation detoriated rapidly and a climate of terror and violence ruled the South. From 1987 to 1989 nearly 30.000 people where killed in this strife only in the southern parts of the country.

The fighting in the North and East between the IPKF and the LTTE and the violence in the South between the security forces and the JVP caused the UNP government to reconsider its policy. President Premadasa renegotiated the *Accord* with India and achieved a withdrawal of the IPKF

36 See C. Wagner, 'Zurück in die Zukunft: Sri Lanka nach dem indo-srilankischen Beistandsvertrag von 1987', *Asien*, Vol. 34 (1990), pp. 22-36.

37 On the development and differences of the various Tamil separatist groups, see D. Hellmann-Rajanayagam, 'The 'Groups' and the Rise of Militant Secessionism', in: C. Manogaran, B. Pfaffenberger (eds.), *The Sri Lanka Tamils. Ethnicity and Identity* (Boulder, 1994), pp. 169-207.

38 See S.J. Tambiah, 1992, pp. 80-90.

39 See A.C. Alles, *Insurgency 1971. An Account of the April Insurrection in Sri Lanka* (Colombo 1979); R.N. Kearney, 'Educational Expansion and Political Volatility in Sri Lanka: The 1971 Insurrection', *Asian Survey*, Vol. 15 , No. 2 (1975), pp. 727-744.

40 See J. Rösel, 'Geheimnis, Terror und der Zerfall staatlicher Macht auf Sri Lanka', in: T. Scheffler (ed.), *Ethnizität und Gewalt* (Hamburg, 1991), pp. 204-220.

in 1990. The JVP rebellion subsided, after its leaders were killed by the police in 1989.

Since that time the conflict is limited again mainly to the north and east. The country is slowly recovering from the economic losses of the late 1980s and achieved economic growth rates of 5 to 6 per cent in the early 1990s. The army was able to defeat the LTTE in the eastern Province, but could not achieve superiority in the north. The LTTE is still controlling the Jaffna district and a large part of the Vanni area. At the same time the LTTE is building up their own police force units and administration in Jaffna. It seems therefore that the division of the country becomes more and more inevitable.

Solutions for the Conflict

The conflict has always centered around the question, how political, economic and cultural claims of a minority can be secured in a multi-ethnic state. What could have been solved with the help of a federal state structure failed because of ideological prejudices. Singer's ironic remark that '...the Sinhalese have simply never understood the concept of "federalism"[41] shows at the same time the different concepts of legitimacy which could not be brought together. The political concept of Sri Lanka being the holy country of Buddhism and the Sinhalese being its chosen people was not compatible with the western concept of legitimacy where a secular state guaranteed equal rights and opportunities to all citiziens independent of their religious or ethnic affiliations.

Therefore decentralization became politizied and the term federalism became 'linked with the issue of separatism'.[42] An ideological contradiction between unitary and federal state developed which could not be solved peacefully, although all proposals centered around the question of federalism or regional autonomy in one way or the other, like the proposals for *Regional Councils* of Bandaranaike in 1957, the *District Councils* of the UNP-government in 1968, the *District Development Council* of the UF-government in the 1970s and the *Development Councils* of the UNP in the 1980s.[43]

The last stage was reached when the UNP and the Tamil representatives agreed, under the pressure of the Indian government, on a *Provincial Council* (PC) system which was set up after the *Indo-Sri Lankan Accord* of

41 M.R. Singer, 'Sri Lanka's Tamil-Sinhalese Ethnic Conflict. Alternative Solutions', *Asian Survey*, Vol. 32, No. 8, (1992), p. 713.

42 K.M. de Silva, 'Regionalism and Decentralization of Power', in: K.M. de Silva, *Sri Lanka, Problems of Governance* (New Delhi, 1993), p. 102.

43 For an overview of this development, see K.M. de Silva, 1993, pp. 99-126.

1987. Special references were made for the Northern and Eastern province to merge into a joint administrative unit until a referendum in the east would be held over the question of a permanent merger. Again it was the opposition of Buddhist groups and the SLFP which caused the UNP to withhold important concessions to the Tamils like a permanent merger of the eastern and northern provinces to form a single Tamil linguistic unit and a devolution of power which included powers on land colonization policies. Therefore neither the TULF nor the LTTE have accepted the Provincial Councils which came into force after the elections of 1988.[44]

Apart from the question of the future structure of the administration, Sri Lanka will face two other problems which can obstruct the peace process. First, it is unclear in which way armed Tamil groups, especially the LTTE, can be reintegrated into civil life. The struggles between the LTTE and other groups like the *Eelam People Revolutionary Liberation Front* (EPRLF) which controlled the joint *North-East Provinical Council* under the supervision of the IPKF in 1989/1990 showed that rivalries among Tamil groups are still virulent. Even if a democratic decision, which groups or parties will represent the Tamils, is taken, one may doubt that violence between the groups will come to an end immediately. Secondly, the course of the conflict shows that peaceful settlements have always been obstructed by opposition parties. Therefore, the perhaps most difficult challenge for the major Sinhalese parties is to end the vicious circle of nationalist Buddhist propaganda being used to obstruct peaceful solution for the sake of getting the majority of votes.

Prospects of a Peaceful Future

In the 1994 elections the *People's Alliance* (PA), a coalition under the leadership of the SLFP, defeated the UNP and won a narrow majority of one seat in the new Parliament. The election was regarded as 'free and fair'[45] and was an important step to reinstall the democratic system which had lost much credit during the quasi-authoritarian rule of the UNP since 1977. This change of government became possible despite the autocratic rule of the UNP, state influenced press and media, widespread accusations of corruption and patronage, civil war and a high level of political violence in the election campaign with 25 death. The high voter turnout of 76 per cent indicates that at least the Sinhalese people had not lost their faith in the democratic institutions. Because of the boycott of the LTTE no

[44] See A. Shastri, 'Sri Lanka's Provincial Council System. A Solution to the Ethnic Problem?', *Asian Survey*, Vol. 32, No. 8 (1992), p. 727-733.

[45] The International Observer Group, *Report of the Parliamentary General Election of Sri Lanka, 16th August 1994* (Colombo, 1994), p. 23.

regular voting procedures took place in the Tamil areas, where the turnout was only 2,3 per cent in the Jaffna district and 25,3 per cent in the Vanni district.[46]

After having initiated peace talks with the LTTE, Chandrika Kumaratunge, daughter of the former Prime Ministers S.W.R.D. Bandaranaike and S. Bandaranaike, won a clear majority of 62 percent in the presidential election in November 1994 with a voter turnout of 70,5 per cent. She achieved her best results in the three districts of the Eastern province - 87,30 per cent of the votes in Batticaloa, 72,36 per cent in Digamadulla, and 71,62 per cent in Trincomalee - where the civilian population had suffered a lot from the war between the army and the LTTE.[47] This was a strong vote for peace even by the local Tamil population of the area, because in the parliamentary election three months earlier the UNP was the strongest party in the Trincomalee and Digamadulla districts. In January 1995 Kumaratunge was able to conclude a ceasefire with the LTTE and her new proposals aimed at a redrawing of provincial and district boundaries in order to create new administrative units in the north and east. Yet, the ceasefire was broken by the LTTE in April and a new round of the civil war started.

But apart from the ongoing civil war, the conditions for a political settlement have become more complicated after the elections. The *Sri Lanka Muslim Congress* (SLMC), which holds seven seats in the new Parliament and is one of the most important coalition partners of the PA, will use its new powers to achieve far-reaching concessions for the Muslims. As a consequence, any peaceful solution must now be acceptable not only to the Tamils and the Sinhalese but also to the Muslim minority, especially in the eastern province where the SLMC has its strongholds.[48]

Conclusion

Apart from the peculiarities of her political development, Sri Lanka can serve as a case for the argument that a democratic system and its institutions alone do not guarantee legitimacy of power. Horowitz made it clear, that 'democracy is about inclusion and exclusion, about access to power, about the privileges that go with inclusion and the penalties that ac-

46 See C. Wagner, 'Demokratischer Wandel und politische Stabilität? Die Parlaments- und Präsidentschaftswahlen in Sri Lanka 1994', *Asien*, Vol. 54 (1995), pp. 35-47.

47 For the district results of the Presidential election, see Embassy of Sri Lanka, Bonn, *press release*, 11 November 1994.

48 On the role of the Muslims and their involvement in the conflict, see C. Wagner, 'The Muslims of Sri Lanka and their Role in the National Ethnic Conflict', *The Journal of Social Studies*, Vol. 58 (October 1992), pp. 92-112.

company exclusion'.[49] Religious nationalist movements who saw the social and economic problems of modernization in an orthodox way, gained more and more influence and demanded special treatment for the majority population. Democratic competition of the major political parties was fuelled by these demands which excluded the minorities who had no opportunity to obtain equal status with the majority population within the existing democratic system. Therefore, the basic consensus of a multi-ethnic society was undermined, leading to an alternative concept of legitimacy: the right of self-determination and a separate state. The case of Sri Lanka shows that the hope that a democratic system will lead to better governance has to be proved anew in every instance.

49 D.L. Horowitz, 'Democracy in Divided Societies', *Journal of Democracy*, Vol. 4 No. 4, (1993), p. 18.

Democratization and the Crisis of Governance in Nepal

LOK RAJ BARAL AND LEO E. ROSE

Democratization requires both the liberalization and the institutionalization of the politics of a country. Governance in a democracy is the capacity to rule in accordance with established rules and procedures. Government is only a tool or mechanism that exercises rule, but the governance 'exercises power'. Thus, if governance and government are adrift in their domains delineated by rules of the game - i.e. the constitution of the state and other statutes - rot begins to appear in the existing political system. Crisis of governance is also a crisis of institutionalization because elites who may once have been instrumental in overthrowing a regime perceived by them as illegitimate become anti-institutional after having come to play an effective role within the democratic system created by them. Parties which fought for democracy and liberalization become vulnerable to the new crises precipitated by their leaders' behaviours, paving the way for their decline and, eventually, for the decay of their institutions. Presenting a case study of Nepal can be an inductive method which may have a wider application, though each problem of governance and democratization is also country-specific. Nepal's experiment with democracy might have its parallels in other countries, but the country's salience cannot be overlooked.

Democratization can also be immediate and transformatory or radical and evolutionary, taking some time to be routinized. The 1990 political movement launched in Nepal was based on the limited demand for a party system. The initiator of the movement was the Nepali Congress party (NC). Its ideological orientation and struggle against the established royal regime (i.e. partyless Panchayat), introduced by King Mahendra after the established parliamentary system in 1960, was not opposed to the institution of monarchy were it conform to the concept and practice of constitutional monarchy as in Britain. The movement leaders seemed to be particularly worried about a possible anarchical situation emerging in the aftermath, once the turbulence of democracy started sweeping the politics of the country. Fearful of the unsettled future trends likely to be generated by a wide spectrum of political forces in an otherwise anti-democratic environment, the NC leaders wanted to put pressure on the stubborn monarch for a swift end of the movement. This way the movement, then picking up momentum as a result of the cooperation of most segments of society and the international community, could be prevented from going out of their control. It was terminated following the King's compromise with the movement consisting of the NC and the United Left Front (ULF), a conglomeration of seven 'communist' groups.

Problems of Democratization in the Post-Movement Politics

The new order produced by the 1990 movement was transformatory in nature despite the continued acceptance of the constitutional role of the King. For the first time, a broad coalition was forged between the movement and the King, producing a Constitution with certain key elements of democratic governance: sovereignty of the people; a multiparty system; constitutional monarchy; and inalienable freedoms of the people. These four elements of the Constitution cannot be abridged by any organ of the government including Parliament, making the People of Nepal the ultimate source of sovereignty. The preamble and article 3 of the Constitution are explicit in articulating this principle which finds its origin in the desire of the Nepalis, 'expressed through the recent people's movement to bring about constitutional changes'.[1]

Yet controversy arose regarding the formulation of people's sovereignty while drafting the Constitution by a Commission formed by the King on the advice of the Interim Government. According to the normal constitutional practice, only a convention approved by a duly elected Constituent Assembly could have been invested with such authority. But since the movement was the source of the Constitution, it has been accepted by a broad consensus in the country, making it the most democratic document Nepal has ever produced. Two parliamentary elections have since been held under the Constitution, giving it a greater sense of acceptance by the people. The movement parties and the members of the Commission tried to put as many constitutional safeguards as possible by limiting and articulating the powers and functions of each organ of the government. The constitution has thus become the instrument to protect democracy from any interventionist force, either the King backed by the military or by other ambitious politicians or groups.

Democratization affects both procedural and dynamic aspects of the political system. The procedural part began with the promulgation of the Constitution in November 1990 and the subsequent parliamentary elections to the House of Representatives (Lower House) and the National Assembly (Upper House), consisting of 205 and 60 members respectively. Numerous laws and regulations were initiated by the Interim and the elected governments thus making the initial transition from a royal regime to a representative democracy smooth and peaceful.

[1] The Constitution of the Kingdom of Nepal (Kathmandu: HMG, 1990).

The process of democratization is underway, but it is becoming increasingly traumatic. Nonetheless, taking it as an inevitable phase of 'second transition' (the first being the interim period) requiring more time to stabilize the process and institutions, the political elites of Nepal are seemingly trying to grapple with new challenges faced by the system. Still, as the nascent Nepali democracy is at a delicate stage of consolidation, it is also demonstrating its capacity to manage the crisis created by the emergent trends of internal and external environments.

The process of democratization and the crisis of governance are also inextricably linked, because the democratic government is expected to conduct the affairs of the state in accordance with the spirit of the established procedures and culture. But such a goal is not possible in a heterogeneous polity in which diametrically opposite political forces have emerged as key players. From a viewpoint of western conventional terminologies, the communists are on the left side of the political divide, while the NC and the Rashtriya Prajatantra Party (RPP, National Democratic Party), form the centrist and the rightist parties respectively. Yet, such a classification is irrelevant because of the very little ideological and functional differences between the three major parties despite the United Marxist-Leninists' (ULM) rhetorics of being radical and progressive. Such a gap between existing reality and its penchant for communism has made the UML incapable of freeing itself from the Marxist-Leninist chrysalis thus giving rise to popular scepticism about its commitment to the four basic principles of the new order as well as to the active role it has been playing within the parameters of the Constitution.

It was also interesting to observe the verdict given to the two principal movement parties in the 1991 election, with the NC becoming the ruling party and the UML achieving the status of a recognized opposition party into the House of Representatives. The results, however, denied a one-party dominant status to a single party. Of the 205 total seats, the NC received 110 seats and 37.75 per cent of the popular votes, while the UML got 69 seats and 27.98 per cent of the popular votes. Later three independents joined the NC, increasing its strength to 113 seats and about 42 percent of the popular votes. The RPP, predominantly dominated by the former panchayat members, won only four seats and 12 percent of the votes.

Such a scenario changed dramatically in the 1994 mid-term polls with no single party getting a clear majority (103 seats) but upgrading the strength of the UML to 88 seats, while the NC was relegated to the second position with 83 seats. The meteoric rise of the RPP was significant, making it one of the three key players, with the RPP a wild-card in the political game. Other small parties like the so-called radical United Peoples Front (UPF), the regional Terai (Nepal Sadbhawana) Party, could not retain their previous position, while a third left party (the Nepal Workers and Peasants Party), won only four seats. Among the seven independents, four were affiliated with the NC, two with the ULM, and one with the RPP.

The party position in the 1994 polls was clear as only five of the 24 recognized parties showed their presence, denying credentials to the rest as recognized parties. Both the 1991 and 1994 elections and the 1992 local elections have established the hold of the three major parties in Nepal - the NC, the UML and the RPP - showing a trend towards a two and a half party system with the RPP trying to overtake its other competitors were the erosion of the NC's popularity to continue in the future. Although it is too early to hazard any guess with regard to the emergence of a three party system as a stable political trend in the country, it can be safely said that no other parties but these three are likely to reverse such a development. The future success of these parties depends on their introspection and coalition building skills within the democratic process. Since the three parties - the NC, the RPP and the Sadbhawana - have formed a coalition government in September 1995 following the Supreme Court verdict to reinstate the House of Representatives, then dissolved by the King on the advice of the UML Prime Minister, Nepali democratic politics has entered a new phase with both hopes and uncertainties.

The two parliamentary elections without any major breakdown of law and order within an interval of three and a half years and the organization of four thousand elective posts at the village, town and district levels (1992) were major achievements of the NC government. In the economic field, the NC government initiated various new measures towards liberalization and market economy to which the succeeding UML government neither showed its strong commitment nor did it declare its opposition to it. Many corporate sectors have been privatized along with the allocation of 71% of the budget for rural development. Keeping an eye on the second mid-term elections in November 1995, the UML government took several populistic policies such as distribution of money to villages, to members of parliament, and to old citizens in addition to a number of other projects announced by the caretaker government. It is interesting to observe that such populist measures were not rejected by the three party coalition government headed by the NC, but it did invent some mechanisms for regularizing as well as streamlining developmental activities at village level.

The NC government (1991-94) also improved relations with India. New agreements were concluded to correct the trade deficit and to promote other sectors of economy. But these measures were overshadowed by intra-party and inter-personal differences that eventually led to the fall of the NC government.

The failure of the NC to continue in power after having received a clear mandate in the 1991 parliamentary elections demonstrated that the historical role played by an organization can seldom provide sustenance for a long period unless the status of leaders is renewed through the processes of democratization, making them accountable and disciplined, and in place within organizations. Lack of such a smooth transformation created some sort of an anarchical situation within the NC. It is an irony that a party with a long struggle for the restoration of democracy had not held organizational elections by 1995, nor had it reformed its 35-year-old party constitution.

Conscious of their historical roles and being perennially guided by a false notion that there was no alternative to their party, the NC leaders were incapable of showing their vision and statesmanship during the years of NC rule. The intra-party conflict that surfaced clearly in the political market place immediately after the formation of the elected government was heightened by personal and ideological reasons. The personal reasons could be attributed to the widening psychological differences between the Prime Minister, himself a novice in the art of governance, and the other equally powerful party leader, Ganesh Man Singh, whose 'situational' charisma had been universally accepted within the country by a wide spectrum of political forces which considered him the 'hero' of the movement. And another powerful personality was the former Interim Prime Minister, K. P. Bhattarai, a member of the triumvirate, as Girija Prasad Koirala had become Prime Minister because of the defeat of Bhattarai in the 1991 elections. These three personalities perceived their own strong roles within and out of government, but failed to establish the much needed coordination between the party and government. As a result, the apex leaders themselves turned into a source of division.

The mistakes made in the process of institutionalizing the NC were related to the endemic conflict between the Prime Minister on the one hand, and the senior leader (Singh) and the party president (Bhattarai) on the other. As a result, the elected government that was considered to be powerful and legitimate was hamstrung when the top leaders opened their ranks on one pretext or the other. Even if the Constitution was not obstructionist because of a clear delineation of power and functions between the King, Government and Parliament, the personality differences considerably affected the efficiency of the Prime Minister who found himself perennially vulnerable to the intra-party feuds fuelled by the two other leaders and their respective polarized rank and file. Thus, owing to the intra-party conflicts the Prime Minister seemed to be more preoccupied with the behaviour of dissident members of Parliament than that of the extra-parliamentary opposition. And the major demand of the dissidents having allegiance to the two leaders was the resignation of the Prime Minister who, ironically, still continued to enjoy an owerwhelming support within the NC parliamentary party. The phenomenon of a majority leader pandering to minority demands set a dangerous precedent for the future.

The situation favouring the elected government was vitiated by the NC dissidents who pulled down their own government when they abstained from vote of thanks resolution in the House of Representatives thus prompting the Prime Minister to advice the King to dissolve Parliament and hold elections in November 1994 in order to get a mandate for what Koirala termed 'stability'. But how such a stability could be insured when his party lacked organizational solidarity or cohesion, a precondition for winning any major election.

Thus, the crisis of governance has its correlation with the crisis of institution-building in Nepal. Now the NC, a ruling party (1991-94), was defeated in the November polls. The politics of compromise and the fear psychology that perpetually haunted Koirala, denied him any initiative within the organization and government despite the fact that he avoided a party-split by bringing all his opponents except Ganesh Man Singh into the Constitutional process despite the electoral setbacks suffered by the NC. The Congress culture becomes an obstruction when the party is in power, a unique phenomenon observed by analysts ever since the beginning of the party's history. Although there have been persistent differences among the rank and file of the party, all seem to be united now at least temporarily. It was more evident when the Prime Minister and his erstwhile dissidents who were the immediate cause of the fall of the government went together during the election campaign as if nothing had happened between them during the period of governance.

The politics of the opposition parties were no less turbulent. The Left groups, working in tandem during their oppositional activities which they had mounted from time to time since the formation of the NC government, seemed to be guided by two opposite strategies. First, the UML behaved as an extra-parliamentary opposition party by resorting to extreme agitational and at times violent street politics, picking up issues based on unsubstantiated sources of information or motivated by anti-NC considerations. They denigrated the Prime Minister by painting him as an 'anti-national' person, bent on selling out the interests of Nepal to India, its southern neighbour. Although the UML stigmatized the NC as a pro-India party, how they would deal with India if they came to power through elections was never considered. As a result of this extreme form of agitation, conducted in the name of 'from parliament to the street', great damage to both life and property had been done. Such an extremist strategy occasionally proved to be embarrassing to the Left leaders whose withdrawal from political brinkmanship became difficult.

Second, although Koirala was head of the prime ministerial system, the Left opposition did not reconcile to his position and failed to negotiate with him on the issues raised by them. Thus, the main opposition party preferred to talk to other NC leaders over the head of the Prime Minister denying the leadership role of the Prime Minister and the spirit of the system. Some NC leaders, who were also not happy with the Prime Minister, took it as an opportunity to score points which, in turn, undercut the role of the Prime Minister.

Politics in Nepal is still based more on personality than institutions; the leadership roles within the government and parties are personalized and lack accountability, and when crises accumulate due to the failure of institutions and leaders, the elected representatives including the leaders of government find themselves stuck with the environment. Such functional and behavioural crises severely hinder the process of institutionalization and legitimization in the country.

Any institutionalization theory suggests that it is, in fact, 'the process by which an organization incorporates its founders' values and aims'. Given the past background of the principal organizations, Nepal had no parties but only movements with a mission of restoring a multi-party system. The theory and practice of political parties began with the promulgation of the Constitution throwing them into the vortex of competitive politics. So they started adjusting to the transformed context of politics and became more systemic in their organization. Both the degree of systemness and of organizational autonomy needed for parties are yet to be seen in the Nepali parties.

If the absence of variable institutions appears as a major crisis of governance, ideological incongruity and persistence of past values and norms are other variables affecting the efficacy of the government. Haunted by the ghost of the past regime and fearing the backlash, democratic leaders count on the role of the King even though his constitutional position should keep him above controversy. Maintaining the King as one of the key players in the present Nepali politics, the democracy-movement leaders including the government are extracautious not to offend the King by avoiding to enter certain domains considered to be exclusive to the Palace. The institution of the Army is one of such vital areas where elected government and opposition parties fear to tread in order not to provoke the King's sensitivity regardless of the Constitutional arrangement of a council for dealing with such issues.

Among other crises, the underutiliziation of foreign resources, low absorptive capacity of aid disbursement, corruption, international agencies and the accompanying 'commission system' without transparency have long-term effects on the development of the country. As a result, a limited group of people having direct and indirect links with the parties or government or other influential non-governmental organizations or individuals have become the immediate beneficiaries. The so-called communist UML was no exception as was demonstrated soon after its coming to power. An end of this development is not in sight regardless of changes in governments and elites.

Absence of a strong political will, attributed to both the vulnerability of elites and to the pulls and pressures exercised for realizing aggrandizement, is another crisis. Nepal's huge water resources, for example, remain unharnessed due to the failures of all variants of governments, as the water issue was overpolitisized by the vested interest groups or power elites during the former regime or by the opposition parties after the 1990 revolution. The constitutional provision that agreements or treaties concerning resources and national borders etc. require parliamentary ratification either by a simple or a two-thirds majority depending on the nature of such agreements between Nepal and other foreign governments, is another hurdle created by the Constitution. Since the Constitution is ambiguous about the method of ratification, and since the parties in Nepal are more inclined to use such a provision as a political weapon against any incumbent government, and particular the NC, no government with a simple majority in Parliament can get through it, let alone a minority government. That the Koirala government suffered humiliation at the hands of the opposition and his critics within the party over an agreement (Tanakpur) concluded with India is a case in point.

Democratization of Nepali politics alone has not spawned a crisis in governance because they are persistent for a long time irrespective of the nature of the political regimes. Lack of political direction in the past and the absence of a culture of accountability persist as if no substantive changes are underway today. Since Nepal's constraints of tradition and history and the underlined authoritarian political culture have also played an obstructionist role towards institutionalization, today's party leaders and their followers seem to be guided by the same old values and norms against which they struggled for a long time. The internecine conflicts within the parties, and especially the NC, are nothing but the manifestation of their lack of adjustment to the new demand of institutionalization that entails both attitudinal change and systemness.

Legitimacy and the Management of Crisis

Nepal's recent exercises in democracy are replete with crises resulting from a new experimentation in the creation of a civil society. The communists were shored up by the other democratic parties in power for nine months but forgot to acknowledge the exceptional character of such a support extended to a minority party to form a government. Anxious to capitalize from its tenure in government, the UML went out of its way for returning to power after the 1995 mid-term polls so that it could change its position from a minority to a majority party.

From the systemic point of view, the UML's decision to go to the polls without facing the scheduled special session of the House of Representatives on 15 June 1995, was a clear violation of Article 53 (3), a mandatory provision given to the members of the House of Representatives, and to which the King cannot also reject. Since the special session was demanded to discuss a no-confidence motion against the UML Prime Minister Man Mohan Adhikari, taking a preemptive step to bypass the special session and vote of no-confidence, recommended to the King to dissolve the House and hold mid-term elections in November. Moreover, the opposition parties led by the NC had given a list of majority members for providing an alternative government after the defeat of the UML through the no-trust motion. But the King complied with the Prime Minister's recommendation for holding fresh polls despite the claim of three non-communist opposition parties and independents that they could provide a stable government.

Although the prerogative of the Prime Minister to recommend fresh elections has been fully guaranteed by Article 53 (4) of the Constitution, what he bypassed was the special session demanded exclusively for passing a vote of no-trust against him. Taking the dissolution issue to the Supreme Court, the three opposition parties - the NC, the RPP and the Sadbhawana - gave a petition to reinstate the House. On August 28, the Supreme Court, pronouncing its majority verdict (8 out of 11), found the dissolution to be a contravention of the Constitution and therefore the House was reinstated in the position it was before the 'unconstitutional dissolution'. Interpreting the Prime Minister's power of dissolution, the Court said:

> 'The power of the PM to recommend the dissolution of the House should not be used to make its powers ineffective, or to ignore the spirit of a responsible government...If the Council of Ministers is allowed to remain in power without facing a no-trust motion, the power to summon and prorogue the Parliament will prove more dangerous than the power to dissolve the House, for the PM may rule in a despotic manner for five years by using his power to summon and prorogue the House. Moreover, His Majesty has summoned a special session of the Parliament on the request of MPs for tabling a no-trust motion against the government. The PM recommended the dissolution of the House by citing this action as one of the reasons. This is contrary to the objectives and basic structure of the Constitution'.[2]

[2] See the full text of the Verdict in *The Kantipur*, 29 August 1995, and a partial translation in the *Nepal Press Digest* (Kathmandu), Vol. 39, No. 36, 4 September 1995.

Expectedly, the UML government was voted out of power on September 10 thus paving the way for a new phase of coalition government of three parties. Of the 205 members, 107 members supported the no-confidence motion. How the new coalition politics works amidst problems of parties and personalities is yet to be seen. Its only alternative is another mid-term poll which may or may not provide a simple majority required for the much touted 'stability'. The Supreme Court's landmark verdict not only put the system on the track but also set some important trends for the resolution of constitutional crisis. First, the general tendency of the political parties to curry the favour of the King for promoting their respective interests has been discouraged by defining the constitutional role of the King. Unless specified by the Constitution, the King 'may offer suggestions, or encouragements to or alert the Council of Ministers on matters of national importance'.[3] It ended the controversy over whether or not the King could exercise his 'discretion' for inviting party leaders to form a government or for dissolving the House of Representatives on the advice of the Prime Minister.

Second, the Supreme Court also defined the role of the Prime Minister and his prerogative to advise the King for dissolution and for holding elections if no party could form an alternate government. Although the special right of the Prime Minister as given in the Article 53 (4) of the Constitution came under heated debates following the UML government decision to dissolve the House without facing it, the Court maintained that it had not interfered in this domain but on the contrary, the spirit of parliamentary accountability has been vindicated. Now no Prime Minister under the present Constitution is expected to ignore the House and take a plebiscitarian approach in the name of a fresh mandate to be taken by a Prime Minister elected by the House.

Finally, setting a precedent, the Court of Nepal maintained that fresh elections could only be held if no parties were capable of forming an alternative government. In the given controversy, unlike the event of 1994, the three parties and some individuals had submitted a list of majority members of the House of Representatives urging the King to invite the leader of the NC to form a government to which the King defied, and to dissolve the House on the 'recommendation' of the Prime Minister.

The Court's verdict was not, however, left unchallenged by the UML. The political system was again in crisis with the UML going against the

[3] Article 43 of the Constitution of the Kingdom of Nepal has focused on the relationship between the Council of Ministers and the King. The duty of the Prime Minister is to communicate to the King on these matters - general administration, bills to be introduced in Parliament, additional information if sought by the King, 'matters relating to existing state of affairs, peace and security in the country as well as political, economic, social, administrative and external relations situations of the country'. And the King's role is to suggest, encourage, or alert the Council of Ministers on matters of national importance.

judiciary when its objective of gaining an absolute majority in the scheduled mid-term elections was foiled. Stunned by the verdict, the UML General Secretary and Deputy Prime Minister said, that the Court decision 'is not consistent with the established precedence, the dignity of the Constitution, and parliamentary and democratic norms and values; it seems to be politically motivated'. Echoing this sentiment, some Indian dailies also censured the Nepali Court for interfering in the 'political' arena. An anti-Court sentiment of the UML got a fillip from these remarks provoking the UML rank and file to go berserk against the Chief Justice and other judges impressing on the people that the communists were indeed bent on destroying the edifice of democracy on the slightest pretext. But this also proved costly for the UML whose democratic credential once again came under close public scrutiny. The non-communist parties by contrast were jubilant about the unfolding developments favouring them, thus prompting them to come out strongly in defence of the Court and the judges who were the targets of the UML. They welcomed the verdict as a landmark event in the history of parliamentary democracy.[4]

During the five-year period of the Nepali democratic experiment, both crises of legitimacy and the mechanisms of conflict management were observed. Crises of legitimacy are endemic to political parties whose leaders, let alone their followers, are yet to be democratized. The UML's defiance of the Court and its move to impeach the Chief Justice and his senior colleague, who succeeded him a month later, on the grounds of the interpretation of the Constitution to its disadvantage has not only eroded its image in the eye of the moderate public but also gave rise to doubt about its commitment to the system. The NC could be equally blamed for undermining its own legitimacy by encouraging anarchical trends within the party. The ideological and strategic fluidity of the UML constitutes a lingering danger faced by the nascent Nepali democracy.[5]

If the temperament of the parties' leaders and other members of Parliament is out of tune with Parliamentary norms, as was witnessed in the NC squabbles, the practice of majority rule would be a sham. It can be only hoped that the parties would refrain from precipitating an internal crisis to the extent they did before, because such a reckless repetition of the old game would damage them as well as the country.

The new situation created after the fall of the UML government was substantively different from the single party governments of the past. But horsetrading demonstrated during the formation of the coalition government in September 1995 failed to convince the people that the alliance partners would be able to hold it together for four years. Raising doubts of

[4] *The Rising Nepal*, and *Kantipur*, 29 and 30 August 1995.

[5] See Lok Raj Baral, 'The 1994 Nepal Elections: Emerging Trends in Party Politics', *Asian Survey*, Vol. 35, No. 5, May 1995.

the fate of the coalition government, the *Times of India* pointed out that the 'return of the Nepali Congress to government, at the head of a disparate coalition united only by its hostility to the Communists, who were expectedly voted out, does not mean that the new team ... is on more stable ground than the earlier ones in the Himalayan kingdom'. Since the coalition was 'skating on a thin majority', its stability would be judged by its own future performance.[6]

Internal conflicts within the alliance partners and personalized behaviour of leaders, however, revealed that the old political culture has survived the fifty year-old struggle of democracy. If the RPP is a conglomerate of former panchayat stalwarts who require to be more disciplined and systemic, the NC needs to set an example by overhauling the party in accordance with time and situation. As of now, no such strategies were forthcoming, allowing the party to be 'hostage' to the 'factional politics' of leaders.

Given the degree of political awareness in the country, any crisis to be encountered by the new Nepali democracy may not be as fatal as some tend to present. Since the consolidation of democratic legitimacy is as much related to the performance of the government as that of the political parties, it is imperative that each party and members of civil society should be more prudent for generating democracy's intrinsic strength and ingenuity. The increase of population due to a variety of internal and external factors and its effects on the environment, economy and social harmony are likely to pose serious challenges to the government in the future. Indo-Nepal migration is one vital issue demanding diplomatic skills for negotiations with India.

How a party in power and out of power makes a difference could be observed by the changed stand of the UML during its nine-month period of governance. The issue of work permit system to be imposed on foreigners (Indians?) was whipped up before it came to power but it changed its position on the issue presumably considering its implications for Nepalis working in India. Prime Minister Adhikari's assertion that even a few thousand Indians could create problems for a country like Nepal while a large number of Nepali migrants could hardly produce any imbalance in India sounded plausible on the eve of his visit to India in March 1995. There are other impending issues between India and Nepal among which the Treaty of 1950 is one. Although the UML's populistic slogans had referred to them on the eve of elections, how it was going to do it alone without India's concurrence was not spelt out. The erosion of legitimacy can be seen at various levels, but discrepancy between slogans and practice is more evident in Indo-Nepal relations. Discussing the role of politicians in power and out of power, one commentator said that the Nepali political leaders do talk

[6] *Times of India*, 13 September 1995.

about the Nepal-India relations at different fora and interviews, but no 'formal agenda has been specified to sorting out the issues'.

One thing is, however, clear that each party or ruler pursues a *status quo* policy towards its neighbours, India and China. So any radical departure from the past relations with India is unlikely. Such indications started coming in soon after the UML took over. What was more problematic for the communist leaders was their overpolitization of Nepal's relations with India and populistic approach to basic issues concerning the peoples of both the countries.

In conclusion it can be said that the conflict and the crisis of legitimacy in Nepal are the byproducts of failures of leaders and parties either in the government or out of it. Lack of confidence, vision and direction of change seems to be producing political crises, raising the issue of the credibility of the system as the whole despite many positive developments that have taken place since 1990. One of such positive aspects was the role played by the judiciary in the management of crises. Nevertheless, political parties, and then the civil society, have crucial roles for taking the country towards stability based on legitimacy. Since Nepal has entered a new phase of coalition politics in an ambience of uncertainty and scarcity, it is difficult to make a prognosis at this stage. It depends on how the parties and their leaders behave and respond to problems faced by the country and democracy.

Indo-Nepal Relations: The Causes of Conflict and their Resolution

SURYA P. SUBEDI

Introduction

Describing the nature of Indo-Nepal relations a scholar and a former foreign minister of Nepal rightly states that '(t)here are few countries in the world whose histories, cultures and traditions have been so closely interlinked for such a long time.'[1] Perhaps, this is one reason why Indo-Nepal relationship is very complex and governed by a number of treaties many of which are now outdated, undemocratic and based on the colonial legacy of the Raj as well as the Cold War. Located between the two giants of Asia, Nepal understandably wants to have a balanced relationship with both.

However, as a land-locked country surrounded by India to the east, south and west, Nepal is virtually dependent on India for her access to the sea and international market. Nepal is a narrow strip across the northern frontier of India, with whom it shares a 500-mile border and this border remains open. Because of this India maintains that the security interests of both countries are 'inevitably joined up.'[2]

This is one reason why since the time of the Raj, the rulers of India, who have regarded the Himalayas as a second frontier under the so-called 'Himalayan frontier policy', have sought to keep Nepal, which lies on the southern slopes of the Himalayas, within the Indian sphere of influence. Consequently, India has used a variety of measures, including the granting of transit facilities, as political leverage, to ensure that Nepal remains under the broader Indian security framework. The resentment on the part of the Nepalese to this policy and India's insistence on maintaining it has been the main reason for frequent serious frictions between these two States. The climax was the 1989 economic embargo imposed by India against Nepal following the expiry of the term of Nepal's trade and transit treaties with India. This essay which concentrates on the legal and political basis of Nepal's relations with India provides a glimpse into the role of international and regional politics in issues of legitimacy - which, in other contexts, is treated as an exclusively domestic problem. The specific case of Nepal is intended to illustrate a general problem: If a government is

1 Rishikesh Shaha, 'Himalayan Impasse: Need for New Perspectives', *The Times of India*, 7 June 1989.

2 Speech of Nehru in the Indian Parliament on 17 March 1950. See A.S. Bhasin, *Documents on Nepal's Relations with India and China 1949-66* (Bombay: Academic Books, 1970), p. 23.

perceived to be too dependent on the government of another state, this may impair its legitimacy at home and abroad.

The crisis continued for over a year and ended only when the Panchayat government that had taken a strong nationalist stand with India was overthrown by a movement in Nepal. It was a movement against the Panchayat system of government organized by various political factions certain of which had received support from Indian political leaders to topple the Panchayat government. For instance, Chandra Shekhar, the leader of an Indian political party which was in the coalition government of India led by V. P. Singh, led an illegal rally organized by the then banned Nepali Congress party in Kathmandu in November 1990 which ended with a pledge to topple the Panchayat government of Nepal. Chandra Shekhar was accompanied by other parliamentarians belonging to the ruling party of India.[3] The movement itself was partly sparked by the scarcity of essential commodities created by the Indian economic embargo against Nepal.

After the overthrow of the Panchayat regime, a new government came to power in Nepal - a government headed by a leader of a political party, Nepali Congress, which critics often characterize as a party lenient towards India. One of the first steps taken by the new government was to normalize its relationship with India. Consequently, the new prime minister went on a visit to India and at the conclusion of his visit in June 1990, he signed a joint communique that sought to limit Nepal's freedom of action in certain foreign and domestic matters. Of course, under this communique India agreed to restore the *status quo ante* to April 1987 in matters of trade and transit.[4] But this was after Nepal had agreed to terms favourable to India in matters ranging from India's security concerns to granting national treatment to Indian nationals in Nepal in excess of any provisions of any treaty that was in existence between the two countries.[5]

This is how most attempts by Nepal to assert freedom of action in matters of foreign policy have ended. In other words, they have ended with the conclusion of treaties of dubious character designed to strengthen India's position *vis-à-vis* Nepal and the 1990 Joint Communique is no exception.

It is understandable that for a country like India, which has gone to war with China on territorial disputes and has not as yet resolved this

[3] See Sunanda K. Datta-Ray, 'Living with Nepal: Must Busybodies Queer the Pitch?', *The Statesman Weekly* (Calcutta), 17 February 1990.

[4] 'India agrees to lift trade blockade from Nepal', *The Daily Telegraph* (London), 9 June 1990. Full text of the Nepal-India Joint Communique is reproduced in *The Rising Nepal*, 12 June 1990, p. 3.

[5] For instance, Nepal agreed to remove Indian nationals from the ambit of the work permit scheme and to grant a number of other concessions to Indian nationals in matters not covered even in the 1950 treaty.

dispute, to demand a degree of understanding of India's security concerns from a country, Nepal, which borders on China but is geographically part of South Asia and has 500-mile long open border with India. But one wonders what are these security concerns of India and how can Nepal avoid undermining such concerns without compromising its own sovereignty and freedom of action?

There are three major bilateral instruments concluded by India with Nepal supposedly to protect the former's security concerns: the 1950 Peace and Friendship Treaty, the 1965 Arms Assistance Agreement, and the 1990 Joint Communique. It is interesting to note that India concluded these bilateral treaties with Nepal when the government in power in Nepal was either in crisis or about to fall or was merely a caretaker government. These are the times when a government is less accountable to the people and has no mandate from the people to conclude a treaty with other states on matters of vital concern to the country. But at the same time such governments are keen to obtain foreign support either to remain in power or to win forthcoming general elections.

While India concluded the 1950 Peace and Friendship Treaty with an oligarchical government in Nepal which was about to be overthrown by a popular movement, the 1965 Arms Assistance Agreement was concluded with Nepal in the aftermath of certain insurgent activities carried out against Nepal from Indian soil by the activists of certain outlawed political parties living in exile in India. Similarly, the 1990 Joint Communique was concluded with the caretaker government of Nepal which had no mandate to conclude any treaty of such gravity.

In short, India has concluded treaties with Nepal dealing with security matters when the government in Nepal, whether it be a Panchayat government or Nepali Congress government, was weak. That is one reason why many people in Nepal adopt an apprehensive attitude not only towards India but also towards their own government since hardly any government of this country of the past, whether it be a Panchayat government or a Nepali Congress government, has cared to take the people in confidence or encourage public debate on vital matters of foreign policy. No wonder why the Nepali Congress government led by G. P. Koirala lost case after case before the Supreme Court of the country on matters relating to its dealing with India. The humiliating setback suffered by the Nepali Congress government in such cases served as a perfect weapon for the communists to brand Nepali Congress as a party lenient towards India during the last general election held in Nepal in November 1994.

Consequently, India, which played a role in the overthrow of the nationalist panchayat regime, had to deal with a Communist government in Nepal which was committed to abrogating all so-called 'unequal' treaties with India. The centrist Nepali Congress party suffered a humiliating defeat, partly because it was perceived by many Nepali people as a party lenient towards India.[6] This is one reason why the Communist Prime Minister of Nepal said that 'We are not part of Delhi's sphere of influence. We are an independent country'.[7]

Although very few people would think that the Communists, who have a much more aggressive nationalist policy, would succeed in asserting freedom of action in matters concerning certain foreign and domestic policy where a less aggressive Panchayat regime failed, the tensions that have resurfaced between India and Nepal are likely to damage the long-term interests of both India and Nepal. It is rather unfortunate that this is happening at a time when all informed observers were hoping that the time had come to model Indo-Nepal relations on the basis of mutual respect, trust and understanding in order to pave way for much more meaningful economic cooperation projects concerning, *inter alia*, hydro-electric power, irrigation and flood control, etc. It is rather disappointing that these two countries have still to deal with rather antiquated treaties and outdated concepts of the Cold War period at a time when old adversaries around the globe are modelling their relations to prepare them for the developmental challenges of the next millennium. What is more, at a time when China can feel safe to supply enriched uranium to India for its Tarapur atomic power plant near Bombay,[8] Nepal and India are still arguing for and against in essence the old so-called 'Himalayan frontier policy of India', and surprisingly enough this issue is still a vote-winning issue in Nepal.

It is in this context that this paper aims to identify and analyse the causes of conflict between India and Nepal and suggest measures to resolve the disputes between the two countries.

6 This party lost votes even in those areas of Nepal which were traditionally regarded as its strong-holds (for instance, the western Terai region) because of the manner in which the Nepali Congress government concluded a hydro-electric and irrigation project agreement (known as the 'Tanakpur Agreement') with India which could have adverse effects to that region.

7 See *Asiaweek*, 30 November 1994, p. 39.

8 See 'Nuclear pay-off: China to supply enriched uranium to India', in *Far Eastern Economic Review*, 19 January 1995, p. 22.

Causes of the Conflict

Problems Surrounding the Security Concerns of India

(1) The 1950 Treaty of Peace and Friendship[9]

The observance of the 1950 Peace and Friendship Treaty has been the matter of acute controversy between Nepal and India more or less since the late 1950s when a 'secret' letter exchanged with the treaty was made public. This letter, together with the treaty between India and Nepal, was signed by the head of an oligarchical government (the Rana regime) that was about to be overthrown by a democratic movement. In its last days in power that government was desperate for foreign assistance for its survival and was prepared to act in tune with New Delhi. Nehru, a shrewd politician, quickly grasped the situation and the opportunity which it offered. That is how the Peace and Friendship Treaty was concluded between these two countries under which India managed to secure terms favourable to it. Muni, an Indian writer, states that 'the Ranas fully accommodated India's security and commercial interests'.[10] Soon that oligarchical regime fell in Nepal. But the treaty concluded by that regime survived and survives till today, much to the discomfort of Nepal.

The principal provisions of the treaty and the letter of exchange are as follows:

Defence and Security

(1) 'The two Governments hereby undertake to inform each other of any serious friction or misunderstanding with any neighbouring State likely to cause any breach in the friendly relations subsisting between the two Governments.'[11]

(2) 'Neither Government shall tolerate any threat to the security of the other by a foreign aggressor. To deal with any such threat, the two governments shall consult with each other and devise effective countermeasures.'[12]

(3) 'Any arms, ammunition or warlike material and equipment necessary for the security of Nepal that the Government of Nepal may im-

[9] See for text of the treaty A.S. Bhasin, *Documents on Nepal's Relations with India and China 1949-66* (Bombay: Academic Books, 1970), p. 32. See for a letter exchanged with the treaty R. Shaha, *Nepali Politics: Retrospect and Prospect* (Delhi: OUP, 1978), p. 252.

[10] S.D. Muni, *Foreign Policy of Nepal* (New Delhi: National Publishing House, 1973), p. 22.

[11] Article II of the treaty.

[12] Paragraph 1 of the letter.

port *through* the territory of India shall be so imported with the assistance and agreement of the Government of India....'[13]

(4) 'Both Governments agree not to employ any foreigners whose activity may be prejudicial to the security of the other....'[14]

Economic and Commerce

(5) 'Each Government undertakes, in token of the neighbourly friendship between India and Nepal, to give to the nationals of the other, in its territory, national treatment with regard to participation in industrial and economic development of such territory and to grant of concessions and contracts relating to such development.'[15]

(6) The two Governments agree 'to grant, on a reciprocal basis, to the nationals of one country in the territories of the other the same privileges in the matter of residence, ownership of property, participation in trade and commerce, movement and other privileges of a similar nature.'[16]

(7) 'If the Government of Nepal should decide to seek foreign assistance in regard to the development of the natural resources of, or of any industrial project in Nepal, the Government of Nepal shall give first preference to the Government or the nationals of India, as the case may be, provided that the terms offered by the Government of India or Indian nationals, as the case may be, are not less favourable to Nepal than the terms offered by any other foreign government or by other foreign nationals.'[17]

(i) Nepalese view of the Treaty

Successive non-Nepali Congress governments in Nepal have every now and then claimed that the 1950 treaty is now an outmoded treaty and derogations from it are commonplace.[18] Since both countries have let many of its

[13] Paragraph 2 of the letter.
[14] Paragraph 5 of the letter.
[15] Article VI of the treaty.
[16] Article VII of the treaty.
[17] Paragraph 4 of the letter.
[18] Speaking to the press on 18 May 1989, the Chief Spokesman of the government of Nepal stated that 'HMG is also carefully considering the observation made by India's External Affairs Minister P.V. Narasimha Rao that instead of accusing each other of violating the 1950 peace and friendship treaty, it would be wise for both India and Nepal to devise ways and means to

provisions fall into disuse in the last 40 years, the time has come to review the treaty and replace it by a new one. One of the arguments advanced by Nepal to make its case against the 1950 treaty is that the government in New Delhi remained silent when Nepalese were forced to leave certain northeastern Indian states, e.g. Assam and Meghalaya in the late 1980s. Given the agreements reached by the central government in New Delhi with various nationalist movements in different federal States of India, it is difficult for India to ensure that Nepalese nationals enjoy national treatment in all parts of India. India should not expect Nepal to conform to a treaty to which India itself is unable to conform. Nepalese officials complain that Indian political leaders tend to forget the sensitivity showed by Nepal to India's territorial integrity and security by maintaining silence during the Gorkhaland movement and the eviction of thousands of Nepalese from northeastern India.

Many Nepalese complain about the influx of Indian labourers into Nepal. It is said that once they come in, it is difficult to distinguish them from the Nepalese people of the Terai region. Some Nepalese allege that bribing local officials, the Indians acquire Nepalese nationality. This unchecked immigration is creating unemployment and brewing resentment within Nepal. It was against this background that the Panchayat government had introduced the work permit scheme for Indian nationals. Analysts have suggested that this move was suspected by India to be a move to identify the vast number of ethnic Indians living in the Terai belt of Nepal. Many Nepalese became unhappy also with the Nepali Congress government for its 'soft' stand on India, particularly for letting cheap, untaxed Indian goods undercut local products. India must realize that these are some of the problems which any government in Nepal will have to deal with.

The government of Nepal states that it is difficult for a small country like its own with a population of 19 million to accord national treatment to the Indians who number nearly 900 million. Hence, Nepal has enacted laws barring foreign nationals, including Indians, from owning land in Nepal. As Nepal borders on some of the poorer parts of India, there is a continuous flow into Nepal of Indian immigrants and labourers in search of work. Some Nepalese have argued that this treaty places an unfair burden on Nepal and gives unreasonable say to India in the conduct of domestic affairs of Nepal: The privileges accorded to the Indian nationals in Nepal under the treaty are not suitable to the present day situation because they

---

remove the distortions or anachronisms of the treaty. As regards Nepal's position we have clearly stated that we are willing to review the 1950 peace and friendship treaty with a view to making it in tune with the time. It may be recalled that the treaty was concluded by India with the last Rana Prime Minister four decades ago in different political, economic and social setting.' See *Nepal and India: Facts and Chronology of the Problem* (Department of Press Information, Government of Nepal), p. 78.

are likely to pose a threat to the sovereignty of Nepal and disturb the social harmony within the country.

A number of arguments have frequently been raised in Nepal to claim that the 1950 treaty has never acquired validity.[19] Among them are the contentions that it is an unequal treaty;[20] a material breach of some of the provisions of the treaty by India has taken place;[21] and there is a fundamental change of circumstances to warrant suspension of the application of the treaty, etc.

(ii) Indian view of the Treaty

India, however, regards the 1950 treaty as valid and insists upon full compliance of its provisions by Nepal. Nevertheless, it emerged from the debate during the 1989 stalemate between India and Nepal that the former, too, was prepared to enter into negotiations with the latter on the whole gamut of mutual relations, including the 1950 treaty. But what India was saying was that because of its 'special relationship' with Nepal it had been very 'generous'[22] to its neighbour in many matters and now, since the latter was intent on changing this 'special relationship', in the view of New Delhi, Nepal was merely another neighbour like Bangladesh and Pakistan, and, thus, not worthy of 'generous' treatment by India. A former foreign minister of State of India, Natwar Singh, who was one of the key players in shaping India's policy towards Nepal during the 1989 crisis, stated that

> 'With Nepal, India has a very special, even unique, relationship... The treaty of friendship of 1950 emphasizes this special and unique relationship. For quite some time the Nepali authorities have been uneasy about some clauses of the treaty and would wish to modify parts of it. By all means. Let both sides sit down to have a second look at it. At the same time, we, as sincere well-wishers of Nepal, should put the facts and realities of life before our Nepali friends. This is precisely what Mr Rajiv Gandhi did when he met King Birendra in Belgrade in September 1989 at the time of the non-aligned

19 See the views of a leading Nepali lawyer, Ganesh Raj Sharma, with *Janamanch Weekly*, Jestha 5-11, V.S. 2051, Kathmandu.

20 H.L. Shrestha, *Some Unequal Treaties* (Kathmandu: Jhilko Publication, 1980), pp. 12-14.

21 An example cited in this regard is India's imposition of a permit system in 1976 for Nepalese nationals intending to visit Darjeeling, Sikkim and Meghalaya. The new regulation placed Nepalese visitors to these districts on a par with other foreign nationals, *The Times of India*, 13 October 1976. This was an example of clear violation of Article VII of the 1950 treaty, which accords national treatment to each other's nationals in several matters, including movement.

22 See an editorial of *The Statesman Weekly* (Delhi), 20 January 1990.

summit. Without violating confidentiality, I can say that what the former prime minister impressed on the king was that it was not the question of one or two or three treaties or even of the 1950 treaty, or the king's proposal for a zone of peace. The real issue was what kind of a relationship did Nepal want with India. That to use an overworked but nevertheless useful Americanism was the bottom line.'

'The choice was to maintain the spirit of the treaty of 1950 after making mutually acceptable modifications in it or go in for a relationship envisaging trade on the most-favoured-nation (MFN) basis as with other countries. Nepal could not abandon the treaty and still enjoy the economic advantages of a special relationship which are not inconsiderable.'[23]

He then concluded that 'both countries must evolve a strategic plus security understanding without any reservations.' This sums up the position held by India during the 1989 Indo-Nepal stalemate. At first sight, this appears to be a fair and frank proposition. But a closer examination of this statement shows us that he was using a language of threat: if Nepal did not elect for 'special relationship' with India, the latter would sever not only the facilities granted under the 1950 treaty, but also the transit facilities of Nepal, the facilities accorded by international law to land-locked States.[24] This is what actually happened during the 1989 crisis. He stated that if Nepal abandoned the 'special relationship' with India it would have

'very adverse immediate and long-term effects, e.g. the advantages of economic, trade and transit and financial aid would evaporate. Fifty lakh [five million] Nepalese living, working, owning property and business, and facing no discrimination would become aliens. Railway freight would go up. Port charges could shoot up. These are just the most obvious examples.'

He should have remembered that by becoming aliens the Nepalese would not *ipso facto* forfeit their property and business and lose their jobs in India. Even in the event of abrogation of the 1950 treaty India would still be under an obligation under international law to treat the aliens fairly and protect their property. It would not be able to deprive the

23 K. Natwar Singh, 'An agenda for talks with Mr Bhattarai', *The Times of India*, 7 June 1990, p. 8.

24 This issue is discussed in greater detail below.

Nepalese of their property and business merely by virtue of the abrogation of any treaty with Nepal.[25] India would be under an obligation to provide international minimum standard of treatment to Nepalese nationals.[26]

(2) The 1965 agreement on arms assistance[27]

In the aftermath of the Sino-Indian border war of 1962 as well as the insurgent activities carried out from Indian soil against Nepal by some Nepalese political activists who were living in exile in India (who were opposed to the Panchayat system of government in Nepal), Nepal and India had concluded an Arms Assistance Agreement under which India undertook to 'supply arms, ammunition and equipment for the entire Nepalese Army' and to 'replace the existing Nepalese stock by modern weapons as soon as available and also to provide the maintenance of and replacement for the equipment to be supplied by them.'[28] Nepal was, nevertheless, 'free to import from or through the territory of India arms, ammunition or war-like material and equipment necessary for the security of Nepal. The procedure for giving effect to this arrangement shall be worked out by the two governments acting in consultation.'[29]

From the Indian standpoint, this freedom, however, did not extend to the import of weapons by Nepal from or through China because it is India which is responsible for the supply of weapons for the entire Nepalese army and replace the existing stock with modern armaments.

However, for Nepal this 1965 agreement no more stands. According to the then Nepalese Prime Minister, K. N. Bista, the agreement was cancelled by Nepal after consulting India some time in 1966.[30] He has said this loudly and clearly more than once. He claimed that India had agreed to the cancellation, a claim not refuted by India. But India said nothing

25 See Article 43 of the Vienna Convention on the Law of Treaties of 1969. This article reads as follows: 'The invalidity, termination or denunciation of a treaty, the withdrawal of a party from it, or the suspension of its operation, as a result of the application of the present Convention or of the provisions of the treaty, shall not in any way impair the duty of any State to fulfil any obligation embodied in the treaty to which it would be subject under international law independently of the treaty.'

26 See generally, Amerasinghe, *State Responsibility for Injuries to Aliens* (1967); Eagleton, *The Responsibility of States in International Law* (1928). Article 9 of the Montevideo Convention on Rights and Duties of States reads that 'Nationals and foreigners are under the same protection of the law'. See also draft Article 5.1 proposed in 1957 by the Special Rapporteur of the International Law Commission on State Responsibility in the *Yearbook of the International Law Commission* (1957), Vol. II, p. 104. The draft Article provided that rights of aliens shall not be less than the 'fundamental human rights' recognized and defined in international instruments.

27 See D.P. Kumar, 'Chinese Anti-Aircraft Guns: Nepal Violated Secret Agreement with India', *The Statesman* (Delhi), 27 May 1989.

28 Paragraph 3 of the agreement.

29 Paragraph 5 of the agreement.

30 *The Rising Nepal*, 25 June 1966.

about the agreement until friction erupted between these two countries in 1989. After 20 years of silence, the Indian foreign ministry reportedly circulated the 'secret' agreement to the Indian media to arouse public support for the actions taken by New Delhi against Nepal.

(3) The 1990 Joint Communique

As stated earlier, this Joint Communique was signed in the aftermath of the 'Cold War' of 1989/90 between Nepal and India. The principal provisions of the Communique on security matters read as follows:

> 'Nepal and India will fully respect each other's security concerns. In this context, neither side will allow activities in its territory prejudicial to the security of the other. The two countries shall have prior consultations with a view to reaching mutual agreement on such defence related matters which, in the view of either party, could pose a threat to its security.'

Other principle commitments undertaken by Nepal under the Communique are as follows:

> 'Restoration of tariff preferences to Indian goods by, *inter alia*, exemption of additional customs duty.
>
> Exemption of basic customs duty on imports of primary products from India as provided for similar products from Nepal imported to India.
>
> Tariff preferences for third country goods should not be such as to be detrimental to the tariff regime for Indian exports.
>
> Removal of Indian nationals from the ambit of the Work Permit scheme.'

Although India also undertook certain commitments with regard to Nepalese exports and imports, what India was actually doing was restoring more or less the same trade and transit facilities that it had been according to Nepal before the 1989/90 economic embargo in return for new concessions from Nepal. This is how India has manipulated Nepal's freedom of transit - a freedom guaranteed under international law. One day India imposes restrictions on the transit facilities enjoyed by Nepal and other day it restores the same facilities in return for new concessions from a panic-stricken government of Nepal. Nepalese leaders were happy just to get the same facilities restored by India without realizing that the implications of other provisions of the Communique tended to tie the hands of Nepal in many matters of vital concern, including security. For instance, the 1990 Joint Communique describes Nepalese rivers as 'common rivers', a concept which is different from the concept of international rivers and could seriously weaken Nepal's bargaining power with India when it comes to negotiating economic cooperation projects regarding the exploitation of Nepalese rivers to generate hydro-electric power or other projects concerning flood control and irrigation, etc.

Similarly, the national treatment provisions of the 1950 treaty had not included employment within the ambit of national treatment to be accorded to the nationals of each other. But the 1990 Joint Communique requires Nepal to remove Indian nationals from the ambit of the Nepalese Work Permit scheme. This is an extra concession secured by India from a weak caretaker government of Nepal in the aftermath of the 1989/90 crisis.

With regard to the provisions of the Communique on security concerns of India, it is not clear what is meant by the term 'full respect for each other's security concerns' in the provision quoted above. Would India not object to Nepal's decision to import weapons from other countries or to conclude defence arrangements with other countries designed to strengthen its security? Or does it simply mean that 'neither side will allow activities in its territory prejudicial to the security of the other'? Or does it mean the following which seems to have been the position of India during the 1989/90 crisis with Nepal:

> (a) Firstly, joint Indo-Nepal surveillance of the border between Nepal and Tibet (which really means China).
> (b) All training of Nepalese military personnel to be conducted by India alone.
> (c) Thirdly, no foreign aided project along the open 500 mile Indo-Nepal border to be implemented without Indian concurrence.
> (d) Nepal must respect property rights of Indians in Nepal and shall not deprive Indians of these rights except under the due process of law; and
> (e) Lastly, all Nepali laws that are not in conformity with the 1950 Treaty of Peace and Friendship will be terminated.[31]

[31] As summarized in a comment on Indo-Nepal relations by Lt. General M. Thomas in the *Indian Defence Review* of July 1990, pp.14-15. His summary is based on Bhabani Sen Gupta's article on Indo-Nepal relations in *Hindustan Times*, 14 May 1990. Gupta seems to have seen a draft comprehensive treaty containing these points which was proposed by India to Nepal during the 1989/90 crisis outlining India's position.

These proposals, as described by Sen Gupta, serve to demonstrate a long-standing Indian insensitivity to Nepal's national pride. He rightly poses a series of relevant questions: How would China react if Nepal permitted Indians to keep an eye on Nepal's border with China? Will they not ask for a similar right of joint Nepal-Chinese eye on Nepal's border with India? What is the justification for the demand for an Indian zone of influence along the 500-mile Indo-Nepal border? On what democratic basis can India demand that Nepal not send her military personnel for training to any country other than India? Who is going to determine which Nepali laws violate the 1950 treaty, an ambiguous and poorly drafted treaty?[32]

Since the 1990 Joint Communique includes certain provisions similar to those of the 1950 Treaty, was this Communique intended to replace the 1950 treaty? The Communique states that '(p)ending the finalization of a comprehensive arrangement covering *all aspects* of bilateral relations, the two Prime Ministers agreed to restore status quo ante to April 1, 1987 in the relations between the two countries.' This evinces that this Communique was meant to be valid for a provisional or temporary or transitional period. Five years have passed since the signing of this provisional Joint Communique and no such single comprehensive arrangement, as envisaged in the Communique, has as yet been concluded between these two countries. Then the question to be asked in this context is: Is this temporary or transitional Communique still valid, especially after the conclusion of separate bilateral treaties on trade and transit in 1991? What is the legal status of this Communique?

From an analysis of the events leading up to the signing of the Communique as well as the provisions of the Communique itself one could arrive at three possible conclusions.

First, since the Joint Communique included all major issues covered by the 1950 treaty, both India and Nepal implicitly acknowledged that the 1950 treaty was now outmoded. It should be noted that both countries had stated during the 1989/90 crisis that they were willing to enter into a dialogue to review the treaty. According to Article 59 of the Vienna Convention on the Law of Treaties, a treaty should be considered as terminated if the parties to it conclude a latter treaty relating to the same subject-matter and it appears from the latter treaty or is otherwise established that the parties intended that the matter should be governed by that treaty. This is the case here. Let us take a provision of the 1950 treaty and its counterpart in the 1990 Joint Communique as an example: Paragraph 1 of the letter exchanged with the 1950 Treaty:

> 'Neither Government shall tolerate any threat to the security of the other by a foreign aggressor. To deal with any such

[32] Ibid.

> threat, the two governments shall consult with each other and devise effective countermeasures.'

A similar provision is included in the 1990 Joint Communique:

> The two countries shall have prior consultations with a view to reaching mutual agreement on such defence related matters which, in the view of either party, could pose a threat to its security.'

Are both of these provisions valid and necessary? If not, which one of these is valid? Which one was meant to govern matters covered by these provisions? A logical answer to these questions would be that it is the 1990 Joint Communique that prevails over all other arrangements made before it on the matters covered by it. Consequently, one would have to presume that those provisions of the 1950 treaty that are similar to that of the 1990 Communique are no longer in operation.

One could argue that the Joint Communique was designed merely to reiterate and strengthen the provisions of the 1950 treaty. If that was the case, the Joint Communique should have made a mention of the treaty somewhere in the text and the Joint Communique should not have envisaged the conclusion of 'a comprehensive treaty covering all aspects of bilateral relations'.

Second, it is also arguable that since the 1990 Joint Communique was meant to be valid for only a short transitional or temporary period, it is no longer valid, especially after the conclusion of two separate treaties on trade and transit in 1991 since the Communique had included provisional measures not only on security matters but also on trade and transit facilities between the two countries.

A third conclusion that could be said to flow from the first and second conclusions is that at present no bilateral treaty obligation concerning security or defence matters, e.g. to inform each other of any frictions with other States or to consult each other on security matters with a view to devising countermeasures or to reach any other mutual agreement on such defence related matters which, in the view of either party, could pose a threat to its security, exists between Nepal and India. In short, it can be argued that the provisions of the 1950 treaty concerning security matters were replaced by the 1990 Joint Communique which in turn has now lost its validity because of its provisional or temporary character.

However, this mere legalistic interpretation of the situation is unlikely to be accepted to India. One might say that treaties are treaties; they stand valid unless terminated in accordance with the provisions of the treaty. Further, a considerable weight of public opinion holds the view that for the sake of maintaining the goodwill that Nepal enjoys among the people of India Nepal should show certain understanding on matters relating to India's security concerns as long as it does not mean compromising its own sovereignty and freedom of action on defence and security matters. It is in this context that the present author has proposed, as we shall see below, a draft framework comprehensive treaty covering all aspects of bilateral relations between the two countries,[33] as envisaged in the 1990 Joint Communique.

The Problem of Free Access to and from the Sea

Principal international instruments concerning land-locked States are the Barcelona Convention and Statute on Freedom of Transit of 1921,[34] the High Seas Convention (HSC) of 1958,[35] the Convention on Transit Trade of Land-locked Countries of 1965[36] and the Convention on the Law of the Sea (LOSC) of 1982.[37] Both Nepal and India are party to the Barcelona Convention and Statute. Nepal is party also to the 1958 High Seas Convention and the 1965 Convention on land-locked States, but India is not party to these Conventions. However, India has just become a party to the 1982 Convention which guarantees the right of free access for land-locked States. In view of the mandatory character of Article 125 (1) of this Convention and the approval of this provision by consensus during the Third United Nations Conference on the Law of the Sea the right of free access as embodied in the 1982 Convention could now be regarded as part of customary international law,[38] binding on all States, including India.

Moreover, a substantial weight of authority supports the view that the right of free access to and from the sea of land-locked States and the principle of freedom of transit are now a part of customary international law, binding on all States.[39] This may be one reason why India acknowledged during the 1989/90 crisis that as a land-locked country Nepal had a right of free access to and from the sea under international law even in the absence of a bilateral transit treaty, albeit the question concerning the number of transit points required for Nepal remained controversial.

[33] See Appendix I, below.

[34] *League of Nations Treaty Series*, Vol. 7, Nos. 1-3, p. 11 ff.

[35] 450 *United Nations Treaty Series*, pp. 11-113.

[36] 597 *United Nations Treaty Series*, pp. 42-63.

[37] UN Doc. A/CONF. 62/122, 7 October 1982.

[38] The Preamble to the HSC states that its provisions are 'generally declaratory of established principles of international law'.

[39] See generally, United Nations, UNCLOS I, *Official Records*, Vol. I, UN DOC. A/CONF.13/29 and Add. 1, pp. 311 ff; M.I. Glassner, *Access to the Sea for Developing Land-Locked States* (1970); V.C. Govindraj, 'Land-locked States and Their Right of Access to the Sea', *Indian Journal of International Law* (1974), p. 190; A.M. Sinjela, *Land-Locked States and the UNCLOS Regime* (1983).

Narasimha Rao, the then Indian Minister of External Affairs, speaking in the lower house of the Indian parliament on 26 April 1989, stated that in 'the field of transit, a landlocked country *has a right* only to one transit route to the sea under International Law.' (emphasis added)[40] This was evidenced by the fact that even in the absence of a transit treaty India allowed, albeit under very restrictive conditions and only through two of the 15 transit routes that were in use prior to the expiry of the old treaty, Nepalese exports and imports to and from third countries. As Nepal had launched a publicity campaign to gain support and sympathy from the outside world in its trouble with India, Indian officials were making strenuous efforts to convey the message that India did not intend to deny Nepal its right of transit even in the absence of a transit treaty.[41]

Thus, since the freedom of transit is recognized in international law, that freedom should be incorporated in a permanent treaty whereby a change of mind of the government in New Delhi or the change of government in India would not affect the transit facilities of Nepal. Since landlockedness is a permanent condition, a treaty dealing with this condition should also be of permanent character. However, one may argue that since the economic activities of Nepal are not static and her requirements as to transit facilities are likely to expand it is not in the best interests of Nepal to conclude a permanent treaty on transit facilities. Of course, legal provisions have to keep pace with the changes in technology and science. Moreover, from a purely legal point of view, too, a permanent transit treaty may not seem to be necessary, if we accept that freedom of transit is established in international law. A freedom already firmly established does not need new documents to establish it. As we stated earlier, since India recognizes Nepal's right of free access and freedom of transit under international law, there is no need to seek India's commitment through a permanent transit treaty.

However, it would be helpful to insert a clause on freedom of transit in a comprehensive bilateral treaty of permanent character such as the one proposed in Appendix I of this paper, spelling out the basic nature of the overall relationship between the two countries and a separate periodic transit treaty that deals with the terms and modalities of transit could be concluded accommodating the needs of any given period of time. In other words, the freedom of transit and the right of free access should be incorporated in a permanent bilateral treaty of comprehensive character and the details on the terms and modalities of the exercise of this freedom and

40 *Foreign Affairs Record*, Vol. 35, No. 5, May 1989, New Delhi, pp. 131 -133.

41 See *The Times of India*, 17 April 1989. But what India was saying was that because of its 'special relationship' with Nepal it had been very 'generous' to its neighbour in extending transit facilities and now, since Nepal was intent on changing this special relationship, in the view of New Delhi, Nepal was merely another neighbour like Bangladesh and Pakistan, and, thus, not worthy of 'generous' treatment by India.

right could be included in a separate transit treaty which could be reviewed periodically without affecting the main framework treaty and in accordance with international custom and practice. This is because the present transit treaty does not go far enough to address the problems faced by Nepal as a land-locked country.

It should be stated at the outset that the new transit treaty, i.e. the one concluded in 1991, repeats, with minor alterations, the provisions of the 1978 transit treaty. The Preamble to the treaty recognizes that 'Nepal as a land-locked country needs access to and from the sea to promote its international trade'. But this recognition is diluted by the inclusion of the principle of reciprocity in the treaty. Article I makes the transit right of Nepal subject to reciprocity, which is not consistent with the very concept of a right of free access of land-locked States. According to Article 125 of the 1982 Convention, the right of free access to and from the sea is not subject to reciprocity; this right is unilaterally and solely available to land-locked States.

Thus, on the surface, Nepal seems to have achieved a satisfactory transit treaty with India since the latter conceded to the Nepalese demand for a separate treaty on transit and for 15 transit routes, in contrast to the stance taken by New Delhi during the Indo-Nepal stalemate that under international law Nepal was entitled to only one transit route; India also agreed to continue to provide overland transit facilities through Radhikapur for Nepal's trade with or via Bangladesh. Nevertheless, the fact remains that the whole exercise on the right of land-locked States during the Third United Nations Conference on the Law of the Sea and the incorporation in the resulting 1982 Law of the Sea Convention of the right of free access of land-locked States does not seem to have influenced the transit treaty concluded in 1991. Nor, apparently, has account been taken of other provisions of the 1982 Convention on the Law of the Sea on land-locked States. For instance, the Transit Treaty disregards not only Article 125(1), but also Article 126 of this Convention. Nepal has secured neither simplified exports and imports procedures[42] nor India's recognition of Nepal's 'right' of free access to and from the sea. Most striking of all is the incorporation of the principle of reciprocity in the treaty. The elimination of the requirement of reciprocity in the 1982 Convention represented a major breakthrough for land-locked States. But if a bilateral transit treaty concluded nearly ten years after the conclusion of the Convention still embodies the principle of reciprocity it could be regarded, from international legal point of view, as disastrous.

[42] See for a discussion on cumbersome customs and transit procedure this author, *Land-Locked Nepal and International Law* (Kathmandu, 1989) ch. 3. Pilferage of Nepalese goods on Indian railways increases Nepalese export costs. According to a survey transit costs consume 8 per cent of Nepal's GDP. See *Far Eastern Economic Review*, 8 March 1990, p. 24.

At first glance, Kathmandu's granting of reciprocal transit facilities to India does not sound disastrous so long as India is interested merely in securing general transit facilities in the event of need. In fact, India too is entitled to certain transit facilities under the general principle of the freedom of transit.[43] But the reality is that Nepal's exercise of the right of free access to and from the sea should not be made dependent on Nepal's granting of similar facilities to India which is not land-locked. It is hardly justifiable to ask Nepal to offer similar facilities in return for something that is available to Nepal by virtue of its land-lockedness. As the 1991 treaty is intended to provide transit facilities to Nepal for her access to the sea, the reciprocity requirement seems, in practical terms, meaningless, since land-locked Nepal, by definition, lacks the means to reciprocate. In fact India's transit trade through Nepal is nil; it does not actually need to use Nepalese territories for its international trade. India seems to have employed this reciprocity clause merely as political leverage.

So far as the Indo-Nepal relationship is concerned, the concept of reciprocity raises numerous issues. As stated earlier, India wishes to tie the transit right of Nepal to other issues like bilateral trade, treatment of Indians living in Nepal, India's strategic interests, etc. Nepal can only hope that India will not try again in the future to put pressure on Nepal by mingling her transit facilities with other bilateral matters. In that case Nepal's right of access will have been strengthened as a legal right rather than as facilities dependent on India's goodwill. For these reasons, it is desirable to include a few provisions on these rights of Nepal in a comprehensive bilateral treaty such as the one proposed in Appendix I.

Exploitation of Water Resources of Nepal for Mutual Benefit

There is yet another dimension to Indo-Nepal relations. Numerous rivers originate in the Himalayas and flow through Nepal to India and ultimately to the Bay of Bengal; they could provide a great deal of hydro-electric power, a cheap and durable form of energy, much needed by both States. It is estimated that Nepalese rivers could generate up to 83,000 megawatts of hydro-electric power,[44] which is more than the combined total hydro-electric power currently produced by USA, Canada and Mexico. For instance, a single hydro-electric power project, the Karnali Project,

[43] Article 2 of the Barcelona Statute on Freedom of Transit provides a general freedom of transit for all States party to it.

[44] 'Only 0.64% of that potential is now harnessed. Foreign consultants say 25,000 MW are easily exploitable if and when India and Nepal reach some agreement on pricing', *Far Eastern Economic Review*, 8 March 1990, p. 26.

would have an installed capacity of 10, 800 MW, the second largest in the world.[45] India has developed considerable interest in these projects[46] but views third party investment in Nepal with suspicion, fearing that Nepal may become a back door for multinationals to India's domestic economy.[47] Obviously, New Delhi would like to see Kathmandu acting in a way which would also benefit India if any gigantic projects like Karnali were to be implemented.

However, many Nepalese take the view that India is keen to exploit Nepal's hydro-power potential to its advantage. Their opinion is based partly on Nepal's experience with the Kosi and Gandak projects in the early 1960s under which India secured disproportionate benefits to Nepal's detriment. It was this hang-up of the past that led to the insertion of a clause, at the insistence of all nationalist forces within Nepal, in the new Constitution of Nepal of 1990 requiring two-thirds majority in parliament to ratify a treaty dealing with the exploitation of water resources of Nepal. The people of Nepal wished to insert a safeguard in the Constitution to prevent successive governments in Nepal from succumbing too easily to external pressure in matters of vital concern. This provision makes it necessary for a party in power to take all other major political parties in confidence before concluding such treaties. This was the mistake made by the Nepali Congress government led by G. P. Koirala, when he concluded the Tanakpur agreement with India in 1992. The agreement was not necessarily an unsatisfactory agreement for Nepal, but the way he handled the whole process was destructive. He tried to conduct everything in a very discreet manner, not informing the people or parliament what he had done or what he was going to do. His attempt to defend the agreement was not only rejected by the Supreme Court of the country but also by the electorate, the majority of whom are illiterate but politically conscious.

Resolution of Indo-Nepal Problems

The first and foremost act that appears to be necessary to resolve all outstanding problems surrounding Indo-Nepal relationship is to democratize it and develop it on the basis of equality, openness, mutual respect and trust. It is necessary to replace certain antiquated colonial style treaties between the two countries. Indeed, the provisions of the 1950 treaty of peace

45 *The Foreign Affairs Record*, Vol. 37, No. 3 (March 1991), p. 35, Ministry of Foreign Affairs, Government of India.

46 See for certain developments in this direction an understanding agreed between India and Nepal, *Nepal Gazette*, Part IV, Vol. 41, No. 36 (1992), pp. 7-10.

47 James Clad, 'GDP set to slump in wake of transit dispute: gasping for breath', *Far Eastern Economic Review*, 8 March 1990, pp. 25-27.

and friendship and the 1965 Arms Assistance Agreement on security matters are very similar, some even identical, to those of the 1923 treaty concluded by Nepal with British India. If Indo-Nepal relations are democratized, it would be difficult for Nepalese political parties to win elections on the basis of anti-India policy and the Indian leaders will also be unable to interfere in the domestic politics of Nepal for their own party political purposes.

Legal arguments apart, one should not lose sight of the fact that the relationship envisaged in 1950 under the Peace and Friendship Treaty of that year has undergone substantial changes over the years. Sunanda Datta-Ray, an Indian writer, rightly advises his Government that Nepal knows that

> 'access to or from a landlocked country is no longer a favour. It knows, too, that colonial style treaties cannot forever inhibit a sovereign nation's foreign policy options or choice of arms supplier. Since there is nothing India can do about these legal entitlements, it might do so with good grace so that at least friendship and influence survive. Ultimately, these will remain our best weapons in the Himalayan Kingdom. We cannot afford to blunt them through the antics of busybodies whose phoney idealism or cynical calculation threatens to spoil the climate for a reconciliation.'[48]

Therefore, it is necessary for both countries to commit themselves to ushering Indo-Nepal relations into a new era of cooperation based on the generally accepted principles of international law, the tenets of non-alignment and the principles of equality and mutual respect to each other's vital national interests. After reading the 1990 joint communique one arrives at the conclusion that it was supposed to be a new starting point in Indo-Nepal relations. It was designed to usher this relationship into a new era of cooperation, since it envisaged the conclusion of a new comprehensive treaty covering all aspects of bilateral relations. But no negotiations are under way for the conclusion of such a comprehensive treaty and no provisional arrangement can last for more than a short period of time. Both India and Nepal should prepare themselves to face the challenges of the next millennium when most regions of the world would have their own trading blocs and stronger economic relations.

The failures of the Nepali Congress government should not be permitted to jeopardize a very important potential for economic cooperation between India and Nepal, especially in the field of harnessing of water re-

[48] See S.K. Datta-Ray, 'Living with Nepal: Must Busybodies Queer the Pitch?', in *The Statesman Weekly*, 17 February 1990, p. 11.

sources because billions of potential kilowatt-hours are running into the sea and water resources, like any other resources, left unharnessed is of no use. Nepal should realize that the unfortunate episode concerning the Tanakpur agreement may discourage India in future and the somewhat slow process of ratification of such treaties of economic significance may prevent other countries from coming to help Nepal in harnessing water resources.

Therefore, what can be stated in conclusion is that the time has come for both Nepal and India to take a careful look at the whole range of treaties concluded between them, and to revise them in the light of the changed circumstances in both domestic and international fronts. On 10 April 1995 the Prime Minister of Nepal, Adhikari, stated that he wanted to review all aspects of relations as well as changes in the trade and transit agreement with India.[49] Earlier, in February 1995 India's Foreign Secretary, K. Srinivasan, had stated that India was prepared to review the 1950 Treaty in case Nepal so wanted.[50] In fact during the Nepalese Prime Minister's visit to India in the spring of 1995, both India and Nepal seem to have acknowledged that it was desirable to review the treaty in the best interests of both India and Nepal.

Nepal needs to nurture the goodwill it enjoys among the Indian people and the Indian political leaders should understand that India has an invaluable asset in the goodwill of the Nepali people. Unless India acknowledges, as argued by Mukerjee, that '(a) strong and vibrant Nepali nationalism is the best possible guarantee that the people will not permit anyone within and outside the country to use Nepal as a cat's paw against India',[51] bilateral matters surrounding Indo-Nepal relations will be exploited by both Indian and Nepali politicians to win votes in elections. India should stop looking at Nepal as India's own backyard. As a country professing to be a leading nation of the Non-Aligned Movement, India should have no objection to Nepal's desire to pursue a policy of non-alignment *vis-à-vis* both of her neighbours.

It is against this background that the present author has proposed a draft comprehensive treaty of permanent character covering all aspects of bilateral relations between Nepal and India. The draft treaty is based on internationally accepted norms which at the same time takes into account the distinct characteristics of Indo-Nepal relations. In other words, it seeks to satisfy Indian concern in matters of security and go a long way to meet Nepal's demand for a treaty based on equality. For instance, Nepal can easily live with certain provisions of the 1950 treaty, especially those

[49] *International Herald Tribune*, 11 April 1995.

[50] *Nepal Press Digest* (Weekly), Vol. 39, No. 9, 27 February 1995, p. 88.

[51] Dilip Mukerjee, 'Himalayan Stalemate: Indian Stake in Nepali Goodwill', *The Times of India*, 4 April 1989.

concerning the requirement to inform or consult each other in the event of any external aggression, in return for other benefits. The obligation to inform or consult each other in the event of an external aggression is an entirely reciprocal obligation that can be found in many treaties concluded between many friendly nations. Diplomacy is about compromise and every state should be prepared to give something in order to gain something. The draft treaty includes provisions, *inter alia,* for cooperation in matters of security and other treaties or protocols designed to implement the provisions of such a framework treaty could flow from it.

APPENDIX I

Draft Treaty of Peace and Friendship between Nepal and India

Preamble

The Republic of India and the Kingdom of Nepal (hereinafter referred to as 'the High Contracting Parties');

Being desirous of expanding and consolidating the existing relations of sincere friendship between them;

Believing that the further development of friendship and cooperation fulfils the basic national interests of both the High Contracting Parties as well as the interests of enduring peace in the region and the world;

Adhering firmly to the basic tenets of non-alignment, peaceful co-existence, mutual cooperation, non-interference in the internal affairs of each other and respect for territorial integrity and sovereignty;

Reaffirming their determination to abide by the purposes and principles of the Charter of the United Nations and the Charter of the South Asian Association for Regional Cooperation;

Having resolved to conclude the present Treaty, for which purpose the following Plenipotentiaries have been appointed:

On behalf of the Republic of India

....

On behalf of the Kingdom of Nepal

....

Who, having presented their credentials, which are found to be in proper form and due order

Have agreed as follows:

Article 1

(1) The High Contracting Parties solemnly declare that there shall be enduring peace and friendship between their two countries and their peoples, each shall respect the independence, sovereignty and territorial integrity of the other and refrain from interfering in the internal affairs of the other.

(2) The High Contracting Parties shall further develop and strengthen the relations of friendship, good-neighbourliness and cooperation existing between them on the basis of the above mentioned principles as well as the principles of equality and mutual benefit.

Article 2

The High Contracting Parties shall continue to strengthen and widen their mutually advantageous cooperation in the economic, scientific and technical fields. The High Contracting Parties shall develop mutual cooperation in the fields of trade, transport, communication, environment and various development projects concerning, *inter alia*, irrigation, river basin development, flood control, and the development of hydro-electric power between them on the basis of the principles of equality and mutual benefit.

Article 3

The High Contracting Parties shall promote mutual relations in the fields of art, literature, education, culture, sports and health.

Article 4

(1) The Kingdom of Nepal shall have freedom of transit through the territory of the Republic of India by all means of transport and the right of free access to and from the sea under international law.

(2) The Kingdom of Nepal shall, in exercise of the freedom of transit and the right of free access, be free to import from or through the territory of the Republic of India arms, ammunition or warlike material and equipments necessary for the security of the Kingdom of Nepal.

(3) Details of the terms and modalities for exercising freedom of transit and the right of free access to and from the sea by Nepal shall be agreed between the two High Contracting Parties through a separate bilateral transit treaty.

Article 5

The Republic of India, in exercise of its full sovereignty over its territory, shall have the right to take all indispensable measures, compatible with the provisions of bilateral treaties existing between the two High Contracting Parties and the principles of international law, to ensure that the freedom of transit and the right of free access accorded by it on its territory to the Kingdom of Nepal does not in any way infringe its legitimate interests of any kind.

Article 6

The High Contracting Parties shall maintain regular contacts with each other on major international and regional problems affecting the interests of both States, through meetings and exchanges of views at all levels.

Article 7

(1) The High Contracting Parties hereby undertake to inform each other of any serious friction or misunderstanding with any neighbouring State likely to cause any breach in the friendly relations subsisting between the two High Contracting Parties.

(2) The High Contracting Parties also undertake to consult each other in the event of either party being subjected to an act of external aggression or a threat thereof with a view to consider taking measures consistent with the Charter of the United Nations and necessary to restore or maintain peace and the security of their countries.

Article 8

(1) In accordance with the traditional friendship subsisting between them the High Contracting Parties undertake not to enter into or participate in any military alliance directed against each other.

(2) The High Contracting Parties shall not resort to the use or threat of force or allow any hostile activities of any form in their territories which are directed against the other Party or which might endanger the peace and security of the other party.

Article 9

The nationals of either High Contracting Party shall, subject to relevant laws and regulations prevailing in their respective countries, have privileges in matters of residence, movement from one country to the other and participation in trade, commerce and industrial ventures.

Article 10

Each of the High Contracting Parties solemnly declares that it shall not undertake any commitment, secret or open, towards one or more States which may be incompatible with the present Treaty.

Article 11

(1) Any differences and disputes arising in the application or interpretation of this Treaty shall in the first place be settled amicably in a spirit of mutual respect and understanding. If within three months of the start of negotiations no settlement is arrived at, then the matter shall, at the request of either party, be referred to the arbitration of three arbitrators chosen in the following manner:

(a) One person nominated by the Government of Nepal;

(b) One person nominated by the Government of India;

(c) One person, who shall be the Chairperson, chosen in common agreement between the two High Contracting Parties.

If the Parties fail to agree on the designation of the third member within a period of three months, the third member shall be appointed by the President of the International Court of Justice. In case any of the Parties fail to make an appointment within a period of the three months the President of the International Court of Justice shall fill the remaining vacancy.

(2) The arbitration tribunal shall decide on the matters placed before it by simple majority and its decisions shall be final and binding on the Parties.

Article 12

This Treaty shall come into force from the date of exchange of instruments of ratification between the High Contracting Parties.

Article 13

(1) This Treaty shall remain in force for a period of 10 years and be automatically renewed for further periods of 10 years unless it is amended under clause (2) or terminated under clause (3) of this Article.

(2) At the end of each 10 years' period this Treaty may, at the request of either party, be reviewed jointly by the High Contracting Parties and if necessary be amended by mutual agreement.

(3) This Treaty may be terminated by either High Contracting Party by giving one year's prior notice to the other.

Article 14

This Treaty shall replace the Treaty of Peace and Friendship of 31st July 1950 together with the letters exchanged thereunder and cancel the Arms Assistance Agreement of 30 January 1965 and the arrangements made through the Joint Communique of 10 June 1990 between the Government of India and the Government of Nepal.

IN WITNESS WHEREOF the aforesaid Plenipotentiaries have signed the present Treaty in duplicate in Nepali, Hindi and English all the texts being equally authentic. However, in case of divergence between these texts the English text shall prevail.

Done in New Delhi this day of ....

....

On behalf of the Kingdom of Nepal	On behalf of the Republic of India

Statements of the Discussants at the Conference on Legitimacy and Conflict

BRUCE BUENO DE MESQITA and SANJOY BANNERJEE

Buneo de Mesquita first turned to Rothermund's paper and commented on the assessment of Indira Gandhi's plebiscitarian campaign of 1971. He would give less credit to Indira Gandhi for this move and rather stress the political circumstances prevailing at that time. The opposition parties were inefficient before 1971, but an Anti-Congress dimension had emerged in Indian politics since 1967 and the events of 1971 were characterised by strategic responses of the Congress to this situation rather than to a redefinition of the rules of the game by Indira Gandhi. He then turned to Rothermund's assessment of Mahatma Gandhi and stated that Gandhi was not adverse to coercion. He then portrayed Gandhi as a game theorist who would always take into account what his adversary would do and would then try to create a situation where he had the moral upperhand and the adversary would be provoked to show his hand by using force. Gandhi wished to demonstrate that the British did not rule India by consent. He failed in demonstrating this effectively, but he did not revise his hypothesis.

Commenting on Mitra's paper and his suggestions for measuring the decline of legitimacy by recording the 'facts' of challenges to it, such as strikes, riots etc., Bueno de Mesquita introduced the example of three contesting parties entering alliances which would not prove durable in 75 per cent of all cases: Supposed one of them (A) is facing an alliance of the other two (B,C). A would make a cost/benefit analysis as he cannot defeat both of them at once. If the alliance between B and C proves to be durable in this case, the war would not break out and thus A's plans would not be put to the test. He further commented on Mitra's game structure with two variables and related it to the level of benefits accruing to the leaders and to the people under different systems of government. In an autocratic system the benefits going to the rulers tend to decrease growth, whereas democratic societies usually enjoy a higher rate of growth. This would benefit both the people and the leaders, but the leaders would, of course, have to think in terms of limited periods in office and calculate the pay off accordingly.

Bannerjee in commenting first on Rothermund's paper stressed the indigenous roots of democracy in India. The British may have introduced Parliamentarism but this does not mean that India also owed the notion of democracy to them which had much deeper roots than those derived from British influence. British education did not have such a widespread impact on India as one would think. He then referred to the reconstruction of the Indian heritage in Nehru's *'The Discovery of India'* and to Mahatma Gandhi's cultural philosophy which created a new bond between the leader and the masses. With regard to the reference to a 'Muslim diaspora' in Rothermund's paper, he asserted that the Indian Muslims were firmly tied to the land of India. With regard to legitimacy he emphasized that it survived the assassination of Rajiv Gandhi. Referring to Rothermund's point concerning the colonial heritage as embodied in the provisions for President's Rule, Bannerjee argued that these provisions stem from a general concern for checks and balances and are not just a colonial hangover. He then pleaded for a theory of legitimacy based on a shared identity and embedded in a cultural process. Legitimacy in the post-colonial society cannot be attributed to a mere aquiescence of the masses.

Turning to Mitra's paper Bannerjee objected to some of the basic assumptions of game theory. He referred to the example of the political situation in Punjab and criticised the stable preference ordering and the irreversibility assumption in game theory. He argued that if the context is changed, the preferences may be reversed. Moreover, in assuming the prevalence of rational choice, no allowance is made for what people think. They may, for instance, misclassify actions.

UTE WACHENDÖRFER-SCHMIDT and SHALINI RANDERIA

Wachendörfer-Schmidt first asked about the impact of the end of the Cold War on the delicate balance of domestic forces in Pakistan. Could this balance be destroyed by changes in the international sphere? Is there a danger of ethnic fragmentation? It is noticeable that there has been an explosion of ethnic conflicts after 1989 and that most of these conflicts have surfaced in Asia. She also pointed out that democracy is not a natural ally of minority rights. There is always the danger of a tyranny of the majority. She also said that she is pessimistic with regard to the effect of local democracy. It will normally not benefit the poor as the redistribution of resources will be in the hands of those who are better organised to achieve their ends.

Randeria started her remarks by questioning the validity of legal discourse which contains no reference to social structure and social movements such as those of women contesting Islamic law and insisting on their rights with regard to marriage and divorce. Referring to Subedi's paper she admitted that the issues raised by him with regard to treaty relations between India and Nepal were a revelation to her. She agreed that fair and just principles should be observed in conflicts arising between nations, but she also raised the question of how to deal with the underlying interests concerning economic affairs and national security. Turning to Sathyamurthy's paper she stated that she agreed with his pessimistic thesis, but she would also like to ask whether the phenomena which he highlighted are peculiar to India or may also be found elsewhere. Finally she raised the question whether the globalisation process does not change the basic power equations at the local level.

THOMAS SAALFELD and LLOYD I. RUDOLPH

Saalfeld referred to the growth of the welfare state in his remarks and then commented on the consociational model of politics and the veto power of the minority which raises decision costs. He mentioned G. Simmel's theory concerning the intensity of social cleavages and the options for bargaining which arise from the criss-crossing of such cleavages. In this context he also pointed to the dynamics of outbidding which can be noticed in the arena of political competition.

L. I. Rudolph mentioned a special characteristic of the Indian political spectrum: there are hardly any parties along class lines, e.g. there is no labour party. But economic issues such as a rise in prices and the fear of inflation do attract political attention. He then referred to the collapse of the Soviet Union and expressed the hope that the Indian state will not collapse in this way but rather show the world its future in terms of multicultural cohesion. He felt that this is more important as the model of the nation-state of the French type has obviously outlived its usefulness as a paradigm of the modern state.

SANGEETA AHUJA

In her statement Ahuja highlighted the role of the army in various conflicts in South Asia. She referred in this context also to Manipur and Nagaland and raised questions about the legitimacy of the army, the line of command within the army and the issue of internal discipline.

CITHA MAAß and WOLFGANG-PETER ZINGEL

The discussants had agreed on a division of labour, Maaß commented on the papers concerning Nepal and Sri Lanka and Zingel on the paper on Bangladesh. Maaß emphasized the difference between Nepal and Sri Lanka. In the latter we are confronted with a crisis of the legitimacy of democracy, as the democratic process has not provided a solution of the conflict which besets the body politic of Sri Lanka and has thus contributed to a crisis of legitimacy. In Nepal, however, democratic institutions are still in a nascent state. In Sri Lanka legitimacy has declined because the Tamil minority has not been encompassed by the democratic process. In Nepal the main problem has been that of transforming an authoritarian monarchy. In Sri Lanka a Western inspired concept of legitimacy had prevailed from 1931 to 1956 which was then replaced by a Buddhist concept. From 1977 to 1983 the main focus of attention was on the preservation of the unitary state. Recently a new phase has begun with President Kumaratunge's endeavour to bridge the gap between the communities. In this way a fourth concept of legitimacy, that of federalism, may finally come into its own.

Zingel prefaced his remarks by stating that as an economist he is not used to think in terms of legitimacy. Conflicts arise in his view from mutually exclusive goals with regard to the allocation of resources. He then referred to A. Sen's theory concerning entitlements and deprivation and stressed that the battle for entitlements usually accentuates deprivation. He then turned to the problem of the legitimacy of international intervention which may be necessary when it comes to settling the shares of river waters which should be due to states like Bangladesh. Even economic aid provided by foreign states may become a source of conflict.

SURYA P. SUBEDI and IFTIKHAR H. MALIK

Subedi pointed out that a constitution may not necessarily be a panacea for solving all political problems. He felt that Shastri had overemphasized the role of the constitution in this respect and warned that if constitution makers try to accommodate too many interests, the constitution may not work at all. He further referred to the problem of the victimisation of politicians once they have lost power.

Malik stressed the role of personalities in South Asian politics and spoke of 'dynastic parties' on the one hand and ethnic parties such as the MQM in Pakistan on the other hand. He felt that the only option of the state is often to watch and wait until the dust settles over ethnic feuds. He argued that in such a context it is difficult to agree with those who say that the state is too centrist in South Asia. He then commented on the difference between religious and ethnic nationalism.

Epilogue

DIETMAR ROTHERMUND

'Legitimacy' proved to be a many splendoured thing in the course of the lively discussions at this conference. Susanne H. Rudolph provided an impressive formula: 'The weak state rests on repression, the strong one on legitimacy'. This, of course, begs the question in which way the strong state acquires legitimacy. It may well be that its ability to maintain law and order is an essential feature of this legitimacy and that coercion plays a decisive role in this respect. How to draw a line between the repression indulged in by the weak state and the coercion exercized by the strong and legitimate state? The type of legitimation, e.g. by conquest, by the grace of God or by democratic process, is of specific concern in this context. If the latter is held to be the crucial one, what about the legitimacy of majority rule in multi-ethnic states? This, in fact, emerged as a recurrent theme in the discussions. All states of South Asia are considered to be nation-states, but all of them contain ethnic or religious groups which demand group rights.

Two methods of dealing with such sources of conflict within nation-states were suggested: (1) the constitutional method of providing an institutional framework which accommodates internal diversity, (2) the method of consociational politics. The first method includes federalism, positive discrimination etc., but it usually comes up against a serious obstacle: the modern constitutional state guarantees fundamental rights to its citizens in terms of individual rights. This is incompatible with an open support of group rights which may even militate against the fundamental rights of the individual citizen. Constitutional frameworks must have a certain rigidity in order to retain their credibility and thus their legitimacy. The second method, that of consociational politics, is more flexible. It calls for coalition-building either among parties or within parties. If it works smoothly, it avoids the contesting of the institutional framework. But consociational politics call for political skills which should not be taken for granted. It is a fallacy to assume that elections are a panacea for all political problems. Elections are like questions addressed to the electorate: if the questions are phrased in a misleading way, the answers are bound to be awkward. If the politicians cannot aggregate interests properly, elections may lead to an articulation of disaggregated interests. In this way the legitimacy of the state which is supposed to be based on a democratic process may actually be undermined by it. The unfinished agenda of this conference would certainly include this point. A closer attention to political management and the rules of the political game could be recommended for further conferences of this type.

Another item on the unfinished agenda would be the economic aspect of legitimacy. It was stated in the discussions that legitimacy is mostly about honour and self-respect and not about economic affairs, but the way in which a political system performs in terms of the allocation of resources is of crucial significance to its legitimacy. Of course, this is related to the issue-consciousness of the electorate. If national honour or ethnic identity are raised as major issues, the test of legitimacy would be in this field. If scarcity and rising prices become an issue, this may determine the degree of legitimacy of the government concerned. It is, of course, also possible to sidetrack an issue, i.e. to harp on honour and identity so as to make the electorate forget about poverty and deprivation. This may mean playing with fire, because, if the issues which have been sidetracked are genuine ones, they may emerge again with a vengeance.

A third point on the unfinished agenda is the influence of exogenous forces on the legitimacy of a given political system. It is convenient to think of such systems as closed ones and restrict the analysis to endogenous factors which uphold or undermine its legitimacy. But outside interference may also help to strengthen the system or to destabilize it. Such interference may be deliberate or unintentional. An outside power may use its secret services to destabilize a system perceived to be its enemy or it may grant economic and military aid to an ally. Such cases of deliberate interference are easy to assess. It is more difficult to deal with unintentional interference which may be as damaging as an openly hostile act, e.g. a power which controls certain resources raises their price in the world market and thus destabilizes the economy of many countries which it does not consider to be its enemies at all. Another complex instance of outside interference are the activities of NGOs which are conceived of as friendly assistance, but may corrupt the elites of a nation and thus undermine the legitimacy of the respective political system.

In giving some thought to this latter instance we may have to revise our straightforward contrast between legitimacy and conflict. Most challenges to legitimacy may be posed not in terms of a direct conflict, but by way of a slow erosion of the elements which support it. In fact, there may be a combination of erosion and conflict which then leads to an unexpected collapse of legitimacy. The recent demise of the Soviet empire provides an object lesson of this kind of coincidence. In South Asia the sequence of events which led to the emergence of Bangladesh also shows a pattern of an erosion of legitimacy which ended in a violent conflict. A study of the erosion of legitimacy would require another conference. At this stage one can only raise the issue which is certainly of great relevance to the present state of affairs in South Asia as well as in other parts of the world.

Bibliography

Alles, A.C., *Insurgency 1971. An Account of the April Insurrection in Sri Lanka* (Colombo 1979).

Almond, Gabriel A., Flanagan, Scott C., Mundt, Robert J. (eds.), *Crisis, Choice and Change: Historical Studies of Political Development* (Boston: Little, Brown & Co. 1973).

Amnesty International, *India, Torture, Rape and Deaths in Custody* (London, 1992).

Anderson, Benedict, *Imagined Communities: Reflections on the Origin and Spread of Nationalism* (London: Verso, 1983).

Anwar Ali (ed.), *Dharmanirapekshata (Secularism)* (Dacca, 1973).

Arora, B., 'Party System and Federal Structures in India: Linkages and Issues', in: T.C. Bose (ed.), (1987).

Asad, Muhammad, *The Principles of State and Government in Islam* (Berkeley and Los Angeles, 1961).

Axelrod, Robert, *The Evolution of Cooperation* (London, 1990).

Aziz, K.K., *A History of the Idea of Pakistan* (Lahore, 1987).

Aziz, K.K., *Rahmat Ali. A Biogography* (Stuttgart, 1987).

BAMNA (Bangladesh Mukto Nirbachan Andolan) (ed.), *A Report on the Elections to the Fifth National Parliament, 27 February 1991* (Dhaka: BAMNA, 1991).

Bebermeyer, Sybil, 'Muslim Nations See Extremism as Main Threat to Stability', *The Asian Age*, 29 Dec 1994.

Bechert, H., 'S.W.R.D. Bandaranaike and the Legitimation of Power through Buddhist Ideals', in: Bardwell L. Smith (ed.), *Religion and Legitimation of Power in Sri Lanka* (Chambersburg, PA: Anima Books, 1978).

Bhargava, Rajeev, 'What is Democracy?', *Seminar* (New Delhi), No. 389, January 1992.

Bhasin, A.S., *Documents on Nepal's Relations with India and China 1949-66* (Bombay: Academic Books, 1970).

Binder, L., *Religion and Politics in Pakistan* (Berkeley, 1961).

Bose, Ashish, *From Population to People* (New Delhi: B.R. Publishing, 1988).

Brams, Steven J., *Rational Politics, Decisions, Games and Strategy* (San Diego, 1985).

Brass, Paul R., *The Rise of the BJP and the Future of Party Politics in U.P.* (Gould, 1993).

Brass, Paul R., *Ethnicity and Nationalism: Theory and Comparison* (New Delhi: Sage, 1991).

Brass, Paul R., *The Politics of India since Independence, The New Cambridge History of India, Vol. IV.1* (Cambridge: Cambridge University Press, 1990).

Breman, Jan, *Of Peasants, Migrants and Paupers: Rural Labour Circulation and Capitalist Production in West India* (Delhi: OUP, 1985).

Brohi, A.K., *Fundamental Law of Pakistan* (Karachi, 1958).

Byres, T. J., 'A Chicago View of the Indian State: An Oriental Grin without an Oriental Cat and Political Economy without Classes', *The Journal of Commonwealth and Comparative Politics*, Vol. 26, No. 3, 1988.

Chakrabarty, Bidyut, 'India's Secularism: Tolerance and Coercion?', in Chakrabarty, Bidyut (ed.), *Secularism and Indian Polity* (New Delhi: Segment, 1990).

Chatterjee, Partha, 'History and the Nationalization of Hinduism', *Social Research* (New York), 59 (1), Spring 1992.

Chattopadhyaya, D.P., 'On the Alleged Unity of Religions', Radhakrishnan Memorial Lecture, Indian Institute of Advanced Studies, Shimla, 1991.

Choudhury, G.W., *Documents and Speeches on the Constitution of Pakistan* (Dacca, 1967).

Choudhury, G.W., *Pakistan. Transition from Military to Civilian Rule* (Essex, 1988).

Conrad, D., 'In Defence of the Continuity of Law: Pakistan's Courts in Crises of State', in: W.P. Zingel (ed.), *Pakistan in its Fourth Decade* (Hamburg, 1983).

Danda, Ajit K., *Ethnicity in India* (New Delhi: Inter-India, 1991).

Das, Veena (ed.), *Mirrors of Violence: Communities, Riots and Survivors in South Asia* (Delhi: OUP, 1990).

Dasgupta, Jyotirindra, *Language Conflict and National Development - Group Politics and National Language Policy in India* (Berkeley, Los Angeles and London: University of California Press, 1970).

Dube, Shyama C. and Basilov, V.N. (eds.), *Secularization in Multi-Religious Societies* (New Delhi: ICSSR, Concept, 1983).

Duncan J., and Derrett,M., 'Social and Political Thought and Institutions', in A. L. Basham (ed.), *A Cultural History of India* (Oxford, 1975).

Easton, D., *A Framework for Political Analysis* (Englewood Cliffs, 1965).

Easton, D., *A System Analysis of Political Life* (Chicago, 1979).

Eller, J. D. and Coughlan, R. M., 'The Poverty of Primordialism: The Demistification of Ethnic Attachments', *Ethnic and Racial Studies*, Vol. 16, No. 2, April 1993.

Engineer, Asghar Ali, 'The Muslim Vote in Maharashtra', *The Hindu*, 19 January 1995.

Frankel, Francine and Rao, M.S.A. (eds.), *Dominance and State Power in Modern India. Decline of a Social Order, Vol.I/II* (Oxford: Oxford University Press, 1990).

Gallard,Keith, *Pakistan. A Political Study* (London, 1957).

Gandhi, Sonia, (ed.), 'Two Alone, Two Together, Letters Between Indira Gandhi and Jawaharlal Nehru, 1940-1964' (London: Hodder, 1992).

Ghosh, Partha S., 'Political Hinduism in India: Genesis, Prognosis and Implications', Occasional Paper of Stiftung Wissenschaft und Politik (Ebenhausen, 1995).

Graham, B.D., *Hindu Nationalism and Indian Politics: The Origins and Development of the Bharatiya Jana Sangh* (Cambridge: Cambridge University Press, 1990).

Gupta, S., 'The Gathering Storm', in: M.M. Bouton and P. Oldenburg, (eds.), *India Briefing, 1990* (Boulder: Westview, 1990).

Gupta, Shekhar, *India Redefines its Role*, Adelphi Paper 293 (Oxford: OUP, 1995).

Gurr, Ted Robert, *Why Men Rebel* (Princeton: Princeton University Press, 1974).

Gurumurthy, S., 'State and Society', *Seminar*, No. 417, May 1994.

Hage, G., Hannemann R. and Gargan, E., *State, Responsiveness and State Activism* (London: Unwin Hyman, 1989).

Hagerty, D.T., 'India's Regional Security Doctrine', *Asian Survey*, Vol. 31, No. 4, (1993).

Held, David, *Political Theory and the Modern State* (Cambridge: Polity Press, 1990).

Hellmann-Rajanayagam, D., 'Tamilen, Tamilsprache und Tamilidentität = Tamilnationalismus?', in: D. Hellmann-Rajanayagam, D. Rothermund (eds.), *Nationalstaat und Sprachkonflikte in Süd- und Südostasien* (Stuttgart, 1992).

Hellmann-Rajanayagam, D., 'The 'Groups' and the Rise of Militant Secessionism', in: C. Manogaran, B. Pfaffenberger (eds.), *The Sri Lanka Tamils. Ethnicity and Identity* (Boulder, 1994).

Hellmann-Rajanayagam, D., 'The Tamil Militants - Before the Accord and After', *Pacific Affairs*, Vol. 61, No. 4, (1988/89).

Hobsbawm, Eric J. and Ranger, Terence (eds.), *The Invention of Tradition* (Cambridge: CUP 1988).

Horowitz, D.L., 'Democracy in Divided Societies', *Journal of Democracy,* Vol. 4, No. 4, (1993).

Huntington, Samuel P., *Political Order in Changing Societies* (New Haven and London: Yale University Press 1st ed., 1968).

Huq, Abul Fazl, 'The Problem of National Identity in Bangladesh', *The Journal of Social Studies,* No. 24, April 1984.

Inden, Ronald, *Imagining India* (Oxford, 1990)
Iqbal, Afzal, *Islamization in Pakistan* (Lahore: Vanguard, 1986).

Jackman, Robert W., *Power without Force - The Political Capacity of Nation-States* (Ann Arbor: University of Michigan Press, 1993).

Jaffrelot, Christophe, 'Hindu Nationalism: Strategic Syncretism in Ideology Building', *Economic and Political Weekly* (Bombay), 20-27 March 1993.

Jalal, Ayesha, *Pakistan. The State of Martial Rule: The Origins of Pakistan's Political Economy of Defence* (Cambridge, 1990).

Joshi, Manoj, *Combating Terrorism in Punjab* (London: RISCI, 1993).

Kangle, R.P., *The Kautiliya Arthasastra, 3 Vols.* (Bombay, 1962), see also Pandurang V. Kane, *History of Dharmasastra, Vol. III* (Pune, 1946).

Kanwal, J.S., *Lhue de Lohe* (New Delhi: Arsi Publishers, 1982) (Punjabi).

Kearney, R.N., *Communalism and Language in the Politics of Ceylon* (Durham, 1967).

Kearney, R.N., 'Educational Expansion and Political Volatility in Sri Lanka: The 1971 Insurrection', *Asian Survey,* Vol. 15 , No. 2, (1975).

Khan, Hamid, *Eighth Amendment. Constitutional and Political Crisis in Pakistan* (Lahore, 1994).

Kohli, Atul, *Democracy and Discontent, India's Growing Crisis of Governability* (Cambridge e. a.: CUP, 1990).

Kopp, M., Müller, H.-P., *Herrschaft und Legitimität in modernen Industriegesellschaften. Eine Untersuchung der Ansätze von Max Weber, Niklas Luhmann, Claus Offe und Jürgen Habermas* (München, 1980).

Kothari, Rajni, 'Decline of the Moderate State', in: Kothari, *State against Democracy: In Search of Humane Governance,* (Delhi: Ajanta, 1988).

Kothari, Smitu and Sethi Harsh (eds.), *Rethinking Human Rights: Challenges for Theory and Action* (Delhi, 1989).

Lamballe, A., *Le Problème Tamoul à Sri Lanka* (Paris, 1985).

Linz, J.J., 'Legitimacy of Democracy and the Socioeconomic System', in: M. Dogan (ed.), *Comparing Pluralist Democracies: Strains on Legitimacy* (Boulder, 1988).

Lipset, S.M., *Political Man, The Social Basis of Politics* (New York, 1959).

Mahmudabad, Raja of, 'Some Memoirs', in: C. H. Philips / M. D. Wainwright (eds.), *The Partition of India. Policies and Perspectives 1935 - 1947* (London, 1970).

Malalgoda, K., *Buddhism in Sinhalese Society, 1750-1900: A Study of Religious Revival and Change* (Berkeley, 1976).

Malik, Y.K. and Singh, V.B., *Hindu Nationalism India* (New Delhi: Vistaar, 1994).

Maniruzzaman, T., *The Bangladesh Revolution and its Aftermath* (Dacca, 1980).

Manogaran, C. 'Colonization as Politics: Political Use of Space in Sri Lanka's Ethnic Conflict', in: C. Manogaran, B. Pfaffenberger (eds.), *The Sri Lanka Tamils. Ethnicity and Identity* (Boulder, 1994).

Manor, James, 'Anomie in Indian Politics: Origins and Potential Wider Impact', *Economic and Political Weekly,* Annual Number, May 1983.

Manor, James, 'Introduction', in: J. Manor (ed.), *Sri Lanka in Change and Crisis* (Beckenham, 1984).

Manor, James, (ed.), *Sri Lanka in Change and Crisis* (London, 1984).

Manor, James, *Power, Poverty and Poison - Disaster and Response in an Indian City* (New Delhi, Newbury Park and London: Sage Publications, 1993).

Manor, James, 'Nehru to the Nineties: The Changing Office of Prime Minister in India', *The Journal of Commonwealth and Comparative Politics,* Vol. 33, No. 2, (July 1995).

Marga-Institute, *The Muslim Community of Sri Lanka* (Colombo, 1985).

Markova, Dagmar, 'Babar's Mosque versus Ram's Birthplace: A Case Study of Misuse of Religion', *Archiv Orientalni* (Prague), Vol. 59, No. 3, (1991).

Masselos, Jim, *Struggling and Ruling: The Indian National Congress 1885-1985* (New Delhi: Sterling 1987).

Maududi, Sayyid Abul Ala, *The Islamic Law and Constitution,* 2nd ed. (Lahore, 1960).

McGarry, John and O'Leary, Brendan (eds.), *The Politics of Ethnic Conflict Regulation* (London: Routledge, 1993).

McGowan, W., *Only Man is Vile. The Tragedy of Sri Lanka* (London, 1993).

Mistry, Malika B., 'Hindu-Muslim Fertility Differentials in India', *New Quest* (Pune), No. 94, (July-August 1992).

Mitra, Subrata K., 'Desecularising the State: Religion and Politics in India after Independence', *Comparative Studies in Society and History,* Vol. 33, No. 4, October 1991.

Mitra, Subrata K., *Power, Protest and Participation - Local Elites and the Politics of Development in India* (London and New York: Routledge, 1992).

Mitra, Subrata K. : 'The Rational Politics of Cultural Nationalism: Sub-national Movements in South Asia in Comparative Perspective', *The British Journal of Political Science,* Vol. 25 (1995).

Moore, M., ''Guided Democracy' in Sri Lanka: The Electoral Dimension',' *The Journal of Commonwealth and Comparative Politics,* Vol. 32, No. 1, (1994).

Morris-Jones, W.H., *The Government and Politics of India* (Wistow, Huntingdon: The Eothen Press, reprint 1987).

Morris-Jones, W.H., 'Shaping the Post-Imperial State: Nehru's Letters to Chief Ministers', in Michael Twaddle (ed.), *Imperialism, the State and the Third World* (London: British Academic Press, 1992).

Mukhia, Harbans, 'Communalism and the Indian Polity', *South Asia Bulletin* (London), Vol. 11, No. 1&2, (1991).

Muni, S.D., *Foreign Policy of Nepal* (New Delhi: National Publishing House, 1973).

Munir, Muhammad, *Constitution of the Islamic Republic of Pakistan* (Lahore, 1976).

Munir, Muhammad, *From Jinnah to Zia,* 2nd ed. (Lahore, 1980).

Murshid, T. M., 'Bangladesh: The Challenge of Democracy - Language, Culture and Political Identity', *Contemporary South Asia,* Vol. 2, No. 1, 1993.

Murshid, T. M., *The Sacred and the Secular: Bengal Muslim Discourses, 1871-1977* (New Delhi: Oxford University Press, 1995).

Naoroji, Dadabhai, *Poverty and Un-British Rule in India* (London, 1901).

Nasreen, Taslima, *Nirbachita Column* (Dhaka: Vidyaprakash, 1991, 1992).

Nasreen, Taslima, *Nashta Meyer, Nashta Gadya* (Dhaka, 1992, 1993).

Nath, R., 'In the Eye of the Storm', *Defence Today,* August 1993.

Nettl, J.P., 'The State as a Conceptual Variable', *World Politics,* Vol. 20, (July 1968).

North, Douglass C., *Institutions, Institutional Change and Economic Performance* (Cambridge: CUP, 1990).

Olsen, B., Sri Lanka, in: P. Baehr, H. Hey, J. Smith, T. Swinehart (eds.), *Human Rights in Developing Countries Yearbook 1994* (Deventer, Boston, 1994).

Oommen, M.A., 'Relative Tax Effort of States', *Economic and Political Weekly,* 14 March 1987.

Pettigrew, Joyce, *Robber Noblemen* (London: Routledge, Kegan and Paul, 1975).

Pettigrew, Joyce, 'Achieving a New Frontier: Rural Political Patterns and their Impact on the Sikh Independence Movement', *International Journal of Punjab Studies,* Vol 2, No. 1, April 1995.

Pettigrew, Joyce, *The Sikhs of Punjab: Unheard Voices of State and Guerrilla Violence* (New Jersey: Zed Books, 1995).

Phadnis, U., *Religion and Politics in Sri Lanka* (London, 1976).

Phadnis, U., 'Sri Lanka: Crises of Legitimacy and Integration', in: L. Diamond, J.J. Linz, S.M. Lipset (eds.), *Democracy in Asia* (New Delhi, 1989).

Ponnambalam, S., *Sri Lanka. The National Question and the Tamil Liberation Struggle* (London, 1983).

Quaid-i-Azam Mahomed Ali Jinnah, Speeches as Governor-General of Pakistan 1947 - 1948 (Karachi, 1962).

Rao, B. Shiva, (ed.), *The Framing of India's Constitution. Selected Documents, Vol. II* (New Delhi, 1967).

Rawls, John, *Political Liberalism* (New York, 1993).

Riker, William and Ordeshook, Peter, *An Introduction to Positive Political Theory* (Englewood Cliffs, N.J., 1973).

Rösel, J., 'Geheimnis, Terror und der Zerfall staatlicher Macht auf Sri Lanka', in: T. Scheffler (ed.), *Ethnizität und Gewalt* (Hamburg, 1991).

Rösel, J., *Sri Lanka. Die Entwicklungshilfe als Druckmittel zur Einhaltung von Menschenrechten* (Frankfurt a.M., 1993).

Rosenthal, Erwin I.J., *Islam in the Modern National State* (Cambridge, 1965).

Rothermund, Dietmar, *Die politische Willensbildung in Indien, 1900-1960* (Wiesbaden, 1965).

Rothermund, Dietmar, *India in the Great Depression, 1929-1939* (New Delhi, 1992).

Roy, Beth, 'Of Cabbages and Kings and Why the Sea is Boiling Hot: How Communities Decide to Fight', *International Journal of the Sociology of Law* (London), Vol. 20, (1992).

Rudolph, Lloyd I. and Rudolph, Susanne H., *In Pursuit of Lakshmi: The Political Economy of the Indian State* (Chicago, 1987).

Saberwal, Satish, *India: The Roots of Crisis* (Delhi e.a.: OUP, 1986).

Sathyamurthy, T.V. (ed.), *State and Nation in the Context of Social Change* (Delhi: OUP, 1994).

Sayeed, Khalid B., *Pakistan. The Formative Phase 1857 - 1948*, (Karachi, 2nd. ed. 1978).

Sayeed, Khalid B., *Politics in Pakistan. The Nature and Direction of Change* (New York, 1980).

Schama, Simon, *Citizens: A Chronicle of the French Revolution* (Harmondsworth, 1989).

Setalvad, M.C., *Secularism* (Patel Memorial Lectures, 1965) (New Delhi: Government of India Publications Division, January 1967).

Shaha, R., *Nepali Politics: Retrospect and Prospect* (Delhi: OUP, 1978).

Shastri, A., 'Sri Lanka's Provincial Council System. A Solution to the Ethnic Problem?', *Asian Survey*, Vol. 32, No. 8, (1992).

Sherwani, L.A., *Speeches, Writings and Statements of Iqbal*, 3rd. ed. (Lahore, 1977).

Shourie, Arun, 'Tada is a Decade Old, So Why has Rao Suddenly Discovered it Must Go Now', *The Asian Age*, 20 January 1995.

Shrestha, H.L., *Some Unequal Treaties* (Kathmandu: Jhilko Publication, 1980).

Siddiqui, H.Y., 'Quest for a Secular Society—Challenge and Response', in Chakrabarty (ed.), *Secularism, Muslim India* (New Delhi), No. 141, September 1994.

Siddiqui, Nafis Ahmad, *Population Geography of Muslims of India* (New Delhi: S. Chand, 1976).

de Silva, K.M., 'Buddhist Revivalism, Nationalism, and Politics in Modern Sri Lanka', in: J.W. Björkman (ed.), *Fundamentalism, Revivalists and Violence in South Asia* (New Delhi, 1988).

de Silva, K.M., 'Regionalism and Decentralization of Power', in: K.M. de Silva, *Sri Lanka, Problems of Governance* (New Delhi, 1993).

de Silva, K.M., *Managing Ethnic Tensions in Multi-Ethnic Societies: Sri Lanka 1880-1985* (Lanham, 1986).

Singer, M.R., 'Sri Lanka's Tamil-Sinhalese Ethnic Conflict. Alternative Solutions', *Asian Survey*, Vol. 32, No. 8, (1992).

Singh, Gurharpal, 'The Punjab Problem in the 1990s: A Post-1984 Assessment', *The Journal of Commonwealth and Comparative Politics*, Vol. 29, No. 2, July 1991.

Singh, Gurharpal, 'The Punjab Elections 1992: Breakthrough or Breakdown?', *Asian Survey*, Vol. 32, No. 11 (1992).

Singh, Gurharpal, 'Ethnic Conflict in India: A Case Study of Punjab', in: John McGarry and Brendan O'Leary (eds.), *The Politics of Ethnic Conflict Regulation* (London: Routledge, 1993).

Singh, Gurharpal, 'The Punjab Crisis since 1984: A Reassessment', *Ethnic and Racial Studies*, Vol. 18, No. 3, July 1995.

Singh, Gurmit, *History of Sikh Struggles*, Vol. IV (New Delhi: Atlantic Publishers, 1992).

Sinha, R.B.N., 'Attitudes of Hindus and Muslims to Family Planning', *The Journal of Family Welfare*, Bombay, Vol. 37, No. 2, (June 1991).

Sodhi, H.S., 'Punjab: The Trendsetter', *Defence Today* (New Delhi), August 1993.

Tambiah, S.J., *Buddhism Betrayed? Religion, Politics, and Violence in Sri Lanka* (Chicago, 1992).

Thandi, Shinder S., 'Counter-insurgency and Political Violence in Punjab 1980-1994', in: Gurharpal Singh and Ian Talbot (eds.), *Punjabi Identity: Continuity and Change* (New Delhi: Manohar, 1995).

Thapar, Romila, 'Religion, Culture and Nation', *Monthly Public Opinion Survey* (New Delhi), April 1991.

Tilly, Charles (ed.), *The Formation of National States in Western Europe* (Princeton: Princeton University Press, 1975).

Tully, Mark and Jacob, Satish, *Amritsar: Mrs Gandhi's Last Battle* (London: Jonathan Cape, 1985).

Upadhyaya, Prakash Chandra, 'The Politics of Indian Secularism', *Modern Asian Studies* (Cambridge), Vol. 26, No. 4, (1992).

Varshney, Ashutosh, 'Contested Meanings: India's National Identity, Hindu Nationalism, and the Politics of Anxiety', *Daedalus*, (Summer 1993).

Wagner, C., *Die Muslime Sri Lankas* (Freiburg, 1990).

Wagner, C., 'Zurück in die Zukunft: Sri Lanka nach dem indo-srilankischen Beistandsvertrag von 1987', *Asien*, Vol. 34, (1990).

Wagner, C., 'The Muslims of Sri Lanka and their Role in the National Ethnic Conflict', *The Journal of Social Studies*, Vol. 58, (October 1992).

Wagner, C., 'Demokratischer Wandel und politische Stabilität? Die Parlaments- und Präsidentschaftswahlen in Sri Lanka 1994', *Asien*, Vol. 54, (1995).

Wariavwala, Bharat, 'Security Issues in Domestic Politics', in : Subrata K. Mitra and James Chiriyankandath (eds.), *Electoral Politics in India: A Changing Landscape* (New Delhi: Segment Books, 1992).

Waseem, Mohammad, *Politics and the State in Pakistan* (Lahore, 1989).

Weber, Max, *Wirtschaft und Gesellschaft* (Tübingen, 1972).

Wilson, Kalpana, 'Class Alliance and the Nature of Hegemony: The Post-Independence Indian State in Marxist Writing', in: T.V. Sathyamurthy (ed.), *State and Nation in the Context of Social Change* (Delhi: OUP, 1994).

Wink, André, *Land and Sovereignty in India, Agrarian Society and Politics under the Eighteenth Century Maratha Svarajya* (Cambridge, 1986)

Wittfogel, Karl A., *Oriental Despotism* (New York, reprint 1981).

Wolpert, Stanley, *Jinnah of Pakistan* (New York, Oxford, 1984).

Wriggins, W.H., *Ceylon. Dilemmas of a New Nation* (New Delhi, 1960).

Index